BOOK OF LIFE

and

The Book of The Kumaras

Sister Thedra

Copyright © 2021 by Halls of Light, LLC

All rights reserved. This book or any portion thereof may not be reproduced or used in any manner whatsoever without the express written permission of the publisher except for the use of brief quotations in a book review.

ISBN: 978-1-7373071-6-7

To the Reader

Please read and review "Divine Explanations" on page 397 for questions and definitions of terms.

This book is only a portion of the precious teachings and prophecies that have been given by Sananda (Jesus Christ), Sanat Kumara, and others of the higher realms, and Recorded by Sister Thedra.

Contents

THE TABLE OF THE LORD 1

OPEN UP THINE HEART 53

THE IMPORTANCE OF THE WORK AT HAND 101

GRACE 157

SUFFER NO MORE 215

THE PRODIGAL SON 265

IT SHALL QUICKEN THEM 321

Mission Statement 390

Sananda's Appearance 391

About the Late Sister Thedra 392

Divine Explanations 397

Other Books by TNT Publishing 408

Esu Jesus Sananda

This reproduction is from an actual photograph taken on June 1st, 1961, in Chichen Itza, Yucatan, by one of thirty archaeologists working in the area at the time. Sananda appeared in visible, tangible body and permitted His photograph to be taken.

THE TABLE OF THE LORD

Holy - Holy is The Word -- Be ye as one blest by The Word - for I, The Lord thy God hast spoken - and thou hast heard Me-

    Now ye shall begin a New part - and it shall form a Great and Wondrous Book - and it shall be called the "Book of Life"- and it shall begin with this page - and many pages shall be added unto it -- And the ones which await The Word shall receive it in portions - as it is prepared and for them it shall be given -- For them which have asked - and unto them - I say: Turn not away - keep thine hand unto the plow - and seek ye favor with Me - for I am come that ye be prepared for Greater things. And I say unto thee - there are none so foolish as he which betrays himself -- For this have I said unto thee - prepare thineself that ye might go where I go -- So let it be as The Father Wills it ---

                                      I AM The Lord thy God

The Word of the Kumara

Beloved of Mine Being:

    Wherein is it said - as thou art prepared so shall ye receive -- It is the law ---

    Now thou hast come unto this Altar - in humility and humble submission - that ye might receive of Me - this communication - by which they might be blest of ME -- Let it be as they are prepared to receive - for each unto his own - each in his own way - and none shall deprive him of his way ---

Now I give unto thee - this Word - and it shall be called "The Word of Kumara" - and it shall be the Word of God - for He hast given unto me that I might give unto thee -- I say it is His - The God of All - The Source of Our Being - that speaketh thru the Kumara which now speaks unto thee -- And it is to be remembered that I take no credit - no glory for unto The Father = God - The Father Who is The "ALL" - The Eternal One - from which all things come - that I give the Glory - the Praise - the Honor ---

Be ye thotful of Him - while thou art in the Way with ME - while thou art in communion with Me - for I say - we shall commune - and He shall give unto us of Himself - that this be done -- So be it as HE Wills it---

I Am but an instrument in His hand - and I beseech thee to give unto Him all the credit - all the Glory -- So be it that He shall Glorify Himself in this His Work---

For the first part - let the other part go first - unto the ones which prove themself - and then this shall follow - and it shall be the one which is added unto the other -- For in no wise shall it differ in Source in Truth - in Doctrine -- Neither shall it be given unto them for entertainment -- It shall be for their upliftment - and it behooves them to consider well that which is given unto them thru this Source---

I say: They shall be blest indeed and in truth - to consider well the Truth herein - for it shall be given unto them in a manner which they can comprehend - and on which they can rely -- So be it that I come that they be lifted up -- So let it be as The Father Wills it ---

Bear in mind - there are none so foolish as he which thinks himself wise ---

Bear in mind - that I am sent of Mine Father even as The Lord of Lords - The host of Hosts - and that I Am One with Him - that we sit in the Mighty Council for the good of all - that we are not alone in this - that ones have been sent in flesh - that the Father's Will be done - that these are the hand and foot of The Father made manifest upon the Earth that His Kingdom be established ---

Now I say unto all - fear not - be ye as one responsible for that which ye do with this Word -- Pass it not unto another - saying: This is thus - and so -what think ye of it? For it shall be given unto thee to bear witness - of this Word - this Work - which shall be accomplished in a short while ---

I am not of a mind to give unto the dogs - the bread I have for the ones which sit at the table of The Lord ---

I am come that they might have the elixir of Life - for it is theirs by divine right - and I say unto the dogs: Depart thou unworthy creatures for thou art me prone to bite the hand which feeds thee - thou unknowing creatures!

I bid thee draw nigh - and hear ye well that which I say unto thee - Yet I shall give unto thee no more than which ye can assimilate - for there is not time to be wasteful - for the time is come when great strength of character shall be demanded of thee ---

<u>The</u> <u>Table</u> <u>of</u> <u>The</u> <u>Lord</u> awaits thine own preparation -- I bid thee go cleanse thineself - and then ye shall enter into the banquet table - wherein ye shall drink of the Chalice - from which He drinks ---

I say unto thee: Give not this Word unto another before thou hast first assimilated it thineself -- Should ye not be at one with it - give it not -- Should ye deny it - give it not - for thou hast no part of it - and thou shall find no reward in it ---

Should ye find it unto thine liking - read it - read it - assimilate it - and ye shall see that which ye saw not before -- For I shall prepare for thee a portion within this Work - which shall be hidden up from the eyes of the unjust and profane -- Let not thine eye be profane - for he which is profane shall not know Me - he shall not bear witness of Me - neither the Word of God - for he is not of God -- Now if ye are not with Me - thou art not with Him - so be it ye shall have no part in this -- So be it I shall give unto the just - and the one which is of Him The Father, The Lord God - The Lord of Lords - The Host of Hosts -- I say unto thee - I come that ye too - might become one with Him ---

We Shall be Heard - Each in His Own Tongue

Sons of God are We -- of the Mighty Council are We -- Of the Mighty Host - are We - and We are qualified to speak this day ---

It is now come when We shall be heard - and each in his own tongue for each unto his capacity to receive ---

Now it is come - when the Host draws close unto the Earth - as the mother unto her chicks - for the Earth stands in peril - and it behooves thee to be as ones alert ---

For all thine learning shall avail thee nought - when it is come that the dragon opens up his mouth to devour thee ---

For thou hast not reckoned with the power which thou hast given him -- It is said - he hast no power over thee - save that which thou hast given him – and it is so ---

Yet thou hast not reckoned with the power of God - The Omnipotent One - The All Wise - The Merciful Father-- It is said: See the hand of God move - See it - and know it moveth! ---

For it shall be as the two edged sword - it shall cut clean - and the plan shall be revealed unto the ones which endure it - for it shall be swift in its action - and it shall be as the balance - for all shall be weighed -- And unto them which are found wanting - I say - woe - woe unto him ---

For long hast the sword been unsheathed -- Long hast it hung in the balance -- Now it shall be slung into space as a mighty force -- And wherein is there a man which shall calculate its force? ---

I say unto thee - no man can calculate its force - its power - its strength ---

No man shall be as free from its thrust - for it shall touch each and every one - and none shall escape its path ---

I say - none shall escape! Yet the law of Truth and Justice shall reign supreme - and unto them which abide by the law - I say - fear not, have no fear - for I am come that ye might know the law - and therein is Mine part -- Thine part is the acceptance of Mine part - Mine gift - for they are given unto saying: "We have not received that which we have asked" -- Yea - Mine children - thou knowest not how foolish thine askings - thine energy wasted on things of the world - when thou standeth on the brink of destruction! Know ye not that thou hast danced to the piper's tune - the fortunes wasted on the idiots delight? ---

For what hast thou asked of The Lord thy God? For what hast thou asked of Him - The One Sent that ye be brot out of bondage? ---

I ask of thee - take ye notice of thine giving -- What hast thou given unto Him - for the sacrifice which He hast made? ---

Poor foolish mortals - take ye heed of thine givings - and thine askings -- Hast thou given in like measure unto His? Hast thou paid an honest farthing for that which thou hast asked of Him?

Pray thou that thou art not cut off - for thine hypocrisy and blasphemy -- I say - see unto thine own preparation - lest thou art cut off in thine wickedness---

Wherein is it said - that ye shall atone for all thine misused energy and willfulness - it is so - for it is the LAW! ---

And no man shall escape it ---

Behold the light of the new dawn - and be ye as one prepared for the new revelation - which shall be given unto thee - and at no time shall it be withheld - when thou art prepared to receive of Me -- So be it that I am prepared to give unto thee in great measure---

Now ye shall put aside thine preconceived ideas and opinions - and ask of The Father - that He send One to give unto thee that which shall profit thee - and ye shall be heard -- So let it be as He Wills it -

Wherein Has He Found the Solution -

Son of God am I - Son of God art thou - and thou art the chosen vessel for this part of this Our Work - and for this shall great things be accomplished -- Yet no man can stand still - and see that which is accomplished - for it is as he progresses unto the greater heights - that he can see that which he hast done - wherein he hast been - and a greater insight where he is going ---

Now it shall be recorded for all that which I now say unto thee - for they which are of a mind - shall profit thereby -- Not one shall be given more than he can assimilate - and it is his nature to hunger -- Yet his capacity is limited - for he so limits himself - by his preconceived ideas and opinions ---

He gives unto himself the lesser part - for he cuts himself off from the greater - for he hast builded his own walls -- Now he shall tear them down - and then he shall be free to move out of his own prison - which he hast created for himself ---

Yet let it be said - many shall build yet other walls - and close themself within - leaving no room for expansion -- Therein is his frailties - his folly - for he thinks himself wise - he thinks he hast found the end of all things! He <u>thinks</u> he hast arrived at the perfect solution of all his torment - all his wants ---

Yet I ask - wherein hast he found the solution - wherein hast he been delivered - wherein hast he found freedom - wherein hast he found peace?

Not within his own walls!

Not within his own power!

Not within his own conceit!

Not within his own church!

Not within his own Country!

Not within his own Council Chambers!

Not within himself!

I say he hast not found the ultimate!

Be it so - that he shall be given as he is prepared to receive - and no more -- Yet I find them impoverished - and starving - yet they do not eat that which is prepared for their strength - for they deny the Source of their Being!

They accept not the BREAD which would be unto them the Bread of Life -- They turn from it - knowing not that they perish without it--

While it is said many times - "Come eat - partake of Mine Cup" - they give no heed unto the call - for they know not the Voice - they have their fingers in their ears ---

Now this is their own will - which motivates them - it is of their own will that they turn away - seeking outward signs and manifestations of wonders -- And these are but the illusions - which shall pass away - and these are the lesser things which are but traps to hold them bound ---

While many shall see - and be illumined - many shall see and not believe -- Many shall see - and know not that which they see -- Yet it shall be given unto them which seek Truth/ Light - to receive as they are prepared to receive - no more - no less ---

Now they shall begin within their own self - within their own household - and therein they shall clean - they shall make clean themself - then their household shall profit by their effort - then the nation shall profit by the household - and the world shall profit by the nation - such is the law - For no light shall be hidden - none shall be lost -- Yet them that hath - unto them more shall be added unto -- Let it be understood that there is no limit within the Light - it is not limited and for that matter - there is no end - no beginning - for there is but One Source - and unto That Source thou owe thine beginning - and in Him thou shall have thine reward -- The end of thine beginning shall be thine reward - for then the Serpent shall have swallowed his own tail -- Therein is thine reward - thine return unto thine Source ---

Be ye blest to return unto IT - for therein is Peace - perfect Peace - and joy divine - worlds without end -- So let it Be ---

To the Prodigal Son

Such is Mine Word unto them - there is but One Door - and it stands ajar -- They have but to turn the Key - for the Key is within their hand. They shall prepare themself to enter - and it is given unto them to have free will - and as they will it - so shall it be ---

Many times - many times - it is said - prepare thineself -- The law is given unto them - the Key is given unto them - yet they stir not -- They give unto Me no credit for being that which I Am - they give no credit unto the Council of Councils - The Great and Mighty Council for their welfare -- While it is given unto them to grovel for a pittance - We proffer Our part - Our Cup -- Our board is a plenty and to spare - yet they reach not a hand to receive of Us - for they are poor of Spirit - and know not that they perish - in the land of plenty ---

I speak unto them which dine on the husks from the belly of the swine -- They have not the taste for greater food - they cultivate the taste for the lesser - I say poor is the one which doth eat with the dogs.

For are they not impoverished - are they not to be pitied - are they not the outcasts - are they not the prodigal sons?

So be it that they shall hunger and thirst for the food from the table which We have prepared for them - they shall eat and be satisfied - for the food I proffer shall satisfy - and they shall hunger no more ---

So be it that they shall forsake their foolishness and they shall learn the way of Righteousness - for this do I speak unto them -- Let no man refuse the Cup I proffer him - for he shall be as one cut off -- He shall close the Door in his own face - and he shall cry out for help - and he shall wait for another day -- I say unto him which doth refuse that which

I proffer him - there shall come a time when ye shall remember Mine Word - and that which I now say unto thee - for ye shall cry for Mine Word - Mine comfort - Mine touch and I shall withhold it - until thou hast learned well thine lesson - and forever made thine own sacrifice - then - I shall take note of thee -- Yet thine waiting shall be long and hard - the nite long - and cold - and no warmth shall ye find - until thou hast atoned for thine wanton - and thine folly -- So be it I have spoken. So let it be ---

The Appointment

Be ye as one which I have appointed for this part - for it is given unto thee to be as one prepared to receive it - and I have tried thee - and found thee trust worth ---

Now ye shall be given an added gift for thine faithfulness - for unto them which hath - it shall be given unto them -- Whose part it is to give unto them - more is given ---

Unto them which is given - more is required - for they which are given - are given that they might give -- Yet when they give not - they are cut off -- So be it I say unto thee - withhold nought which is given unto thee for them - and ye shall know that which is for them ---

While thou shall too know that which is given unto thee for thine own preparation ---

Now it shall be given unto thee to be as Mine hand made manifest unto them which have not - and unto them - I say: Poor in spirit art the ones which have not - yet they shall be offered the gifts of Spirit --

While it is given unto the poor of spirit - I say - they know not the Good Gifts of Spirit - they have not tasted of the fruits of Spirit - therefore they are impoverished and they know not the joy of sharing the fruits of the Spirit ---

Let it be said - that they shall will to partake of such fruit as I speak of - for it is thru and by the fruit of Spirit that they shall be nourished - for from the root cometh the fruit - and it is free unto all whichsoever hunger for such gifts as shall be nourishment unto them ---

While many ask for the fruit - and reject the Spirit - I say - the fruit of the Spirit is the nourishment - while the Spirit is that which brings forth the fruit -- And to reject that which brings forth the nourishment is liken unto the fool which hast no part of the Cup which holds within it the Living Water -- Let him also accept the Vessel - and likewise he shall receive of the Fruit ---

So be it that I Am but the Vessel of Mine Father - for I too am Sent of Him that a Greater Work be done -- So be it and Selah ---

Hold out thine hand - and I shall give unto thee a part- yet ye shall be as one willing to receive Me and of Me - for I am not an intruder - I bestow not Mine gifts upon the rebellious - for I am prepared to go the last mile with the ones which are of a mind to accept Mine Gift - they are perfect gifts - given of The Father - and unto Him all the Praise and the Glory-- So be it these gifts are too numerous to mention - and too few prepared to receive -- I bid thee open up thine hand and prove Me. Yet ye shall have clean hands - for I give not of Mine gifts unto the ones of dirty hands -- I prepare a table before thee - and I bid thee come and partake of all Good things prepared for thee-- Yet ye shall first groom thineself - ye shall cleanse thineself - and present thineself as a fit subject - that ye might receive of Me - for I am one of The Host - and I bid thee come and partake of the feast -- Yet none enter which are filthy and unjust -- While the Sun shines on the just and the unjust alike, the Banquet is prepared for the just - and they only can enter into the banquet chamber - for therein ye will find only the just and prudent - for therein is wisdom -- So be it that this table is spread before the just and the unjust - yet the unjust shall look from afar - while they shall not enter in -- Hear ye that which I have said - and ye shall profit thereby - So let it be -- For this have I spoken ---

The Holy Sacrifice

Fortune thineself the Good Gifts of God -- Fortune unto thineself joy that thou hast not known - for the joy of Service rendered in His Name and for His sake is the reward of the Initiate -- And unto thee I say - bring unto The Father thineself as a living sacrifice -- Offer up unto Him thineself in Holy sacrifice - that He might do His Work thru thee and by thee ---

Let no man take from thee thine divine inheritance - for each hast an inheritance - and it is earned thru and by the Holy sacrifice - which is thine own self will - and it shall be as an acceptable gift - for none other is required of thee - none other acceptable unto The Father ---

So be it - I ask of thee nought - I accept nought save thine willingness to accept Mine Gift - which I proffer thee -- Yet should thou turn from Me - I shall give it unto another - and he shall profit thereby - for I am a filled One - I give because I do not contain all that I have -- I say Mine nature is to give - I keep nought for Mineself - for

Mine Cup is filled from the fount of Living Water - it flows freely and gently - therefore it never ends - neither does it stagnate -- I am fortuned to be One which stands before the throne of The Most High Living God and I am not given unto withholding - yet I know where to give - and when it is wise -- For the one so prepared stands as one willing to receive - and there is no rebellion within him -- He hast won his Victory over his own will - and he stands as a servant - ready to do the Will of The Father which hast sent Me -- It is by His Grace that I am come --

I come bearing Gifts - and they shall be becoming unto Me - for I shall not be ashamed of that which I offer unto thee - for I know the worth thereof -- And at no time shall I give unto the fools Mine priceless Gifts -- I say unto thee - be ye aware of the Gifts which I hold within Mine hand - and ask not for more - until thou hast first learned to use that which thou hast been given --

Ye shall stand before Me as one naked - shorn of all thine laurels - as one prepared to accept the new -- And unto thee I say - let it be thine own will that ye shall surrender up - for ye barter not with another's will - ye make no bargains with Me - for I am not of a mind to bargain. I am not of a mind to take the time to bargain - for time runs out - and shall I find thee wanting? I ask of thee: Shall I find thee wanting? Bring thine gift unto the Altar of The Most High Living God - and it shall be acceptable unto Him - then ye shall be as one prepared to receive Pearls without price --

So be it and Selah --

Thine Time is Nigh Spent

Wherein has thou brot thine gifts - wherein hast thou given unto The Father the Gift which He asks of thee - Wherein hast thou devoted thineself unto Him ---

Hast thine time been profitable unto thee - hast thine time been well spent ---

I say unto thee - thine time is nigh spent -- Think ye well of Mine questions - for they are well put ---

I ask of thee - ponder well these Mine questions for it shall profit thee much ---

Now ye shall stand as one which hast been shorn of all thine glory, all thine laurels - and they shall avail thee nought - for ye shall be as one accountable for all thine energy - all thine deeds - all thine words - and ye shall account for each moment - each day - and the nite shall be as the darkness heavy about thee - for it shall hang heavy over thee -- And it behooves thee to give of thineself that The Father's Will be done and it shall be as nothing thou hast done - for thou hast not as yet devoted thine hands - thine feet unto Him - thou hast words of thine own - thou hast reserved for thineself a seat in the place of the dragon for thou art not devoted unto the Whole -- Thou art not as yet willing to follow where I lead thee - for thou art as one looking backward -- Thou - O man of Earth - feign wisdom - thou art not looking where I point -- Thou art as the fool riding the back of another - looking backward ---

I say - look ye forward - and see ye the way I point unto thee -- I say - arise ye - man of Earth! Come forward - and be ye spared from a fate worse than death ---

I have prophesied - I have pleaded - I have sibored thee - I have given unto thee the law -- I have given Mineself in sacrifice - that ye might know that which I know - yet ye turn from Me - seeking of men, asking of them - while I say unto thee - Come - accept Mine Word - trust in Me - accept Mine hand - yet thou fearest -- Oh poor in Spirit - think ye that I am impoverished? Seek ye what? Look ye for what? Ask ye for what? Think ye Me a fool? -- I say unto thee - I know thine needs, great as they are - I know them - and I am prepared to fill them -- Could thou but know that which I am prepared to do ---

O man - I speak unto thee in Great compassion - Great Love - and with Great Mercy - for Mine Father hast sent me that ye might be lifted up -- It is by His Grace - His Mercy that I am come ---

Let thine heart be cleft - let it be softened - let it be the Chalice - that I might fill it - for I have for thee the Elixir of Life - the cure for all thine ills --

So let it be that I have spoken -- Let it be that thou has received Mine Words - for this are they given---

I am Mindful of Their Sufferings

Say unto them - that the way hast been made clear - and they shall walk within it - there is no other way that they might return unto their rightful estate ---

They are but outcasts - until they - of their own free will - place their feet upon the path - and walk the strait and narrow way - which leads unto their Victory ---

Their Victory depends upon their own effort - their strength of character - and their part which is their preparation ---

Their preparation is their part - while Mine part is to point the way and remind them that they error not ---

I say - I am commanded by law to remind them - I am come that they be reminded of their short-comings - the error of their way -- I come not to comfort - neither to give unto them poultices - I come that they might know the cause of their ills - their sorrow ---

Wherein have I been unmindful of their suffering? Yet it is said they seek relief from their suffering -- Why then - do they not accept the freedom I offer unto them - there is nothing so free - nothing so permanent - as the freedom I offer ---

Yet why do they wait -- For their waiting they shall suffer more - for their refusal they shall suffer yet greater torment -- Yet they wait! - Blest are they which come when called -- Blest are they which come unto Me - for they shall know peace -- For Mine Peace I shall give unto them ---

Let it be said - that they have but made a mockery of Mine sayings, they believe not that which I say unto them - they ask of man that he bless them - They ask of man his opinions - and they believe Me not!

One Shall Take Up His Cross

Sayeth I - The Lord of Hosts - the time is come when one shall take up his cross and follow Me - one which hast given unto Me his will - and which hast within his hand the Golden Key -- He shall walk in Mine footsteps - he shall blaze forth a path - that others might follow after him ---

This one - I have given Mine Seal - I have blest him - I have given unto him the Word - and I have called him out from among them - and he hast heard Me - and answered Me -- Now I shall lead him into the path of righteousness - and I shall deal justly with him ---

Yet I shall not allow him to deal with worldly things - I shall demand obedience and sacrifice of him - and he shall walk upright - and give unto Me his undivided attention -- For I shall have no rebellion within Mine house - I shall place before him many stumbling blocks - and he shall be sorely tested - and he shall weary of his lot - yet I shall deal with him in love and mercy - for he is Mine - he hast given unto Me his heart - and it is softened - and I shall abide with him - for I know him for that which he is -- He hast no other desire other than to serve Me - and serve Me he shall -- He shall be diligent in his service - and he shall find joy in serving Me -- He shall be a shining lamp - as a beacon set on a hill -- And they shall know him as the one called - and he shall be obedient unto the law -- And he shall not betray himself - so be it ---

I have spoken of one which shall come --

So let him come for I shall bring him --

It Behooves Me to Warn Thee

By the Mercy of The Almighty Allwise God - Our Father - I am permitted to speak unto thee this day -- I am permitted to say unto thee that I am He which hast been unto thee Benefactor and Sibor -- And for this hast thou been spared - for in time past - thou hast stood on the brink of destruction - and I have drawn thee back - as one which knows not the dangers -- For it is by Mine Grace that ye stand upon solid ground - for had I not interceded for thee - thou should not have footing upon the Earth ---

Now - it is again come when ye shall be called upon for thine all - for thine very soul shall be demanded of thee -- Thou hast not reckoned with thine destiny - thou hast not known that which thou hast fortuned unto thineself in thine unknowing ---

Yet I say unto thee - the time is short and thou art not wont to hear that which I have to say - yet it shall be said - over and over - for it behooves Me to warn thee ---

For from the beginning I have watched thee - and I have given unto thee in a measure - that which should profit thee - Yet thou hast not given of thineself in Wholly surrender - thou hast gone thine way in rebellion - and thou hast set up idols and worshiped them - thou hast ran after strange gods - and they have led thee into the pit ---

While there are ones entrapt - I say unto them: Look - see ye that thine salvation is nigh - see the hand that proffereth thee thine freedom.

Know ye that thou art entrapt! Know ye that thou art entrapt!! ---

For I see thee as a bird with a broken pinion - and thou canst not raise of thine own power -- Yet I come unto thee in great love and compassion - that thine wounds might be healed ---

While I say it is given unto Me to have great compassion upon thee, I say ye shall first give unto Me credit for being that which I Am - and ye shall reach out thine hand - that I might touch it - and ye shall know that ye have been touched ---

Ye shall allow Me to touch thee - and then I shall administer unto thee - and ye shall be as one alert - and then ye shall be as one prepared to give unto Me - that which I ask of thee - and it shall be no more than is required of thee -- For it is lawful that ye make sacrifice for that which the Father hast for thee-- He hast Willed unto thee a fortune far greater than the Princes' of Earth - for He hast given unto thee His Name. He hast fashioned thee in His own image - and He called His image good -- And thou hast forfeited all that He hast given unto thee. Now I see thee as one bowed down in sorrow - want - and as one dejected - yet He hast given unto Mine keeping that which ye shall be given - when thou hast picked thineself up and shaken off the dust - and prepared thineself to receive that which I have kept for thee ---

For as the Mighty Council hast made known unto thee - it is as a body - a Council - which sits in Council for the good of all - and nothing is hidden from Us We know the law - We abide by it - We are one with it - and We are well qualified to counsel thee-- We are the Ones appointed by The Greater Counselor - and He hast All Authority - All Time -- All Space is His to command - and He hast the Power - The Power of All Power - for none is Greater than He -- And for that reason We are come - that the Earth and Her children be lifted up ---

I say unto thee - thou hast sung thine song - and thou hast given no heed unto the tune thereof -- Thou hast paid a ransom for the discord thereof - for thou hast sold thine inheritance for a poor penny -- Thou hast squandered a princely fortune - and danced unto the piper's tune - while the city hast fallen into ruins ---

Now it is time to become sober - and stand upright and ask of thine own soul: Where am I going - where didst I come from - what is mine inheritance - and how shall I claim it? Then ye shall be as one given in proportion unto thine capacity -- Such is Mine Word unto them which have ears to hear -- And unto them I say: Arise! Arise! Seek the Light and it shall not be hidden from thee -- So be it ye shall have assistance, for this have We of the Mighty Council spoken out this day -- Peace unto thine soul forevermore---

Every Tongue Shall Confess Mine Name

Say unto them - Mine time is come and the day draws nigh - when every tongue shall declare Me - The Lord God - the Host of Hosts - the King of Kings ---

Every tongue shall confess Mine Name - and every eye shall see - and they shall sing praise unto The Lord God - they shall cry out: Hail! unto the King! Hail unto the King of Glory! He Is Come!! ---

Now it shall be a glad day - and every one shall lift his voice in a loud shout - Hail! Hail the King of Glory!

For they shall know that the day of their deliverance is come - and they shall be glad ---

Blest be the ones which come - for they shall behold Me as I Am - for they shall be as ones delivered up - and they shall know ME ---

I say they shall know ME as I Am - and they which know Me shall know The Father which hast Sent Me - so be it and Selah ---

I say - they which know ME shall know Mine Father - for The Father and I are One--

And at no time shall they be deceived - for I Am The Son of God - and I come that they be <u>not</u> deceived by the deceiver - which is abroad in the land ---

I say - I Am Sent that they be not deceived - for the deceiver is abroad in the land - and he is want to hold them bound ---

Be ye as ones prepared to receive Me and of Me - for I shall go forth declaring the Truth - and I shall be as one of flesh and bone ---

I shall walk as man - speak as man - and I shall do a mighty Work and ye shall speak Mine Name with thanksgiving - and with reverence, for I come unto thee in love and Mercy -- For this do I say unto thee - be ye as one prepared to receive Me - for I shall prove Mineself - I shall show Mineself to be all that I claim - yet I say: Be ye alert - and seek the Light - and it shall not be hidden -- I say - ye need go neither to the hills - or the scenic places to find Me -- For many shall say - look here, look there - yet I know wherein I shall find thee - and I am come as a thief in the nite - and no man can follow Mine flight - for I shall move quickly -- I shall be here - I shall be there - and there is no place I cannot be - for I am not limited to time - place - space - or body of flesh-- I say flesh shall have no power over Me -- I shall be swifter than the eye - I shall be more powerful than thine weapons - I shall be unto thee all things - for have I not said: I am The Sent of God - bringing with Me Great Power and Strength -- And the Authority given unto Me of Mine Father maketh Me <u>all</u> <u>powerful</u> -- And no man shall unsheath his sword before ME - for I say - his weapons shall be as nought - for they shall fall from his hands as the rain from the leaf -- I say: Be ye as one prepared to receive Me - for I come swiftly - so be it and Selah ---

The Reward Follows the Gift

Sori Sori -- Hold ye the Light -- Pass not thine gift unto another - for it is greater than thou hast imaged -- Thou hast asked nought in return for the gift so generously bestowed upon thee - yet thy reward is great indeed -- Fortune unto thineself the greater reward - for there is indeed a great one stored up for thee - let no man rob thee of it ---

While there are many which shall sing thine praise - there are ones which shall attempt to take from thee thine crown -- They shall attempt to destroy thine work - and cast thee out of the House of the Lord - yet they shall fail - utterly - for they shall drink of their own cup which they have prepared for thee -- Give unto them nought which they can use against thee - yet they shall be responsible for "The Word" - which hast been given unto thee for them - they shall spit upon it - and they too shall answer for their actions ---

For think ye We know them not? While it is given unto thee to see but one face - We see both - I say they have two faces - and they deceive Us not! ---

Give unto all which asketh - forch nothing upon them - let them ask and then ye shall respond unto them with love and compassion ---

While there are the traitors - I say some shall come humbly and quietly - seeking Truth - Light - and comfort -- These shall receive without stint - and they shall be found worthy of Our attention - and they shall receive that which they prepare themself for to receive---

These shall be as the faithful servants -- These shall believe in the Word - and they shall take heed of it - and live the life which is asked of the candidate -- They shall pay the price exacted of them - the sacrifice of their own puny will - of the self - which is self-sacrifice ---

Let them come - let them ask - let them go - let them prove themself for surely they shall -- It behooves Me to speak unto thee thusly - that ye may be prepared to receive them ---

Receive them in the Name of The Most High Living God - and ye shall stand blameless before Him -- Let thine light so shine that they might see it -- Yet the traitors shall see not - for they are blind unto the light - for the darkness comprehends not the light---

So be it that I Am with thee

Unto the end --

There Shall Be Changes

Be unto thineself true - and look deep within thine own closet - and see that which thou hast stored up -- And know ye that thou art responsible for what ye find therein-- For no man shall let thine profit be his - he shall neither take away - neither add unto thine store - for each is responsible for his own closet ---

I say - now it is time to cleanse it out - for ye shall find it most profitable indeed ---

Hast it not been said - there shall be changes - and is it not so? ---

I tell thee - thou shall not take one iota of thine possessions with thee - and thou shall not be as one admitted into the Holy of Holies unclean ---

Thou hast laid up treasures upon the Earth - where moth doth eat - and wherein they become legirons - and now that they are more than legirons - I say unto thee - give unto Me credit for knowing that which I see - and that which I say -- Ye shall be as one free from all attachment, all loves - all things included - and ye shall stand ready to go forward - and nothing shall hinder thine progress -- Let it be swift - profitable - for it is said - no man shall stay thine flight ---

O man - hast thou not learned the lesson of preparedness?

Hast thou not suffered vainly - hast thou wanted more - hast thou not found the futility of waiting?

I say unto thee - give unto The Father thineself - and He shall deal justly with thee - for is He not Merciful and Loving always ---

I say unto thee: He knows thine every need - thine every want -- While thine wants are the poor part of thine need - yet that which is needful thou shall have - indeed that which is needful thou shall have - for it is the law that ye learn thine lesson well ---

For this have I spoken -

I AM Sanat Kumara

The New Order
Take the Beam Out of Thine Eye

Wherein hast it been said that one shall be raised up - and that one shall do a mighty work - is it not so?

I say it is so - so let it be as The Father hast Willed it - for it is by His Will that this work shall be done - and it is now begun - and great shall be the accomplishments thereof -- No man can measure the magnitude of its accomplishments - for it shall continue thruout many generations yet unborn ---

Now I say unto thee - of this generation - be ye warned aforehand - that this is the day when one is Sent - when One walks amongst thee - and One which hast come into thine midst that ye be lifted up -- Yet ye shall put on thine fine raiment - and purify thineself - cleanse thine house - and prepare thineself that ye might receive Him - and of Him - for He shall be the one which thou hast waited for -- Let His appearance not deceive thee - for He cometh as a thief in the nite - He sends no card before Him - that ye might give unto Him hospitality - not acceptable -- For I say - He shall know thee even before He knocks -- I say - He shall need no porter - He shall need no one to announce His approach - for it is said: "He comes as a thief in the nite" -- He hast come - yet He shall seek out them which hast prepared themself for to receive Him ---

He shall be as one of flesh and bone - yet He shall be no part of flesh and bone - for He is free of ties - any earthly ties -- No tie binds Him - save His love for the Earth and Her sons ---

I say: Be ye watchful -- And too - I say: Ye shall entertain angels unaware - for they are too - come that this be established the "New Order" ---

Hold thineself in readiness - for thou knowest not the hour of His approach - Behold in Him the Light - and know ye Him by the Light - Yet I say unto thee - take the beam from out thine own eye - that ye might see His Light - and by thine light He shall find thee -- Seek not in the dark places for Him - go not unto the far places - for He knoweth wherein thou art ---

Show forth thine own light and He shall follow it - He shall be drawn unto it -- So be it that I have spoken unto them which have a mind to hear - and they shall hear - and they shall profit for the attention given unto Mine Words - for thine reward cometh not without obedience - it cometh not without sacrifice --

So be it that the sacrifice shall be acceptable unto Him - He asks nought save thineself as a living sacrifice ---

So let it be acceptable unto Him ---

The Ancient of Days
Tidings of Great Things to Come

So be it that I am come - on behalf of a world in chaos - for the chaos is great - the darkness overpowering -- Now I stand with outstretched hand that I might assist - and at no time shall I give the bitter cup -- Let it be understood that I am come at The Father's command - and at no time shall I betray Mineself or Mine trust ----

While I am the Ancient of Days - I Am the Worthy Grand Master of the Inner Temple - and I am aware of thine needs - for great is the darkness! Great thine needs!

While We of The Mighty Council - come bearing tidings of Great things to come = of the coming or the King of Kings - the Host of Hosts, the Lord of Lords - We bear tidings of great joy -- We give unto thee the lessons - the great laws - and We give unto thee that ye be strengthened in thy weak parts - and no place can ye be that ye cannot be found ---

Hast thou not heard the glad tidings: Hail! Hail! He is come - the King of Glory! Hast thou not heard? ---

Be ye blest to hear - for the Sound shall permeate the Cosmos: He is Come - He Is Come! Let thine heart be quickened - let thine eyes be made to see - and ye shall be blest ---

Lift up thine eyes and give thanks unto The Father Which hast Sent Me ---

There are none which seek the Light which shall not find ---

I say: Watch! Look! Listen! And ye shall see - ye shall hear and know - for ye shall be quickened ---

For this have I spoken - and I am speaking ---

Let it be for thine own sake that I say unto thee: Look - See - Hear and be ye at Peace --

The Proclamation
To Go Forth

Stand all ye at attention -- Give ear unto the proclamation which goes forth this day - for it shall be as hast not gone forth from the Mighty Council before---

Yet the time is come when it shall be proclaimed - and it shall be done - and no man shall stay the power of this proclamation - for it shall be such power as to make man's power of no consequence - and at no time shall this power be nullified ----

The power of the Light shall be sent forth - and man in his blindness shall be made to see the manifestation of this power - and he shall know his own weakness - that he cannot stand against such power ---

The purpose of the manifestation - is that man might come to see - that man might come into the light - that man might become that for which he is sent into the Earth from the beginning ---

Think ye not that God is a revengeful God -- He is Merciful - filled with Mercy - and a Loving Father-- Yet I say - it is now necessary to give unto them such manifestations as shall awaken them -- And their sleep shall end - they shall arise! and awaken from their lethargy - their sleep - they shall be as ones called forth from the dead - and they shall arise - and they shall see and know that they have slept overtime ---

They shall cry out - and they shall be heard - yet there are ones which shall wait - and these are the ones which have not seen - which have not heard - for there shall be ones which put their fingers in their ears - that they might <u>not</u> hear - they shall close their eyes that they see not - and these shall wait -- They shall wait - and it shall be long and sad - for long shall they wait ---

For it is said - there is a season into all things - a time of sowing - a time of gathering in - it is the law -- They which refuse to hear - heed - this call which hast gone out shall WAIT -- So be it they shall desire that their torment and waiting end - for none shall bring them against their will -- It is given unto Me to see them wail in outer darkness - while the call reverberates thruout the Cosmos: Come! Come unto ME! and let thine waiting be no more -- These which come shall be free of their bondage - and they shall be glad -- So be it I have spoken out of the Light - by the Power of The Lord God Almighty - and thou hast received Me and thou hast comprehended that which I have said - yet ye know not the magnitude of the POWER-- Such is Mine Word unto them which doth receive it unto themself: Prepare thineself this day - for tomorrow bringeth great change -- Who amongst thee can say that which ye shall do - that which ye shall see - that which ye shall endure that which ye shall become --

So be it I AM

Sanat Kumara

Stand Up and Be Counted

While it is said that there shall be changes - it is Good - for progress is change - and change shall bring progress -- For this hast it been said: Prepare thineself - for it is well that thou art prepared - for therein is wisdom ---

Wherein art thou prepared for the changes which shall come about. It is given unto Me to know that which shall come - and it shall be for the good of all -- For this hast the Mighty Host drawn nigh unto the Earth ---

For this hast thou been counselled by the Ones of Higher Realms.

Bear in mind that We of The Mighty Council are not of the Earth - We are the Guardian thereof ---

We know Her need - and likewise thine needs ---

Now ye shall be as ones prepared to receive in greater measure - for this is Mine Word unto thee: Measure well thine own stature - and be ye as one honest in the measure thereof - for it is given unto man to measure the stature of his brother by his own -- He hast not the mind to see himself as he is - he gives unto himself great glory - and praise - while he gives unto his fellow man the bitter cup - he sets himself over his brother - and oppresses him - and takes from him his bread - and then calls him foolish ---

He sets up his own laws - and asks that the oppressed bow down unto them -- He prepares a portion for his enemy - knowing not his enemy -- For it is said: He hast served well the dragon - which is of a mind to hold him bound in bondage -- Yet he gives unto him that which he demands of them -- They forfeit their inheritance that he might be served - they bow down before him - they crawl on their belly before him - and give unto him that which he asks of them - and they find themself entrapt - then they cry: Lord! Lord!

Wherein have they denied the dragon

Wherein have they given of themself that he be satisfied

Wherein have they denied him - wherein hast he freed them

Now I say unto them: Thine time is come - ye shall stand up and declare openly whom ye shall serve-- Ye shall stand up and be counted.

Whom serveth thee

Whom shall ye serve

Where doth thou stand - O man

For it is said: There shall be a great power flood the Earth - and no man shall stand against it which serves the dragon ---

It is clearly and justly stated - that the darkness shall be put to flight. The Light shall consume the darkness -- For this hast the Word gone forth from out the mouth of God ---

So let it be well with thee --

Amen and Selah --

Ye Shall Account for Thineself

Hasten ye - make ready thineself - for the hour approaches - when thou shall be called forth - and ye shall stand as one before the mirror - ye shall face thineself - ye shall account for thineself - and ye shall see thineself as thou art - and no time shall ye deceive thineself ---

For the day of accounting shall be upon thee -- It shall be the day of a meting out - and ye shall see that which thou hast accomplished in the time which hast been allotted unto thee ---

Now I say unto thee - the time cometh swiftly - when thou shall atone for all the energy which thou hast misused - all that which thou hast said - done - and that which thou hast failed to do -- For the day to of accounting is upon thee - let it be profitable unto thee ---

While I say unto thee - prepare thineself - I say as thou art prepared so shall ye receive - so let it be - for it is the law ---

While there are none to sacrifice for thine own misdeeds - many have made the supreme sacrifice - that all men be lifted up - for when one Son is risen - and he finds such joy as man hast not known - he hast no other thot than to assist the one which seeks the heights - which seeks his own salvation - while he walks blindly - bound in flesh ---

I say: Blest is the one which walketh after righteousness - for he shall be lifted up ---

Hear ye Me - and know ye that I Am One of them which have made the SUPREME SACRIFICE - for this am I prepared to assist thee -- For this do I know that - which thou canst become - and it is said: No man knowest that which he shall become ---

So be it that thou art not self-sufficient - yet the law forbids Us - the Ones which hast prepared the way before thee - to give unto thee of Ourself - until thou hast prepared thineself for to receive - for We cannot give unto thee more than ye canst bear ---

Now I say: When thou hast prepared thine own self - We shall know when thou hast paid the price - and when thou art prepared We shall know wherein thou art - and therein We shall find thee -- So be it and Selah ---

Be ye as one sobered - and fear not - for I say unto thee: Thou art not alone - for Mercy and Justice shall be meted out unto thee -- So be it I am within the place wherein all things are known - and I see it as done ---

So be it the time runneth out - and it is Mine part to speak unto thee and to give unto thee this part - for I am responsible for Mine part - and I give forth of Mineself in love and compassion - that all men might be free of bondage -- So be it that I am One of the Council which sits in council for the benefit of mankind -- Think ye that thou art far ahead of thine Elders - thine Benefactors? ---

I say unto thee O man of Earth - thou shouldst do well to harken unto Mine Words - and be ye as ones alert - fashion no legirons for thineself - cut away that which thou hast fashioned - and give not unto thine brothers - that which thou wouldst not like - for it shall be fortuned unto thee to drink of the cup which thou hast prepared for thine brother. So let it be - according unto the law ---

He Shall Know the Mysteries

One shall be raised up in this day - and he shall be given his Royal Raiment - and he shall walk in the Way of the righteous - he shall partake of the Rites of the Order of Melchezedek -- He shall be given the right to partake of the Rites - for he shall be as one prepared - he shall be as one which hast earned the right to participate in the Holy Rites -- He shall be as one given the Breast Plate of Silver - Gold - Emerald and Pearl -- He shall wear upon his brow a Star- and he shall know the Mysteries from the first unto the last - for there shall be nothing hidden from him ---

So be it I shall place upon his head a Crown - and he shall wear it in honor - and he shall Glorify The Father which hast sent Me - for I am come that this might be accomplished -- So be it for the good of all.

I have spoken unto thee that ye be prepared - for such is thine part and at no time shall ye be found wanting - for I say unto thee -

I Am with thee unto the end -

Order is God's First Law

Order within - Order without - and thru it shall be the sign of the Son of God - for this hast the Sons spoken out that there be order --

Now it is said: "Order is God's first law" - it is so -- Everything according to its own order ---

The order of the day - is chaos - for from out the chaos shall come progress - for out the chaos - comes progress -- As the seasons follow each other - progress follows the chaos ---

While thou seeth the chaos - thou seeth not the progress -- Yet it is said thou art part of the progress -- Thou art part of the chaos - and therefore thou art part of the progress ---

Be ye as one which hast part in the progress - and weary not of the chaos - for it is but the cleansing out of the debris of ages past - and it is given unto thee to have part in the cleansing -- Fear not the appearance of the cleansing - let it be - and grieve not for the part which is fortuned unto him which hath another part -- Yet it is said - ye shall fortune unto thineself "Good Gifts - and ye shall set thineself apart - and drag not thine legirons with thee -- For this hast thou had a part in the chaos - and for this hast thou been confused therein -- For this is it said: Turn unto the Light - seek ye the Light - and cut away thine legirons ---

Mine hand I extend unto all - yet I say unto thee - be ye as one which can comprehend Mine Words - for I speak unto thee - none other. So be it that I know of that which I speak - and I say unto thee: Ye shall be reminded of these Mine Words - and at no time shall I give unto thee foolish sayings ---

Blest is the one which hears that which I say unto him --I say: Cast from the call the filth - all the legirons - all the opinions - all the preconceived ideas of the Light - and of the WORLD - for thou hast been led by the blind - and they have been led by the blind -- Therefore it is come when the forces of Light shall be released in great measure - and it shall be as nothing seen by man - for it shall bring great fear -

great joy - great suffering - great affliction - great relief - freedom - and the oppressors shall have their day - likewise - the Sons of Light shall have theirs -- So be it the battle of Light vs - darkness ---

It is said: Choose ye this day which ye serve - choose ye this day - for the morrow cometh swiftly and surely ---

Be ye as one prepared ---

I have spoken - let them hear that which I have said - for I have come that they might hear --

So let it be known - that which I have said unto them--

There are No Gifts So Great

Look not unto thine laurels O man - for thine laurels shall be as coals upon thine head -- I say look not unto thine laurels - for they shall weigh heavy upon thine brow ---

Many a man hast had his crown taken from him - yet I say unto thee no man shall take from thee thine inheritance ---

Too - it is said - ye shall prepare thineself for to receive it -- Let it please The Father Which hast Willed unto thee thine inheritance - let it please Him to give it unto thee - for it is not spent - it awaits thee - no other shall take it - none other shall claim it - for each unto his own -- Each is known - each one unto his own - for none are overlooked - none are forgotten ---

Therefore I say unto thee - there are no gifts so great as that which awaits thee -- Ye shall ask The Father for that which He hast Willed unto thee - and ye shall accept it in His Name -- And ye shall put aside all thine puny ways - all thine former idols - all thine pettiness - and stand as a little child - humble of heart - pure and chaste - and ye shall have within thee no conceit - no deceit - no hatred - no bigotry - no animosity -- No part of thy puny self shall remain - for thou shall stand shorn of all thine self-glory - and thine old self -- This shall pass from thee and thou shall put on the Royal Raiment - and prepare thineself to be brot into the Inner Chamber wherein ye shall see the Glory of The Lord - and ye shall sing praise unto His Name - and ye shall be glad -- Let it be - for this I have spoken - for I am the One which hast answered the call - "Let there Be Light" and I Am come that IT BE --

So be ye blest thereby -

O - Wanderers in Darkness

Sorely oppressed are they which hast given unto man power over them for they have trusted in the frailties of flesh - they have been as the "foolish Virgins"-- They have found - wherein they have sought relief there hast been no relief - they have given credit unto him which hast sorely oppressed them ---

Wherein hast flesh comforted the Spirit of man

Wherein hast he found comfort - surely not in flesh - for the flesh is like unto a yoke upon him - it weighs heavy upon him

Wherein hast he been free from the oppressor

Wherein hast he been given his freedom

Wherein hast he sought freedom - wherein hast he given thot of his Source

Wherein hast he been prepared for his freedom

Wherein hast he given unto himself the bitter cup

Wherein hast he asked of The Father his freedom

Yet it is said: Ask and ye shall receive - yet ye shall ask with thine whole heart - mind - and soul - ye shall be as one mindful of that which ye ask - and be as one prepared to receive it -- And it is given unto thee to pay the price for thine asking -- While no price is too great for that which is offered unto thee for the asking - I say it is given freely -- While thou hast offered up thine puny prayers and petitions - thou hast not given of thineself - that which is asked of thee -- That is the only sacrifice demanded of thee - this is the sacrifice required of thee - this is the price which is asked of every one which asks of The Father -- Such is the Kingdom of Heaven - such is the gladness of His Sons - and such is the gladness of each and every One - which hast held out a hand unto thee in love and mercy ---

I say unto thee - O wayward ones - O wanderers in darkness: - bound in flesh art thou - and weary of thine burdens art thou - and thine lamentations art heard - and pity is thine plight -- Yet thou hast not prostrated thineself in Holy Adoration before the Throne of The Most High Living God - thou hast not brot unto Him the sacrifice asked of thee - of frail man - which walketh in darkness ---

I say: Behold before thee - the Light - for It lighteth thine way - It maketh strait the Way of The Lord and It hath all power - both in Heaven and Earth -- It revealeth unto thee all mystery - It revealeth unto thee all things - both seen and unseen -- It bringeth thee out of darkness. It beareth thee up - and It sitteth thee on the right hand of God The Father - and It giveth unto thee the right to call thineself a Son of God and It giveth unto thee the Royal Raiment-- And the force of the mighty waters shall roll over thee - and ye shall stand and bear up - and ye shall know thineself to be a Son of God - ye shall know as a Son -- All mystery shall be revealed - and nothing shall be hidden - for it is given unto Me to know - for I Am The Worthy Grand Master in the Inner Temple---

The Price Required

While it is now come that I have declared unto thee these things - it behooves thee to hear that which I say - for I am not afar off - in some remote corner -- I am not of the dead -- I Am He which is Sent of Mine Father - like unto Mine beloved Brother Sananda -- I come as He - with Power and Authority - for indeed We are One - We are not divided -- And for that matter We are One with The One - The Father - which hast sent Us ---

He hast sent Us - that there be Light - and We come at His command. He hast said: Let there BE Light - and We are come that there BE Light -- Let It be as He hast commanded ---

For this is Mine part - this is Mine Word - and WORD shall be as the WORD - It shall endure - and It shall lose none of Its Power - It shall not return unto Me void - for It hast gone out of Mine mouth as It hast gone out Mine Father's in the beginning ---

While He hast endowed unto ME the Power of the WORD - HE hast given unto thee power to receive it ---

He hast given unto thee the ears to hear - and He hast brot thee forth as a living soul - and placed thine feet upon terra-firma - and blest thee with great and good gifts -- What hast thou given in return -- What hast thou offered unto Him - what hast thou asked of Him for the good of all -- What hast thou brot unto Him as thine tribute -- Oh ye faithless - slothful servants - Oh ye laggards; hast thou been so dull as to offer up unto Him the lesser gifts - the things which thou hast found worthless that thou hast been given of the ones of like kind -- These are but trappings - and they are not of any value unto Him - for <u>all</u> things are His - and He is not of a mind to accept the lesser gifts -- He hast asked of thee: "Bring unto ME thine HEART - thine SELF - for I am the Giver of all good and precious gifts -- Give unto ME that which is Mine and I shall give unto thee that which is thine"-- So be it the Light which is His shall light the way before thee -- Hear ye that which I say unto thee and ye shall be blest to hear -- For this do I say hear ye Me ---

So be it I Am come that

Ye be blest -

Hallowed is the Ground

Hallowed is the ground upon which ye stand -- Hallowed is the path thine feet follow - for it is said unto thee that the Lord God hast passed this way - it is so - and He hast gone the way before thee -- Now He but bids thee follow in His footsteps - for He knows the way - and He hast pointed out the pitfalls -- He hast said unto thee: Thou art within thine right to give unto Him credit for knowing the way - for hast He misled thee? Ne'er hast He misguided thee.

I say unto thee - nay and nay - for He hast come that ye be lifted up and I say He is prepared to give unto thee as He hast received - and He hast received His inheritance in full ---

Be ye as one which shall receive of Him - as He hast received of The Father which hast Sent Him --

For this hast He come ---

I come that I might bear witness of Him - I come that ye might be given thine inheritance in full -- Hast thou reckoned the value of it -- Hast thou calculated thine inheritance in full -- Is there one amongst thee that can comprehend the fullness of his inheritance? ---

I say: No man walking in flesh - as flesh - knoweth the untold measure of such inheritance - for man hast not seen - neither hast he dreamed the likeness thereof - for he hast not the capacity to comprehend ---

Therefore I say unto thee - be ye as one about thine preparation - yet ye shall not give unto thineself the bitter cup - conjure not the portion which would be unto thee a pitfall -- Conjure not the part which poisons thine own cup - for it is said - thou shall drink of it - and let it be sweet in thine belly-- Wast it not said that one would be sent to give unto thee as thou art prepared to receive - so shall it be-- Let it be well with thee - and fortune unto thineself the greater part ---

Such is Mine Word unto thee this day --

The New Government

Harken all ye which have eyes to see - all which have ears to hear - for this day hast there been one sent into thine midst - for to do a great and mighty work - which shall profit thee ---

That work shall be a new work - and it shall bring about the new government of the world - for the government of men's affairs -- The government of men shall be unlike that of their affairs -- For man shall learn obedience unto the first law - then they shall set up laws by which they shall govern their affairs---

Then they shall be ethical in their dealings one with the other -- They shall know that which is the "First law" then they shall deal justly with each other in all their affairs ---

This then - shall bring about a new government - which shall be set up and it shall be for the most part directed thru and by - the one of which I have spoken ---

He shall move silently - and fortunately <u>unknown</u> by the populace for long hast the populace been hostile unto the One Sent of God ---

It is long that He - hast awaited this time - when He might find the few which is prepared to receive Him - for He knows well that the populace is unprepared for His coming ---

He knows well - that He is not alone - that He hast the assistance of the Great and Mighty Council - that We of the Council are with Him - that We are at His command - for He is Ours - He is with Us - of Us - and One with Us - We forsake not our own ---

Let it be said that - "One with God is a majority" in thine world is it not so! ---

I tell them of a surety - that one man which is Sent is a majority - for it shall come to pass that He shall bring about greater changes for greater good for the many - in less time than all the wayward populace in darkness -- So be it I know of which I speak---

Now ye need not speculate upon him - his identity - his whereabouts for I say unto thee - he shall not reveal himself unto the traitors - for his mission shall be finished - and he shall return even as he went - and no blood shall stain his pure garments which are spotless -- So be it I have spoken of one which is in thine midst this day - and his work shall be as none of thee is capable of accomplishing - for thou hast not prepared thineself -- Few - are capable of receiving him - or of him ---

He hast given no sign of his coming - for he hast come as a thief in the nite -- He hast come to find thee eating and drinking - sleeping and given unto riotous living -- Thou art dancing unto the fiddlers tune - while He is about The Father's business ---

Now I say unto thee thou faithless ones: Dance on! Dance on! - for thine hour hast come -- Thine hour hast come when ye shall prove thineself - on this very day -- Ye shall accuse Me of being amongst the gods of the pores - the gods of the ancients - the idols - the necromancers - the spirits of the dead -- Yet - I say unto thee - thou art not qualified to name ME - for Mine Father hast sent ME with power and authority - to give unto them which are prepared to receive Me and of Me - and I say unto thee: It matters not that ye be one of them - for I shall do Mine Work - nevertheless it behooves thee to ponder well this - which I have given for the good of all -- So let it be as ye will it - for none shall give unto thee more than thou canst bear - it is said - We forch not upon thee - ye shall awaken in due season - So let it be ---

I AM

Sanat Kumara

He Hast Been Robbed

Fortune unto thineself the Gift which is Willed unto thee from the beginning -- Ye shall accept it in the Name of The Father - Son and Holy Ghost -- Now I ask of thee: Knowest thou The Father - The Son, The "Holy Ghost"-- Wherein hast thou Known These - Yet are They not ONE-- I ask of thee: Knowest The Father - Knowest The Son - Know ye The Holy Ghost ---

I say unto thee: The Holy "Ghost" - is The Mighty Council -- For hast it ever been - and this Name hast long been given unto the body of The Council - the Body which IS - The Council -- And it is thru this Council that the Spirit of God Worketh with man - the <u>Host</u> which hast been called "Ghost" -- While it is so little understood by man - and because of his dogmas - he hast not been given great revelation - he hast given unto man power to take from him his birthright -- Yet I say he shall come to know that he hast been robbed - his "Pockets picked" and he is left impoverished in a desert land ---

Yet it is said: There are greener pastures thou knowest not of -- Let it be for thine own sake that I bid thee come forth - as one fearless and obedient - unto the call - it shall be unto thee great strength - and ye shall be glad ---

Let it be said that the Great and Mighty Council shall pour out upon thee Great Light and revelation -- So be it ye shall come to know the true from the false-- I say - ye shall prepare thineself for the greater part, so be it the law --

Let it suffice that ye receive as thou hast prepared thineself to receive -- Yet it is given unto Me to say unto thee - there is One amongst thee - that shall find them which are prepared to receive the greater part. So be it that I know Him - and that which it is about -- Therefore it behooves Me to say unto thee: Blest are they which seek Him out - yet ye need go not to the sea - the mountain - neither to the plains - for He shall find thee by thine light --

So let it shine forth that all might see it - and be drawn unto it ---

The Word Sayeth:--
Mighty is the Word and Great the Power Thereof ---

Let it be recorded this day - that which The Word sayeth - for the WORD hast proceeded out the mouth of God - and become manifest in the first magnitude -- It is pure in Its Essence - the Essence which is the first magnitude - uncontaminated -- It is The Power of God – unstilled, unchanged - uncontaminated ---

So be it that The WORD sayeth: Be ye still and know that I AM - that I AM - and that thou art - and from the same Breath have we come into being - from the same Source - from the same Power -

Therefore we are One in essence - there is no difference in essence While it is given unto Me to be of the greater power - the greater light, greater knowledge - for I am nearer unto the Throne of God - I say unto thee: Thou hast proceeded from out the Throne of God - thou hast gone forth as one made manifest thru and by the spoken Word -- Thou hast become a living soul - and thou hast been given individuality thru and by the WORD -- Hear ye that which I say unto thee - and ye shall be glad - for unto them which hear shall be given in greater measure.

It is given unto thee to be walking - step at a time - and as thine stride expands - so shall thine power increase - thine power of comprehension - so let it be ---

For the child shall grow into maturity - ere he receives a man's wage so shall his strength suffice the labor given -- The labor to be done shall be as his strength is equal -- So be it that he shall be given in compensation unto his ability -- I say - unto his preparation he shall receive -- So be it that his ability is apparent unto Us - therefore he is given no more than he can bear -- So be it I am speaking unto them which have heard that which I say - yet it is the law - applicable unto all ---

For this is the law - and all come under it ---

Book #2 of The Kumaras

Beloved of Mine being -- I have given unto thee the part which is for them which art want to hear – It is for them - and in no wise is it to be forched upon the willful ones - which would but spit upon them -- Forch not upon them one word - for it is the way of the unknowing ones and it is said they shall ask - they shall be as ones free to ask - yet they which ask not - in no wise shall be given -- For as they are prepared - so shall <u>they</u> receive -- When they are prepared they shall find - for they which seek the Light - It shall not be hidden from them - so be it the law ---

While it is given unto thee to be Mine hand made manifest unto them for these parts - it shall be accounted unto thee - and ye shall profit thereby for not one servant shall go unaccounted for -- Now it is said - that ye shall begin the Second part of this - Book of the KUMARAS -- Let this be as book No. 1 - and the following shall be No. 2 -- So be it it shall be in greater numbers - or greater volume - so let it continue from hence as the Book of The Kumaras -- Such is Mine Word this day.

The Plowman Hast Come

Let this word go forth unto all men this day - and it shall fall upon fertile soil and take root - for the soil is now fertile - and the water is prepared. The plowman hast come in their season - the sowers in their season -- Now I say the ground is prepared - the season come - and a mighty onrush of the Waters shall come forth - and the seeds shall take root and flourish for a season - <u>some</u> shall wither and die - some shall endure and these shall yield up a mighty harvest -- For the time is short - liken unto an hour of "The Day" and it shall be given unto thee to be part of this day - part of the sowing - part of the reaping -- Let not thine roots perish - for I say unto thee - thine roots shall be deeply planted in the soil which shall be watered from on high -- Let them take nourishment then - and flourish - and bring forth great harvest - and it shall profit thee ---

For all men shall be lifted up in due season - and he which hast not prepared himself this day - shall await his time - for there is a season unto each and every one - and he shall not be forgotten -- Yet sad is he that sleepeth - for he hast not as yet heard the Word - so be it he shall - in the day allotted unto such things -- So be it that his awakening shall be rude and harsh - for he hast slept while the Sun shines -- Now the call hast gone out: Awaken! and the fields call forth - and the season approaches - and the Sun shineth forth in His glory - and the workers are found eating and drinking - the sleepers sleeping - the laggards dancing the piper's tune - and heeding not the call - shirking all responsibility - making a mockery of Mine Words - and bringing forth great chaos from out the greater chaos --

So be it they are unaware of their responsibility - they assume not their responsibility - therefore they shall be cut off -- They shall not share in the harvest of the workers -- It is now come when the workers shall be brot forth in great number - and they shall sing forth the song of praise -- Their labor shall be the labor of love - their burdens shall be light - and they shall be made to rejoice - for they shall know wherein they labor - they shall know the fruits of their labor - and they shall be glad -- So be it I have said it - and it is so - for I Am the One Sent that this day bear fruit - it shall bear fruit of a new kind - and the father shall know his child - and the mother shall suckle her babe ---

So be it and Selah -

I AM

Blessings Too Numerous to Number

Be ye as one responsible for each word - each deed - and at no time shall ye give unto thineself the bitter cup - for it is given unto thee to drink of thine own cup -- Prepare not the bitter cup for another - for surely ye shall drink of it --

Let it be sweet and ye shall drink of it with gladness and joy ---

Hast it not been given of the Host that which satisfies - and that which sustains thee -- By the hand of God hast thou been fed - by His hand hast thou been led out -- And it is given unto thee to be as ones unmindful of thine many gifts - and thine many blessings -- So be it that all thine blessings canst not be numbered - wherein is it said: Ye shall number them by tens and ten times ten - for they shall multiply - and they shall be too numerous to count – for I say unto thee - thou shall be given in greater measure - and no man can measure the gifts which shall be bestowed upon thee - for it is said the treasury shall be opened up unto thee ---

I speak unto them which serve the Lord thy God - for He hast said that His servants shall be exalted over all the Kings of the Earth - for they shall inherit the Kingdom of God -- So shall it Be ---

Blest are they which inherit the Kingdom - for they shall abide in the house of the Lord forever ---So shall it be -Amen - and Selah -

Many Sent to Assist

It is said and truly so - that there are many which would trip thee up - and it is given unto Me to know them and wherein they are -- Yet it is said that they which seek the Light shall find - and the Light shall not be hidden from them - while they shall first seek the Light - and all things shall be added unto them ---

Be it so that there are many sent to give assistance unto them which seek - yet the One Sent shall ask nought save obedience unto the law - and He shall not trespass upon their will -- He shall hold out a hand - and He shall give unto them as they are prepared to receive - and for them many gifts are prepared -- Yet it shall be their part - to prepare themself for to receive the priceless gifts which are prepared -- So be it these gifts are bestowed upon the just and righteous - and none shall be given out of season - for each in his own time -- The time of preparation is now - the time of receival follows the preparation - so be it and Selah.

Honor the WORD - praise the Name of The Father Solen Aum Solen - unto Him all the Glory - and the Honor -- Unto Him all power, unto Him all thanksgiving - all praise ---

Let it be recorded for all time to come - that when he gives unto The Father his Heart - his hand - his will - he hast made a covenant with Him The Father - and it is said that there are none so sad - as them which betray their trust - themself - for it is come when each and every man shall stand naked before the Throne of The Most High Living God and account for himself -- And no man shall be unto him his porter - for he shall stand as his own witness - he shall stand face to face with himself - and he shall not deceive himself - he shall be his own judge - he shall be his own liberator - and he shall see himself as he is -- So be it that each and every one shall account for himself -- So be it I know - for I see from afar - and I know - for it is given unto Me to be within the place wherein all things are known -- So be it I am One with The Father Which hast empowered Me to speak unto thee thusly: - "Holy - Holy - is The WORD"

So be it and Selah --

OPEN UP THINE HEART

For this part - let it be written - that all might bear witness of this Mine Word - for it is given that they might know that which I say unto thee. It shall be recorded - that it go within the records - and none shall add to or take away - from or to this portion -- It shall be exactly as I speak it - and there shall be no errors therein ---

By Mine own hand have I given unto thee Mine blessing - I have established such communication with thee as is necessary -- I have given unto thee in great volume - yet it is not finished - neither have I closed Mine mouth - for I shall speak aplenty this day -- When the time comes that they hear that which I say - I shall give unto them in great measure -- Yet unto them which close Me out - it is given unto them to close the door upon themself - for it is said: "Open up thine heart that I might come in" - and I shall give unto thee that which thou art prepared to receive - It is so ---

Now for the time at hand: - This shall be the beginning of a great and wondrous Work - a Work which supersedes that which hast gone before - and it shall be equal into the book of the Herald of Light - for it shall herald the coming of the Light - and it shall be the forerunner of a greater Work which shall come forth from this Source - and thru this Source ---

It is prepared and it rests - and it shall go forth in the time which is near - and it shall be finished in a time which is appropriate - and in no wise shall it be interrupted - for it is of great necessity - and of great import -- So be it that ye shall stand at attention - and ye shall know the call - and at the call ye shall hasten to gather up thine pen - and record that which I say unto thee -- Let it be a service rendered for the good of all ---

So be it I shall speak unto thee on the morrow--

All Mystery Shall Be Clarified

By the Word shall it be made known that which shall be -- For the Word shall declare the forecoming events - and time shall be in its season - and the first shall be last - and the last shall be first -- So be it that all mystery shall be clarified - and that which hast been a mystery - shall no longer be a mystery ---

Before the coming of Great events - there is always One sent to proclaim the event -- Yet likewise another comes - and he proclaims another - therefore the mystery -- For as the false one would confuse - tear down - he mimics the real - and he gives of himself unto the confusion - that they be confused ---

Let us make clear the Word - for this is the time of clarification -- There hast been much confusion in the world of men - concerning the coming events - and it behooves Me - to say unto thee - the confusion is not within the Great and Grand Plan - it is within man's minds - for they are divided against themself - they are filled with fear and misgiving - they are prone to doubt and anxiety - they are not stable -- They run after signs and wonders - they are born of anxiety - and fear. Now let it be said - that they which have asked for Light shall be at peace - and peace shall first be established within them - and they shall turn from the world - seeking no more the way of man - and they shall devote themself whole-heartedly unto the Light - they shall follow It - and be led out of bondage ---

For this do I now speak unto thee - that they might be led aright - for many have followed the will-o'-the-wisp - the dreamers - and the fortunes of men which are in bondage -- They fear the Light - while bowing down before the idols which hold them bound ---

Now this day - be it such as they can comprehend - and say unto them in Mine Name - that they shall arise! No longer shall they crawl upon their bellies before their idols - they have but to stand upright - walk upright - and see the Light -- For it is now come when many shall expound great theories - and with great - lengthy and flowery sermons declare unto thee their wisdom - yet shall they tell thee thine destiny - thine end? Wherein hast they been schooled that they have become so wise - think ye that there is one amongst thee that knows thine destiny?

Wherein is he - wherein is the prophet which knows what ye shall do - for hast thou not free will - hast thou not been given the greatest gift of man - hast thou not been given in greater measure - and knowest ye the fullness of thine gift - for it is said: "Ye know not that which ye shall become" - it is true - for thou knowest not ---

While it is said - offer not thine gifts unto idols - and give not unto them which doth make a mockery of The WORD - it is said: They know not the results of their mockery - for they are bound by the dragon -- They seek in the dark - they have as yet - not known the first law - that of obedience - that of love -- And the way of the Initiate is both Love - and obedience - for the LOVE of God The Father makes of them obedient servants - they question Him not ---

Yet they - follow blindly the dragon - questioning not his motives - for they are want to measure his motives by their own measure -- They ask for bread - he gives unto them a stone - and they are wont to believe it bread - while they are impoverished - and sad indeed are they. They are not mindful of all the gifts which hast been bestowed upon them by The Father which hast given unto them life ---

Let it be said - they shall be mindful of their gifts - and they shall rejoice for them - for HE hast given unto them in great love and mercy.

So be it and Selah --

Last Rites

Hold ye the light that they might see their way - for it is given unto them to stumble in the dark - wherein they find no light -- The light shineth forth - yet the darkness comprehends not the light ---

Wherein is it said - that great Light shall come forth - which shall consume the darkness - it is so -- So shall it be - and man shall behold it - and he shall be as one illumined - and he shall go forth as one which hast been made new -- At no time shall man be destroyed without a hearing - for he shall be given that which he is capable of receiving -- And when he is no longer capable of receiving - he shall be given the last rite - and it shall be as tho he had never been - he shall go out into the outer darkness and be no more -- For it is every man's right to return unto his rightful estate - and for that hast the Word gone forth: "Come Home - Come Home" ---

Let the word go forth in all its power - all the magnitude - and let them which are prepared - be brot in - such is the chosen - they are prepared -- So let it be -- For this have We of the Mighty Council spoken out - that they be prepared ---

Now a great and mighty Light shall arise amongst thee - and it shall shine forth brighter than the noon day Sun - and it shall be beyond mortal eye to behold it - for it shall be as no man hast beheld with mortal eye - and It shall set aside all law of Earth - It shall nullify the law of Earth - and the Sun shall give forth no light in comparison - for It shall outshine the noon day Sun -- It shall be the One which hast stood above all -- And it shall be given unto them which endure the Light - to be caught up in It - and they shall no more be seen of man - for man could not behold the Light which they are within -- For they shall be caught up within the Light - and they shall no more return unto their dwelling places - for no more shall they be bound in darkness ---

Let it be said - that they which are prepared - shall be caught up with the Light - which mortal eye cannot see - for eye could not look upon such Glory -- It is given unto Me to know such Glory - for I am in the midst of The Glory of The Lord - and I am come that ye might know as I know ---

Such is Mine Word unto thee this day -- Accept it and be glad --

Light - The Source of Man's Existence!

Light is Light - and Its power shall be unto all men their existence for without the Light they would not exist ---

While it is said that they are in darkness - it is because of their own unknowing - for the darkness knows not the Light -- While The Light knows the darkness and the cause thereof - the cause being man's willfulness and man's sores -- Man hast brot upon himself all his woes and sorrow - for his disobedience unto the law ---

While the law is given unto him - and he walks not accordingly - it is but his own willfulness which brings about his sores - his tribulations.

Heed ye then the law - and walk ye in the Light - and no more shall ye be bound in darkness ---

Think ye that thou hast known the fullness of thine inheritance - think ye that thou hast known the depth of sorrow - think ye that thou knowest the density of outer darkness? ---

Nay - man of Earth - thou hast not known the intensity of the Light in Its first magnitude - neither the density of the darkness - which shall be the lot of them which are cast out ---

For there are ones which shall be cast into outer darkness and these shall wait - These shall wait - and sad shall be their lot ---

It is given unto them which know - to give unto thee the word - the law - a helping hand -- Why dost thou turn from them which would give unto thee of the Living Water - so be it I am come that ye be brot out of bondage ---

O man - think ye - thou art not in bondage --

Think ye thou art free --

Think ye that thou art wise --

Think ye that thou diest in thine wisdom - that thine learning is sufficient unto thine salvation - that thine light is sufficient - that thine works - yea - even unto thine "Good Works" - it is not so - for thou hast found thine reward in thine boasting - and in thine own echo - of thine boastings ---

Now thine laurels shall fade away - thine garments of luster shall tarnish - and fall as rags about thee - and ye shall stand shorn of all thine vain glory - and ye shall see thineself as thou art - for there shall be no secret closet within thine house - wherein thou canst hide thine nakedness ---

I say - ye shall stand naked - and ye shall see thineself as thou art - O man - will thou not see that which thou hast done - thou shall see – indeed thou shall behold all thine deeds - and ye shall father thine children - and I say unto thee thine children shall lie in thine bed to torment thee ---

Arise! Upward! and onward forever - and let not thine feet hold thee earth-bound -- Cut away thine legirons - and pick up thine feet - let them be swift to come - let them be light as wings of light - for they shall be light - when thou hast forsaken thine own way - and asked the Father God - Solen Aum Solen for the Light -- He - shall send a host unto thee that ye be loosed - He shall send unto thee A Mighty Host Which shall bear thee up in the day of thine afflictions --

So be it I have spoken - unto them which have ears let them hear - So let it be --

Mystery of the First Mystery

Let it be said - that he which shall receive of ME - hast received the Mystery of the first Mystery - therefore I say unto thee - prepare thineself to receive ME and of ME - for I give unto thee as thou art prepared to receive ---

I say - behold the WORD - let It be ever before thee - and It shall be unto thee thine Shibboleth - and it shall be thine Shield -- And the Light shall be unto thee thine light - and ye shall walk therein knowingly - and ye shall not fall -- So be it I am come that ye be prepared for that which I hold within Mine hand - and no man shall take by force - that which I hold within Mine hand - for I yield not unto them Mine power - Mine part -- Mine gifts are numerous - and priceless. I say - ye know not that which I have for thee - for thou couldst not envision that which I hold for thee ---

Yet when thou hast come of the age of accountability - thou shall claim all that The Father hast endowed unto thee - then ye shall stand before Him as a Son - ye shall stand as in shining armor - for ye shall wear the Royal Robe - and the SORE shall be no more - and all thine sins shall be blotted out and remembered no more - So be it and Selah.

I say ye shall become of age - the age of accountability - then ye shall know thine gifts to be priceless - and ye shall number them one by one - and ye shall hold high thine head - and wear thine Crown with dignity -- Ye shall wear the Crown and it shall be unto them a sign that thou hast been born of the Light - that thou hast received thine Sonship.

Sufficiently Warned

Hath thou not been sufficiently warned - that ye might be spared greater suffering and misery - hast thou not to been given the law whereby ye might be prepared ---

It is now come when great changes shall take place - and ye shall be part of the changes - let it be for the better -- For thine own sake have We of the Mighty Council said many things designed to awaken thee ---

Yet the sleepers sleep!

Wherein is it said: The hour draws nigh - when ye shall go out of thine dwelling place - to return no more.

Wherein is it said: that two shall be at the well - one shall be taken, one left ---

Wherein is it said: that - ye shall no more spin - ye shall no more give unto thineself the Bread of thy labors - wherein is it said - thine time is come - and I ask of thee - thinkest thou - thou art above the law?

The law is explicit - and it is clearly stated - and presented unto thee that ye be prepared for the many changes ---

Hast it not been said - that there are none so sad as he which betrays himself - or - his trust ---

Too - it is said: As thou hast prepared thineself - so shall ye receive. Now when thou hast prepared thineself to receive the fullness of thine estate ye shall be given - and no man shall take from thee one iota of thine fortune – so be it - it is thine by Divine Inheritance - and unto thee I say: When thou hast grown unto the age of accountability - thou shall receive thine inheritance in full ---

Such is Mine Word - unto them which have ears to hear let them hear --

I Speak of Freedom

There are but few which have gone out of the body - prepared to walk the Royal Road - and for this do I say unto thee - great is the provision provided for them which shall yet go the Royal Road -- And these shall be the ones which shall take with them the body - which is of flesh -- Yet it shall be as purified Light Substance - it shall lose its density - and it shall be as a body of Light Substance - it shall be as the Light - and its substance shall be of Light Substance -- For it shall be changed in the twinkling of an eye - it shall need no resting place - for it shall have no need to rest - for it shall weary not.

I say it shall be as wings of light - it shall go - and come swiftly - it shall know no time space - neither distance - for time shall be no more. Distance shall be as nought - and it shall be unlimited. This therefore is freedom - freedom from bondage - therefore I speak of freedom - and that which shall be given unto few - yet it shall not be given unto all - for not all - are to go the same way -- Others shall go thru the gate of death - others shall depart unseen - unheard - and be no more seen of man - leaving behind them no tracks - no paper - no word - for their flight shall be as the eagle - and it shall be noiseless and without herald. I say others shall go out with great cries of agony upon their lips - and great shall be their suffering - yet their suffering shall be unto them their atonement - and their reward earned -- Their suffering shall be remembered no more - and great shall be their joy - for they shall return no more unto the world of darkness - wherein they shall have their memory blanked from them -- They shall be given a place in the Sun - and they shall sing glad anthems that it is finished -- Judge no man by his stature - for his stature is not measured by a rule - it is not given unto man to know the stature of another - for he wears the veil - as a shroud about him - covering his nakedness - yet I know him in his nakedness -- I say I knew him ere he took upon himself the veil/ the shroud -- For this do I say that he hast come into the world of darkness as the second death - and the second death shall be overcome - and it shall be as the first - for it shall be as the resurrection of the soul - It shall be reborn - and it shall become a Son of God.

And so shall it be - So be it – by the Grace of The Father

Solen Aum Solen

Amen

The Greater Limits

So be it that there is no time in the realm wherein I abide-- Let Us call it seasons and for that it hast been called "Time" - yet time as man calls it - exists not - for We of the Greater Vision - see that which hast been accomplished times ago - and know that which shall be done in "times" to come - so far as thou art concerned ---

Yet man being the ruler of his destiny - he hast free will - and it is given unto him power to exercise it - for it is HIS and no man - shall take it from him -- Yet he shall go so far and no farther - for he dare not pass his limits -- There is a limit - so far as he hast prepared himself - he shall go - and no farther - for his Guardian knows his limits - and he is held within that limit - for his own sake - until he is further prepared for yet greater limits --

Therefore, it is said: "Prepare thineself for the greater part" - and therein is wisdom ---

No man passes his limits unprepared - yet thru his willfulness - he bringeth upon himself his own limitations - his own boundaries -- For it is said: One stands ready to give unto him assistance in his ascent-- Hold ye fast unto the Light - and let not thine feet drag - lift them up - and do that which thou art given to do - and make ye haste - for it is said - the time is come when ye shall be called - and ye shall be glad for thine preparation - and at no time shall ye rebel against the law - for the law is given for thee - for thine own benefit -- For thine own sake hast it been given unto thee - and man's judgement - his opinions and pre-notions shall be as nought - for it shall not change the law one iota for the law of which I speak is unchangeable - it is not to be changed. Therefore let it be said - that the "Son of God" cometh not to change the law - rather that ye might understand the law -- Therefore We of the Mighty Council - counsel thee: Be ye alert - and obey the law - and ye shall be given as thou art prepared to receive -- So let it profit thee to heed - receive counsel of Us - of the Mighty Council - for We are alert unto thine every need - be ye also alert unto thine own needs - thine weakness - thine strength shall be multiplied - that ye overcome thine weakness - when thou hast asked Our assistance for the good of all --

Yet thine weakness lies within "Self" - it is for self that the weak asketh, these are want to see their weakness - while the strong and pure of heart ask for the fellowman - they ask for the good of all - therefore they are stronger -- They are given as they are prepared to receive - for they are of the Light - they know that they are one with their fellow man - therefore they limit not themself - they bring the Greater Gifts unto the Altar - they render up the self - they give of themself in sacrifice - they give the supreme sacrifice - God's Gift unto them --- This he shall use as He Wills - for the good of ALL -- And that gift they shall be multiplied ten thousand times ten thousand times! And it shall serve as their own award - their crowning Glory - for The Father shall make of it their Royal Robe -- This is their reward for the sacrifice of self will - the gift which HE can use to fashion Greater Mansions of The Kingdom of God ---

I Shall Prove Mineself

Be ye as the mouth of Me - and speak forth the words which I shall put into thine mouth - and it shall be unto thee great strength - for this have I prepared thee ---

I say unto thee - thou shall speak the words which I shall put into thine mouth - and it shall profit thee -- For as thou hast proven thineself I shall make of thee Mine mouth made manifest in flesh - for I say unto thee - I am in need of thee -- For I see them crying out - and they are but babes - they are weak - and weary -- They as yet have not grown in strength - that they might stand on their own feet ---

Yet I say unto thee Mine Beloved - they shall not ride thine back - for they shall grow strong - and become of age - and they shall walk upon their own feet ---

Let it be said that none shall put words into Mine mouth - none shall proclaim falsely - to be Mine "Mouth piece" - for I shall spew them out.

I have given unto thee the WORD - and the power - and the Authority - that thou hast earned by thine sacrifice and obedience unto the command ---

Now let it be recorded that which I say unto thee - that they bear witness of Mine Words - then I shall prove Mineself ---

Now it is said: I shall put Mine Words into thine mouth - it is so - yet no man shall come seeking of thee favors - for I say - I shall not permit this - for I shall give not unto them which seeks for self -- I shall not satisfy their curiosity -- I shall put Mine Words into thine mouth as it pleases Me - and not to satisfy them -- Neither shall I give unto them comfort - neither shall I pity them - yet I shall deal justly with them - and have mercy upon them - for I say unto thee - it is now come when I shall demand of thee greater things - greater devotion - Greater Strength - Greater Stature ---

And greater shall be thine strength - and thine reward - for as thine strength is spent - so shall it be renewed - and let it be -- For this do I say unto thee - pick up thine pen - and let us begin the greater part -- Let it be said that this is but the beginning - so be it I know - and I say unto thee - it is but the beginning ---

Mine Hand Shall be Strong and Sturdy

By Mine hand shall this Word be written - for I shall direct the hand and I shall speak aloud the Word - and it shall be heard - and there shall be no errors herein - for Mine hand shall be firm and sturdy ---

Therefore I say - none shall say it is not so - neither shall they deny Mine Authority - for I shall offer unto them no signs of Mine Authority. the WORD shall be Its own authority ---

Let It go forth this day - as the WORD - and It shall hit Its mark - It shall find Its mark ---

There are many which are prepared to receive It - and therein they shall find strength - they shall find great Light - and thereby they shall be strengthened -- So be it that they shall come into great learning - for the WORD shall expand Itself - and multiply - It shall be unto them both food and drink ---

So be it - I say unto them: There are none so sad as them which blaspheme against The WORD - The Power of God - Which hast sent forth The WORD ---

I say - they are the ones which betray themself and their trust - for "THE WORD" is given unto them - that they might profit thereby - yet when they blaspheme against - and defile It - they but betray themselves, therefore they come under condemnation ---

There is put before them the Word - The Law - and when they do give it unto the dogs - they have denied themself the reward thereof ---

I say unto them: Blaspheme not against The Word - hold It sacred, defile It not - bind not thine own hands -- Yet ye shall apply the Law unto thine own self - and when thou hast become efficient in the law - then ye shall be prepared to say unto thine fellow man: "It is Good! for I have tasted thereof" - then ye shall be as one prepared to say unto them: "I see - I hear - I know" - and then ye shall be as one prepared to go forth and give unto them the Glad Tidings: "HE is Come - The King of Kings - HE IS COME! THE LORD OF LORDS - THE HOST OF HOSTS" ---

For then ye shall be as one appointed - as one called out - as one brot out - and ye shall then speak with Authority - for ye shall be touched -- Ye shall be as one ordained - and thereby given the power and authority - to speak for the Order of Melchezedek - and it is given unto ME to be the Host of the many members of that Order - for I am the one known as the Most Worthy Grand Master of the Inner Temple and I preside over the lesser Orders of the Temple -- I am sent from out the Inner Temple - that this might be accomplished-- Yet I give not unto the profane - the "Secret Password" I pass it in unto them which prove themself worthy ---

Wherein hast thou proven thineself worthy to receive the "Key" of the Mysteries -- Yet it is said - that all Mysteries shall be revealed unto them which prove themself worthy - it is so - so let them prove themselves.

For this is this word given unto thee for them ---

Forch not the WORD upon them - let them come of their own will and partake as they are prepared - for the babe shall have his "Bit" - his "Bottle" - while the older - stronger ones - shall come unto the banquet table - and dine sumptuously and be satisfied -- Therefore I say - let them find their way - let them have - as they are prepared to receive.

So be it there are many which are hungry - yet they know not where the table sitteth - they look afar - hither and yon in their confusion - they are as unstable - they waver between the dark and the light - they run up and down - saying their rigamaroles as puppets - knowing not that they are the puppets - for they are the pawns of a society - corrupt unto its core ---

It is said: Come ye out and be ye separate - dare ye put on the Armor of God - and dare ye be as one separate from them! for I say - they are as the traitors - they are the whoremongers - they are the thieves and robbers - they are the purveyors of lies - they are the infidels - they are the poor in spirit ---

And they are the cast outs -- Be ye as one which can stand alone - and declare thine own freedom -- Be ye as one which hast heard the call - and answered it - for this hast it gone forth this day -- Arise! Alert thineself - prepare thineself for the Greater Part --

Amen and Selah -

He is the...

For this part let it be given unto them that they might know that which I say unto thee -- There is but One Lord God - which is The King of Kings - and The Host of Hosts -- He is The One Sent - Over All - and above all - for He is the One "Mighty and Strong"-- He is the one which hast given the law unto Moses - in the beginning - He is the One which spoke unto the Children of Israel - He is the One which hast fashioned the Temple of the Inner Sanctuary -- He is the One which heads the "Mighty Council" -- He is the One which is Head of the Order of Melchezedek ---

For He is the First Born - and therefore He is First Begotten of The Father ---

None other hast that station -- This makes of Him the First in line of His Father's Children - of His Father's offspring - and this makes of Him the Son of God -- For that hast He first received His Inheritance in full -- For this hast He first come forth from out The Father - from Him hast He gone out first - as a Son - as the First Born hast He gone forth ---

Now it cometh the time when there shall go forth again - the same Son of God The Father - as a Mighty and Powerful Power - as a Great Light - and IT shall cut away the darkness -- It shall be unto the forces of the darkness - their banishment -- For the forces of darkness shall no longer bind and torment a people which seek the Light ---

And I say unto thee this day: I see them crying out for the Light ---

Be ye not deceived - they are weary of their lot - and these shall be unbound - yet I say unto them: Weary not of thine search - for it shall end - and thine reward shall indeed be thine liberation -- Thine time shall come - and ye shall be glad for thine search - weary not ---

Yet ye shall tire not - for thine waiting shall be according unto the law - and no man - shall hasten the day of thine unbinding - neither shall he add unto-- Thine days shall end - and the Word shall be fulfilled-- As I have spoken - so shall it be - for I know whereof I speak.

Let thine waiting end in thine Victory - then ye shall hear the glad cry: Hail! Hail unto the Victor - for thine waiting hast ended in Victory!

The Victor

Hail! Hail! Unto the Victor!

For he cometh forth as one which has overcome - he cometh forth as one arrayed in Light -- He raiseth on wings of Light - he bears the authority of his own Name -- His number is written upon his garment - his authority is within the Word of his mouth - for he hast the authority within his mouth -- He hast the rod within his hand to give and to receive -- He hast the reign over the world - he hast learned that which hast been said unto him - he hast overcome ---

He hast become one with the Light which hast become his Vesture. He hast control over the elements - for he hast become ONE with The Light -- He hast won his freedom thru and by his application of the law. He hast at last been delivered out of bondage - for he hast overcome his bonds ---

He hast sought his freedom thru application of the law - he hast sought his freedom in the Light - he hast asked of the Light - and he hast received of the Light ---

So be it he cometh forth as one on wings of Light - that he might receive his eternal Sonship - that he might be numbered with The Host. So shall he be - for he hast prepared himself that he might be numbered amongst them ---

He hast been unto himself true -- He hast been faithful in all commands -- He hast fulfilled his covenant - and He hast been as a faithful and true servant of the Light ---

He hast given of himself that he be prepared - he hast given of himself in selfless service - asking nought for self - yet he hast been as one rewarded for his efforts that others be lifted up ---

He now stands as one arrayed in garments of Light - brighter than the noon day Sun - Such is his Light - such is his Garment -- He wraps himself about within the Light and becomes One with IT ---

Such is the one which returns this day - such is his reward for service rendered unto the Light -- Faithful in his time - faithful in his word - faithful in his bearing - and rewarded in his righteousness ---

So shall it be - so shall it ever be - be it so -

So shall it EVER BE -

As a Mighty Beacon

Be ye as one which hast Mine hand upon thee - and I shall bless thee. With Mine own hand shall I bless thee - and ye shall bring forth the Light which I give unto thee -- For I shall send forth a Light which shall shine forth as a Mighty Beacon - and It shall be seen from afar - and they shall see it -- Some shall fear - and return unto thee no more - some shall be drawn unto it - and they shall abide in the Light - and they shall be glad ---

It is said - that there shall be One Sent - and it is so - and that One shall do a Mighty Work - and He shall be as One prepared - for He hast had the Mystery which no man hast performed before Him -- He hast the power to perform that Mystery - and it shall be done in the Name of The Most High Living God - and it shall neither be spoken or written for it shall be for the Just alone - and that fortune belongs unto One alone - and He is the one to come ---

Harken unto Mine Words: He is the One to come - for He shall come unto thee - and HIS coming shall be as none other ---

Such is Mine Word unto thee Mine Beloved ---

Yet <u>they</u> shall bear witness of this Mine testimony unto thee ---

So be it I AM Sanat Kumara -

True Freedom

Be ye, as one lifted up - for by Mine own hand shall I lift thee -- And it is given unto Me to be the Most Worthy Grand Master of the Inner Temple - and I am prepared to give unto thee that which I have kept for thee - and I shall withhold nought ---

Blest are they which are lifted up --

Blest are they which receive of the greater part --

Blest are they which walk knowingly - for they are free to go and come - they are unbound -- No longer are they bound unto the Earth no longer do they come under Earth's laws, they are unbound - free - free to go and come - free to go into any region - any kingdom - any place. And they are not bound by place - time - space - neither the lack of power - and authority - for they have the power - and the authority -

So be it and Selah ---

Now ye shall give unto them this Word: When one hast completed his mission - his time is fulfilled - he hast obeyed the law - and surrendered up his Will unto The Father - The Giver of ALL GOOD GIFTS -- He then hast qualified himself for his inheritance - and he hast been the inheritor of The Kingdom - which he - Son of God – receives. He hast fully prepared himself - by and thru the Grace of The Father.

For The Father hast sent a Son - that he might know the way - and it is clearly stated that He Is the Way - and He is the Wayshower - and none enter save thru Him ---

So be it that there shall be a great onrush of Waters - and the Spirit shall be poured out upon thee - and ye shall bring forth great Light - and ye shall be unto them Mine hand and Mine Voice - for I shall speak the Word - and ye shall hear it and record it - for them which shall be as ones prepared to receive it - so be it - and Selah ---

Hold thineself in readiness - and I shall speak unto thee - and ye shall be acceptable unto Me -- So let it be as The Father hast Willed it.

Hast Thou - ?

Let the word go forth this day - as it is written -- And as they are prepared - so shall they receive - and each in his own tongue ---

I say unto them: The time of consideration is come -- Consider well from whence cometh thine strength - thine benefits - all thine blessings.

Think ye that ye are sufficient unto thineself?

Think ye that ye could sustain thineself - should the hand of God be stayed?

Think ye that thou couldst find comfort in thine own accomplishments?

Think ye that thou couldst maintain thineself - should the Sun fail to give unto thee light? - should the rain not fall?

Think ye well of thine blessings - what consideration hast thou given?

What thot hast thou taken of thine Benefactors?

Hast thou been reminded of them this day?

Hast thou taken thine ease - without thot of them which have no ease - hast thou forgotten the sick and the dying?

Hast thou administered unto one of these?

Hast thou given thot of the ones imprisoned for Mine sake?

Hast thou given thot for the ones which hast given themself in Holy Sacrifice - hast thou given thot of them which hast gone the last mile for thee - for thine sake - hast thou given unto them thot this day? - I ask of thee? ---

Be ye aware of thine Benefactors - and suffer them not grief - for they are aware of thine plight - they weary not of service on thine behalf. So be it I know them which serve thee - and their untiring efforts that they might give unto thee a helping hand -- I say - be ye aware of their assistance - and ye shall be blest -- So be it and Selah --

? - ? - ?

Has thou set thine borders strait???

Be ye as one filled with the Spirit - for I say unto thee - the Spirit shall be poured out upon thee - and ye shall be as one prepared for the WORD which shall go forth -- And it shall be given for the good of all yet ye shall receive it -- For their sake shall it be given unto them -- Yet there shall be witnesses of the Spirit - which shall be poured out upon thee - for they shall know that it is the Spirit which giveth the WORD.

Now let it be said: that they shall receive it according unto their preparation - according to his own understanding -- And it shall be no less for their lack of understanding - yet it shall profit them to ponder that which is said herein - for there shall be given many things which they are want to know -- Many things shall be revealed unto them which <u>see</u> that which is said herein - for there shall be hidden up from the profane - many things which shall be shown unto them which hath eyes to see ---

For hast it ever been that THE "WORD" is hidden from the profane and the eye of the pure in heart - shall be opened and they shall see -- And many shall give unto them a part - and the parts shall be placed together - and these parts shall comprise the Whole -- And for this do I give unto thee Mine part - which shall be added unto the other parts - for I am One which hast awaited this day - when I might speak out for the good of all ---

It is now come - and yet I find them asleep - eating - drinking - and indulging the senses - making war upon their brothers - and bowing down unto their idols -- While I am speaking unto thee - and while thou art recording Mine Words - I see them as demon possessed - waging war on their fellow man - and therein is their own downfall -- I say unto them: He which take up arms against his brother - shall perish - it is the law -- I say it is the law - and the law shall not be set aside for any man, nation - country - or the punishment thereof be escaped - be he of any color - nation - or creed - for the just takes not arms against his brother. Let him which bears arms against another - say unto himself "This is mine brother" - this is mine BROTHER - and I am his -- And let him consider well his cause - for it is said: "Ye shall not kill" - ye shall neither buy - sell - or carry arms against thine brother - so be it -- It is said - and it is given unto Me to know whereof I speak - for I know the law - and man comes under this law of which I speak ---

It is said: Bear ye no malice - bear ye no hatred-- And unto them which are filled with hatred - I say unto THEE: Thou art as guilty of the crime as tho thou carried the weapon -- Yet is thine hatred and malice more poisonous than the armaments - I say: A thousand times more dangerous - yea - a thousand times! ---

Hear ye Me - and be ye thotful therefore - of thine own closet - of thine own garment - is it spotless? ---

I ask of thee - art thine hands clean - art thou clean? Satisfy thine own self and answer ME - Art thine hands clean -- Point not thine finger unto them - art thou his keeper - hast thine house been set in order?

Hast thine borders been set strait - Hast thine obligations been met, hast thine part been met - hast thine part been without question ---

Hast thou stood as one spotless before men.

Hast thou stood as the one without blemish - while that which ye are called to do - thru and by - the Offices of The Great and Mighty Council ---

First - thine complete surrender of thineself - thine will - and then ye shall be given an assignment - and ye shall be first appraised of that assignment - and ye shall choose if it is thine Will to accept - or reject it ---

So be it that I speak unto them which have ears - let them hear -- Unto them which have a mind to serve - let them serve in the Name of The Father - Son and The Mighty Council ---

So be it - and Selah --

Living Words

Be ye as one for which these words are given - for I speak unto thee - that YE might be prepared for the greater part -- I say it is for thee that these words are recorded -- Not for the generations which follow after thee - but for <u>thee</u> in this day - at this time -- Yet I say they shall aptly apply unto the generations which are to come - or follow thee - for I say unto thee - they shall not be void by time - neither man's laws or opinions - for they are LIVING WORDS ---

This Word which I shall give unto thee - this day - is: Be ye as one receptive unto he Word - for it is for <u>thee</u> - and as thou art prepared - so shall ye receive -- Hold ye steadfast - and be ye as one sober -- And let no man trip thee up or turn thee aside - for there are many pitfalls - and they are carefully hidden - that ye might be entrapt -- I say: Walk ye with sure step - follow ye the Light -- Ask of <u>no</u> <u>man</u> his opinion - neither his blessing - for I say unto thee: The Father is The Source of All Light - the Cause of thine being - and He knows thine need -- And He is the source of All supply - and for this hast He sent His Sons forth that ye might have that which is needful unto thine learning - unto thine preparation ---

Yet ye shall make thineself receptive unto the Light - and ask of The Father that He give unto thee comprehension of the Light ---

Know ye that He is the Giver of All Good gifts -- Yea - He gives and He takes - for He is the beginning and the end of His Work ---

He is the Author and the Finisher of His Work -- He sends out - He brings back - and so it is - worlds without end ---

Wait not for another - for I say unto thee - come forth - declare thineself - fear not - give unto no man the power to stay thee for it is now come when ye shall stand up and be counted ---

I ask of THEE: Where goest thou? ---

Hast thou heard that which hast been said unto THEE? - "Prepare Thine Self" -- For it is now come - when ye shall give an accounting of thineself - for none other shall answer for thee -- Think ye - that thou art not responsible for that which ye do with this MINE WORD - for I say unto thee - thou art responsible - for I have spoken unto thee O reader for I know thee -- I know into whose hands these Mine Words shall be placed - and I know the responsibility of each and every one which handles them - for there is a responsibility which goes with The Word - and it behooves ME to warn thee ---

I say: It is not by "Accident" that these Words are placed within thine hands - for there are many which are sent to accompany them on their way - that they are put into thine hands -- Think ye not- that they are given willy-nilly - unto thee -- They are given with great concern for thine own welfare -- with much consideration and preparation ---

Think ye not that there is no design - no plan!

For there IS a design and a PLAN -- I say unto thee - be ye alert - accept that which is given unto thee in love and Mercy ---

So be it - I Am One Sent of The Father

Obedience

So be it that I shall speak of obedience - that which is required of thee. And it behooves Me to speak of thine shortcomings ---

When it is said: "Prepare thineself"- it is the obedience unto the law which is required of thee - obedience unto the Word as it is spoken - or written -- It is the first thing that the Initiate learns - the wisdom of obedience unto the law - the wisdom of application of the law -- And he sets about his own preparation without the prattle which is given unto most men which know not the wisdom of Silence ---

He keeps for himself that which is given for him -- He walks humbly - justly and quietly among men - and he gives not the part designed for him - he boasts not of his progress -- He gives credit where credit is due - and he wearies not of his trials - for they are many ---

He gives justly unto all men - he waits not for them to ask his blessings -- He blesses them by his preparation - the preparation of himself -- For inasmuch as he is lifted up - all men shall be lifted up - for his light shall shine forth as a beacon set on a hill - they shall see it and be drawn unto it -- He shall put on the Armor of Light - and no evil shall attend him - for he shall be cleansed - and he shall wear pure garments - and be sealed with the Light – so be it and Selah ---

I say it is now come - when one shall go forth - and he shall be as one prepared to do that which he is given to do -- He shall wear pure linen - and they shall not be stained -- Neither shall he have the blood of the Saints upon his hands - for his hands shall be clean - his hands shall be spotless -- And he shall be free of all corruption - and he shall walk amongst thee as one without blemish - for he shall be spotless!

I say - he shall come unto thee in such manner - and ye shall accept him as one of thee - for he shall come in an incorruptible body - and he shall give unto thee that which is given unto him for thee - and he shall bless thee by his presence - so be it and Selah. He is One Sent of God the Father -- So be it as He Wills it --Amen and Selah -

Let Them....

See ye the hand of God move -- It moves majestically and with precision -- It moveth with surety and with power -- I say - the hand of God moveth with swiftness and power ---

Let them see the movement thereof-

Let them see!

Let them Behold the Glory of The Lord – for

He passeth amongst thee --

Let them behold Him - The Lord of Lords -

The King of Kings - The Host of Hosts --

Let them sing the Anthem: "Hail! Hail! - The

Lord of Lords IS COME - Hail unto HIM"

Let them come forth and rejoice

for He is COME ---

I say: Let them come forth and rejoice - for they shall know Him - and they shall be glad ---

Let them join in the glad anthem -

Let them come unto Him and be touched -

Let them gather round about and hear that which He says unto them.

Let them prepare to receive Him and of Him - for He shall know them - and it is given unto Him to be the One Sent of the Father - that they be brot out of bondage -- Yet sad shall he be which is found wanting - for he shall be as one dejected - for he shall hear the words: "Depart! ye know Me not - thou slothful and dejected" -- He shall be dejected for his slothfulness --

He shall be turned away for his slothfulness - for he hast not prepared for the day of the Coming of the Lord -- He shall remember that which hast been said unto him -- He shall cry out: My Lord - have I not sought thee out? See me - here I am -- Lord I come forth - see me. Here I am -- And He shall answer him - "Ye slothful man - in the time of thine wonton I spoke unto thee - and ye rebelled against Me -- Now ye stand in need of ME -- Ask of thine friend - let him give unto thee drink - let him give unto thee bread - yet shall thou hunger more -- Let him give unto thee drink and thine thirst shall not be quenched -- Yet thou hast spat upon Mine servants - thou hast belittled Mine Sayings - and now thou dare come as one subservient asking favors of ME -- What hast thou done to ask favors of ME -- Show ME thine hands - thou unclean wretch -- Thinkest to deceive ME"? Thus shall he flee - and hear within his ears the ring of the Words: "Depart from Me thou slothful" ---

He shall remember well the Words - which hast been spoken truly and justly ---

For none shall be brot out which are unprepared ---

O - man - hear ye these words which I say unto thee - they are for thine own ears -- Let them fall gently upon thine ears - and may The Lord God have Mercy upon thee ---

The Most Worthy Grand Master Speaks

Be ye as the hand of ME made manifest - and say unto them in Mine Name - that I am the "Most Worthy Grand Master" within the Inner Temple - wherein Our Father abides ---

I speak unto them with the Authority and sanction which He hast given unto Me ---

He hast given unto Me sanction to speak unto thee thusly: --

Be ye as one prepared - for the time is now come when ye shall be called out -- And it behooves thee to be prepared - for it is given unto thee to be as ones in lethargy -- Thou art prone to wait -- Thou art indifferent unto that which is said unto thee -- And it is given unto Me to see thee running to and fro - as ones in confusion - art thou not in confusion?

Now I say unto thee - thou shall be <u>still</u> - hear Me - and listen well unto that which I say - for I am not to be turned away as an imposter.

I am trust worth - I give unto thee that which shall profit thee - ye shall be as one prepared to receive it ---

Fortune not unto thineself the bitter cup ---

I say unto thee: I Am Sent of Mine Father also -- I am come in love and compassion - that ye might be spared ---

Let this be said now - that the putting off of the body of flesh is not the end -- I ask of thee: Knowest thee thine end? Seest thou thine end?

I say unto thee - it hast not as yet appeared unto thee - that which ye shall become - for no man knoweth the end ---

Be ye as one prepared to receive that which I bring for thee - and I shall give unto thee in great measure - in greater measure shall I give unto thee ---

I say: Prepare thineself for to receive ---

Yet I say - give unto Me credit for being that which I am - and fear not that thou hast not known Me - for I say unto thee - thou knowest not the lesser advisor - the lesser emissaries - the ones which hast given their all that ye might have light ---

Ye give unto them no credit - no credence for being that which they are -- They are no less for thine unknowing - for they are no less for their martyrdom -- While they have suffered great indignities of men - they were not turned aside, they proved themself worthy of their reward.

I say - thine thinking hast not been unto thee light -- Thine learning surely hast not been great wisdom -- Thine opinions hast not liberated thee from bondage ---

I ask of thee: Why deny Me - when I come unto thee from out the Realms of Light - wherein all things are known? ---

I say unto thee - and I speak unto thee - and it shall profit thee to hear Me out ---

Bear ye in mind that ye shall stand face to face with thine own self and ye shall give an accounting of thineself - none other shall answer for thee - none other shall be responsible for thee -- Ye shall come alone and ye shall stand as one naked - ye shall bring with thee nought save thineself -- It behooves thee then - to be as one clean - without blemish. And ye shall have no false gods - for I say unto thee - there is but One God The Father which hast sent Me -- Behold His hand move - and see the movements thereof --

I Am He which is The Most Worthy Grand Master -

Mighty Onrush of Power

Let these Mine Words go out unto all the LANDS OF THE EARTH - for it is now come when there shall be a Mighty Onrush of Waters - and they shall cover the Earth - and wash clean the old -- The old shall be cleansed and the Earth shall stand refreshed - and the ones which have been true unto their calling shall come forth as ones prepared for their new part ---

For think ye not that there shall not be changes - for think ye that We of the Mighty Council Sleepeth! ---

I say We sleep NOT! -- We are about The Father's business - and no man shall be unto Us a barrier -- For We go forth as a Mighty Army prepared to do battle---

We carry the "Rod of Power" "The Shield of Light" "The Armor of God"

So be it We come in His Name - and We shall know no defeat ---

Think ye that man is the author of this Work? Think ye that it is the work of man?

I say unto thee - prove thineself correct - and I shall bow down before him which is the Author of this Work --

Let him come forth - and I shall declare him wise - and I shall award him according unto his good work ---

I say unto thee O man - thou hast not seen the finish of Mine Work. I am not finished -- Be ye not so foolish as to take Me lightly - for I am not to be taken lightly -- For I come unto thee from out the Realm of Light ---

I am One with Mine Father which hast given unto Me sanction to speak unto thee thusly -- Therefore I say unto thee: Heed Mine Words - and be ye blest --

For this have I spoken unto thee thusly.

Therein is Thine Reward

Be ye as one prepared to go the last mile - for therein is thine reward - therein is thine safety - therein is thine end - and thine sojourn shall end in thine Victory -- For there are none overlooked - they are remembered with longing - they are as ones away - and they are not forgotten ---

I say unto thee: Thou hast gone out from thine place of abode - thou hast wandered long - and far -- Yet Our love hast followed thee - and we have held thee fast in thine time of unknowing ---

We have bent down - We have stretched out our hand - and We have offered unto thee Our love - Our assistance -- We have bowed before thee in holy supplication - that ye might arise and come forth as one prepared to partake of thine inheritance ---

So be it We give of Ourself in selfless sacrifice that ye might come into the fullness thereof -- So let it be as thou shall will it -- Yet I say unto thee this day - thine inheritance awaits thee - ye have but to claim it in the Name of The Father Which hast sent Me -- I tell thee of a surety He hast kept for thee a princely fortune - and no more shall ye go into bondage - no more shall ye want - when thou hast accepted the fullness of thine Inheritance -- Let it suffice that We are aware of the fullness of thine Inheritance - for We have received Ours in full - therefore We are fully qualified to speak unto thee thusly ---

Ask of no man his blessing -- Ask of no man his opinion - for he too is bound in darkness -- Let it suffice thee that The Father Knows thine needs - and from Him comes all good gifts -- And all thine sores shall be healed by and thru His Grace ---

So be it I know that Grace and I am Glad ---

Let Us Speak of Fear

Let the record be set strait -- I am the One Sent this day - that this be given unto them which are want to learn of ME -- I say I have a part for them - and it - shall profit them to accept it - for it is given unto Me of The Father which hast sent Me ---

There are none so foolish as the one which thinks himself wise -- Therefore I say unto thee: Be ye of a mind to learn - and for this have I come - that thine capacity be expanded ---

Now let Us speak of fear -- Fear is but thine own imaging - thine own darkness - thine own fear - it belongs not unto the light -- Yet ye fear the Light -- I ask of thee: Why fear the Light? ---

When thou art bound by thine own darkness - thou art not of the light -- It is said: Come ye forth out of darkness - see ye the Light - walk ye in It ---

Yet ye turn away - crying out for man's opinions - that he pass judgment upon thine Benefactors ---

Will thou O man - learn that thou hast been bound by thine dogmas and opinions - and that thou art tied unto them? ---

I ask of thee: Wherein hast these things freed thee? ---

I ask of thee: Wherein hast these dogmas and creeds profited thee?

Hast they given unto thee comfort? Hast they freed thee of thine bounds - by which thou art bound?

Now I ask of thee: Thinkest that the Son of God is lesser than that which hast bound thee? O – man, wherein art thou bound ---

I say unto thee: The Son of God speaks out on thine behalf - that ye might awaken unto thine plight - and come forth as one awake - and as one prepared to receive the greater part -- Let it be said - that thine legirons shall be cut away - and thine hands shall be untied - when thou hast responded unto the call: "COME" -- Yet ye shall not turn aside - neither look back - for a man which shall put his hand to the plow and turneth back - is worse than an infidel -- So be it that he shall be called unfit to till the fields ---

I say he shall be lower than the beast - for he shall lose his inheritance - so be it -- I say unto thee - consider well this day which way ye shall go - choose ye wisely - and may The Father have Mercy upon thee ---

I Shall Cause a Manifestation

Such is Mine Word unto thee this day - and it is given for the good of all -- It is given that all might be blest - for it goes forth upon the eth - that it might find its mark ---

I say - I breathe forth the Word - and it shall find its mark - and it shall not return unto Me void ---

Such would I give unto thee this day: Mine time is come when I shall cause a manifestation unto man -- I shall bring a manifestation forth - such as man hast not known - and I shall cause him to become aware of the manifestation -- He shall be aware of it - for I shall cause him to be aware ---

He shall behold the power of "The Word" for I shall speak IT with power and authority - and IT shall take form - and IT shall be as nothing man hast known ---

He shall stand in wonderment and awe ---

He shall be frozen in his tracks - for he shall have great fear within him ---

He shall run and hide - he shall fall down on his face and cry out - Lord! Lord! Have Mercy! - for he shall be as one fearful -- It is said unto "them" - "fear not" - for great things shall be revealed unto them which fear not ---

I say unto them: Prepare thineself that ye be prepared for the greater part -- Think ye that ye know the Greater Part? Think ye that ye <u>know</u> the Greater Part?? ---

I ask of thee: What think ye that I say unto thee?

Think ye that I speak idly? It is not given unto ME - to make idle talk - for I am not so foolish ---

I Am about My Father's business!

I say unto thee: "Be Up and about thine preparation" - for the time comes swiftly when ye shall be faced with thine foolishness ---

I say: "<u>The Time Swiftly Comes</u> - when ye shall be FACED WITH THINE FOOLISHNESS" ---

Be ye alert - fear not - know ye that there is nothing to fear -- Walk ye in the Light - let IT be thine Armor - and ten thousand shall stand watch over thee -- Let thine tabernacles - thine temples - thine edifices of harlots - fall into ruins - yet I say unto thee - no harm shall come nigh unto thee -- Put on the Armor of God - and ye shall not fear - for there shall be a Host that ye be protected -- Let thine own hands be clean -- Let thine light so shine that it be seen - and by thine own light shall ye be found ---

So let it be - for this have I spoken -

Mysteries

What hast been said is not new unto thee - yet thou hast not learned the meaning of that which hast been said -- Much hast been said concerning the "Mysteries"-- Yet there is no mystery other than thine unknowing - It is said: "All things shall be recalled unto thine memory"- and it is so - so be it as thou art prepared to receive ---

Wherein is it said: That there shall go forth a great light that shall bring Great Light unto the Earth- and know ye the meaning thereof?

I say unto thee - thou knowest not the meaning thereof - for it is as yet not revealed unto thee - it is as yet a mystery ---

It is said: None pilfer the mysteries of the Inner Temple - and it is so - for I am the Most Worthy Grand Master of the Inner Temple - and I Know the Works therein - and I am the Guardian of the Mysteries - and I give not of the Mysteries unto the unjust and imprudent -- I give unto them which are found trust worth - and I say unto thee - I am not deceived - I am not to be taken unawares ---

So be it I have spoken -- Let them which have ears hear that which I say.

Be ye - blest to hear - for I Am the One Sent that this be done this day--

Thou Art Not Alone

Forget not that thou art not alone - thou art not alone - I say unto thee - thou art NEVER alone ---

So be it thou art the one which hast prepared thineself for to receive this part - and I am prepared to give unto thee in abundance -- So be it I am He which is sent that this be done ---

I come in the Name of Mine Father Solen Aum Solen-- I say unto thee - it is now time that thou be given in greater measure - for the time is come when the multitudes shall be awakened - and they shall find their dreams shall torment them - ere they arise from their slumbers -- They shall sicken of their unknowing - they shall cry out for light ---

Yet in their confusion - they shall find no comfort -- They shall be as ones prepared - for they shall establish peace within themself -- And it shall be established that they might be given the greater part ---

They have wearied of the Word: "Prepare" - yet they shall learn well the wisdom of "Preparation" - for none receive the fullness of their estate unprepared ---

I say: This is the whole of OUR MISSION - that <u>THEY</u> be prepared. Yet they play unto the piper's tune - while We give unto them Our love - and Our hand in compassion ---

They turn from the Light - seeking solace in sleep - and in the dark.

While We give unto them of OURSELF - that they be brot out of bondage - they ask not of The Light - they seek not The Light ---

They feign wisdom - and speak of the Light - as tho they were authorities on a subject which no man can define ---

They feign compassion - and they spew words of hatred from their mouth ---

They say their rigamaroles in pious fashion - and send their sons into battle with <u>their</u> blessing ---

I say unto thee - what "Sin"! What pity!

What fools they be - and what the consequence!!

They shall come to know! I hear them say: It is necessary that we send our sons - for we are the power of the world ---

Yea - we are the <u>power</u> of the world!! I say unto them: Ye FOOLS! Know ye not that thou hast <u>no</u> powers -- That which hast been entrusted into thine keeping shall be taken away - for thou hast been slothful in thine stewardship - thou hast been unto thineself traitor - thou hast betrayed thineself - thou hast been as the one laggards - and unfaithful in thine trust -- I say unto them: Ye shall be removed from thine high places - wherein thou hast been as the shiftless servant - lax in thine application of the law -- Thou shall be removed into a far corner - and seen of men no more -- So be it I have raised Mine Voice against thee and I am not finished -- For a generation shall be raised up which shall overthrow thy temples - and be as the ones sent - for I say unto thee - ye have forfeited thine estate for a poor penny ---

Hast it not been said: "Pity is he which betrays himself"? So be it I shall speak again - and it shall profit thee to hear Me out.

Each One Shall Read His Record

Let them which would deny Mine Word - come forth and speak - for I shall hear them -- Let them which would deny that which I say - speak and I shall hear him ---

For I am aware of them - yea - before they have spoken -- Yet it behooves Me to warn them: That which they say shall be as the open book - and they shall be faced with their foolishness - their folly -- I say each and every one shall read from his record - and he shall stand face to face with himself - and he shall see wherein he hast denied THE WORD - and that which he hast brot upon himself -- For he shall be as the judge - and the law shall deal out justice -- The law shall be the law and none shall set it aside - or make restitution for him ---

It is said - that there are none so sad - as he which betrays himself - so be it -- It is given unto Me to know - for I am over watchful - I am not in anywise in lethargy -- I have been at Mine Work for many a time and therein is a greater time than thou canst calculate -- Thine time hast now come when ye shall come to know wherein thou art bound -- I say thine limitations are many - why? -- Thou art bound in the Earth for a reason - for a season - and thou hast not known wherein thou art bound, wherein thou art - neither by what thou art bound ---

Wherein art thou bound? Knowest wherein thou art?

O man - I say unto thee - thine limitations art many!

Thou art limited in thine unknowing - thou art limited for thine unknowing -- There is the story - which thou art want to know ---

I say - thou fearest to know the story - I hear ye say: I do not want to hear - for I believe not -- Unto thee I say: Thine unbelief hast been thine own - undoing - thine unknowing changes not the law -- Be ye as one prepared to learn of Me - and I shall give unto thee a part which I have kept for thee - it shall profit thee to receive it -- So be it and Selah.

Condemnation

Hast it not been said - that all things shall be revealed in the season allotted unto such - and it is so -- There is a time of going out - and a time of coming back - and it is given unto man to be as ones on their return - no more shall he turn back ---

For it is given unto him to progress - as the poor in spirit shall be taken out - and the strong shall remain -- As the fortress shall they build the new -- They shall constitute the fortress ---

The ones which are firmly planted upon the "Rock" shall find their endurance as the Rock - they shall not be blown by the winds - and the waters shall wash over them - and they shall endure all the storms - and they shall not be moved ---

For theirs shall be a solid foundation - which shall be as the Rock.

For the "ROCK" is the foundation of the Church which shall raise up in their midst ---

They shall see their foundations crumble into decay - and their temples shall fall at their feet -- Their altars shall lay in ruins - and they shall cry for their idols - yet I say unto them: Weep not - for no more shall ye set up thine, places of idolatry - no more shall ye bring up a generation of harlots -- I say unto thee O man: Thou hast brot forth a generation of harlots and bastards -- Thou hast forfeited thine inheritance - and thou hast called thineself "Christians"---

I say: Thou art no Christ-ians - thou art as the ones which sleep with the pigs! ---

Thou art asleep! Thou art as yet not awake! Thou hast been guilty of fornication - thou hast plundered the word of God" ---

Thou hast given unto the ones which ask for bread- a stone - and thou hast taught false doctrine - in the Name of the Allwise - All Mighty God - and His Son Sent of Him -- Thou hast been as the drunken - thou hast defecated in thine own bed ---

Thou hast been as the bride without the bridegroom-- Thou art now in disgrace - I say thou art now an outcast - cast out in dis - Grace - without Grace -- Thou standeth in want - poor - of Spirit - impoverished and wanting for bread - cut off and crying in thine affliction -- I say unto thee: Thou standeth naked - thine nakedness showeth - thine shame exposed ---

Thou poor of Spirit - I say unto thee: Thou art as the outcast in thine nakedness - thine shame - thine disgrace - for thou hast betrayed thineself and thine trust ---

So be it I have spoken plainly and fearlessly - and according unto the law - for this am I sent -- I am come by THE AUTHORITY and THE POWER of The Allwise Almighty Father which hast given unto thee being--

The Royal Raiment

Hast it not been said that the day draws nigh - when there shall be a great light flood the Earth - it is so -- And the light shall consume the darkness - and there shall be peace amongst men - for they shall know Peace - for Peace shall be established within them ---

Now it is said that there shall be great changes - and change is good so let it be -- For this are We prepared to send forth Great Light - Great Strength -- And there shall go forth a Fiat - new unto man - and he shall stand as <u>one</u> - and he shall know himself to be ONE ---

Therefore there shall be no more war - no more hatred - no more malice-. No more hatred shall man know - for he shall be One with <u>all</u> men -- He shall be as One of mind and spirit -- He shall kill no more - for he shall be as one wise -- And he shall not eat of the slain - neither shall he grovel for his bread - for he shall be as one with the Elements and he shall take from the Elements that which is needful unto him -- He shall not want - for his wants shall be supplied ---

He shall take from the Elements his bread - his drink -- And his clothes shall be of the etheric substance -- He shall wrap himself about with substance taken from the eth - and he shall be as one garbed in the finest of raiment -- He shall be as one prepared for that which awaits him ---

I say: This is the inheritance of man - when he hast become of age And he shall walk as one sober - and he shall know that he is A Son of God - and he shall wear well his Royal Raiment - so shall it be --

The New Fiat

Be ye as the hand of Me made manifest unto them - and say unto them in Mine Name - that this is the day of salvation - this is the time of preparation ---

There shall go forth from out the Mouth of God - a New Fiat - and it shall be obeyed - it shall be as the "New Fiat of God" -- For He hast set up His Kingdom - and He hast filled His Kingdom and it is now come when He hast prepared another ---

And it shall likewise be filled -- Yet the Work shall be finished ere the Kingdom is filled -- I say it is now come - when the Sons of God which sleepeth - shall awaken and come forth as ones awake -- They shall be as ones prepared that they shall come into the New Kingdom ---

Too it is said that: "I shall go to prepare a place for thee" -- It is prepared - and now is the day of the fulfilling -- The Kingdom of God shall now be established within the new place and them which doth awaken shall be brot in - and they shall stand as Sons of God arrayed in the Armor of God - and He shall give unto them their Royal Crown - and they shall wear it in honor and with dignity.

They shall stand before Him as ones prepared to receive of Him their Crown - their Inheritance -- They shall be glad for their preparation -- Yet I say - thine waiting hast been long and hard -- Yet thine Victory won - the time shall be as nought ---

I say unto thee: Awaken this day unto thine Inheritance - come forth that ye might claim it - in the Name of The Father Son and Holy Spirit.

Be ye prepared to give unto Me more time - and I shall give unto thee greater than thou hast received - for it shall take more time - and I shall provide thee the strength and the energy -- So be it I shall be as thine Sibor - and I shall sibor thee in the things which shall be new unto thee - and it shall be given unto thee in simple language - understandable unto the least of them -- They shall be as the ones prepared to receive it - for there are ones which await this part ---

I say unto thee - be ye about The Father's Business - for thou hast a calling - and it behooves thee to be about thine Calling - Let us begin this part with The Word - - and they shall come to know the meaning thereof -- So let it be unto thee Great Light ---

Wherein is it said - ye shall receive in Greater measure -- So be it and Selah ---

Close this first Book with these Words:

Sheloheim Adomni

THE IMPORTANCE OF THE WORK AT HAND

Hast it not been said - that one shall come unto thee and give unto thee that which is prepared for thee ---

It is now come when there is great necessity for this part - for it is the time for the Work which hast been given unto Us to do - to be done. Yet it is necessary for them which have answered the Call - to step forth as ones prepared - and at no time shall We fail in Our part -- For it is given unto Us to Know the importance of the Work at hand - and by no other means can this Work be accomplished. -- It is necessary that the ones called and chosen - be about the business at hand -- And for this do I say unto thee - ye shall give unto Me time for this part which I have now prepared for thee ---

Ye shall receive it in the Name of The Father Son and Holy Spirit - so be it and Selah ---

Ye shall change no Word - ye shall not edit it - ye shall let them have it as I give it unto thee - and I say unto them - change not a Word. Yet I see them pilfering and distorting the Word which I give unto thee. Yet I say - woe unto him - for he knows not the law -- It is said many times "There are none so sad as them which betray their trust - none so foolish as he which thinks himself wise" ---

Let him which have ears hear that which I say unto him:

Be ye blest to accept of ME the Word which I bring - and I shall give unto thee a part for thine own - separate from theirs - this I have saved for thee -- Ye shall receive it in the Name of The Father Son and Holy Spirit - Amen and Selah ---

Hold ye steadfast and waver not - for I am about to give unto thee that which hast been kept for this time ---

It is said - that there shall be great revelation for them which are prepared to receive -- And unto them let it be said: Thine capacity shall be increased - and thine opinions shall count as nought -- So be it I speak unto thee of many things - and unto thee I say: Thine preparation is Greatest of them all -- It is for this that I now speak - that ye be prepared for a Greater capacity - a greater revelation -- I say unto thee: Turn not away - discount not the Words which I say - for I am The One Sent that this Work be done NOW.

For this am I prepared - for this is My Priestess prepared - and it is given unto Me to prepare her - and put Mine Words into her mouth - and she shall speak that which I give unto her to say - and she shall not be given unto flattery or charlatanry -- She shall be as the Voice of Me for I shall be unto her that which is necessary -- She shall wear with honor and dignity - the wreath of laurels which I shall hold over her head - for I shall give unto her that which I have kept for her - and no man shall take from her one part - one parcel of her Inheritance -- For it is so written that she shall receive her Inheritance in full - so be it and Selah -- I am come that it be so - so be it and Selah --

Law and Order

This shall begin the next Book of this part - and it shall be that of Law and Order -- This shall be unto them their law - under which they come now - and in the time ahead -- They shall know the law under which they come - and it is for their preparation that it is clearly defined -

clearly prepared for them - and given unto them -- For this is not a new law - a new part - it is that which wast given long ago by One Sent -- Yet they have chosen to go the way of flesh - obeying not the LAW. For this have they fortuned unto themself much torment and suffering and anxiety -- While they have not obeyed the law - the law exists - and is no less in operation -- They shall now know wherein they have transgressed - wherein they have failed ---

This then shall be made clear unto them -- They shall be as ones prepared to face themself - and account for their actions/ deeds - and that which they have said -- They shall be as ones prepared for the day when they shall go into another place of abode - and they shall know the law thereof - for it shall be given unto them aforehand -- Yet it is said: They shall have the mind to learn - and pity is he which refuses to learn -- This is the time of learning - and it is given unto Me to be given this part - that they might know well that which shall be given unto them to do ---

Yet they shall not ask that they be given the way which they would have ---

They shall accept that which WE of The Mighty Council deem wise for they know not that which they have in store for them ---

As little children - they ask for things - which are not for them - not theirs - and that which would but torment them ---

They have as yet not become aware of the need - which would be unto them their benefits -- They know not that they are in want of the things which have provided them for their progress ---

I say - they desire the things of Earth -- They seek power/ prestige/ sympathy/ glorification/ thanks/ praise - and they fail to realize these things are not the real part of their preparation - nay - nay - they forget the way in which the Initiate walks ---

They go into the market places seeking <u>things</u> perishable - made of man - forgetting these are not the things which would be unto them comfort --- They think to comfort themself - they seek comfort for self, forgetting the ones which are tormented by hunger -- They minister not to the dying - they feed not the ones which cry for bread - they ask for themself -- They seek out the ones in high esteem - that they be looked upon with esteem - they say that which man is want to hear - that which pleases his fancy - that which agrees with his policies that which causes him to be looked upon as WISE -- And then he becomes convinced of his own wisdom ---

Now I say unto them: They shall indeed be brot to account for their foolishness - their childishness -- They shall come to know that they buy and sell in vain - for their barter shall profit them not - for the <u>things</u> which can be bartered - sold - or bought - shall perish and be no more for they shall be of no account ---

These things which hast comforted them - shall no longer comfort them - for they shall not take <u>one thing</u> with them into their next abode.

Yet I say unto them: They shall free themself from <u>all things</u> - yea father - mother - sister - brother - son - daughter and household -- For they shall enter into their next place of abode - empty of hand - and free of all legirons -- They shall be as ones bare -- They shall not bring with them <u>one thing</u> - one possession -- They shall be stript of all associations - all past glories - and they alone shall be responsible for their preparation ---

For We of The Mighty Council have given unto them from the beginning the LAW - and they have been sent forth from out the Mouth of God - that they might Glorify Him in the Earth - yet they have lost their way ---

For this are We now sending forth The Word - the Messengers - the Emissaries anew -- We are crying out - for this is a New Day -- A New Dispensation is given unto them - and it too shall end -- Therefore it is said: Arise and come forth - for it is the Day of Awakening ---

Such is Mine Word unto them -

So be it and Selah

Other Realms - Other Laws

Thine part is to be mindful of the LAW - to apply it unto thineself -- And be as the one responsible unto the LAW - for thou art bound by the LAW --

The LAW differs in each realm - and therein thou art given the Law by which thou dost exist within it---

Yet it matters not what Law each realm hast - while thou art yet bound within the realm of man of Earth ---

While it is given unto thee to be Earth-bound - thou art under the law governing Earth and Her inhabitants -- Yet it is said that as thou art prepared - so shall thou receive -- As thou progress into yet realms unknown unto thee - thou shall come under yet Laws unknown unto thee ---

While it is given unto Us of The Mighty Council - to be above the Law of the lower realms - it is given unto Us to be qualified to direct thee aright – that ye too come into the place wherein there is no limitation - wherein there is no bounds - no boundaries - no sorrow - no longing -- Hast it not been said that thou shall be unbound - it is so. And it is given unto Us to know such joy -- It is given unto Us to see by the misery and sorrow of them bound in darkness - It is for Our Knowing and Our Love for thee - that we give unto thee a hand - that ye too be lifted up ---

Let it be for thine own sake that ye give ear unto Our Call - for I say unto thee - it is "Real" - it is R E A L ! ---

Thou hast fancied the Call something else - something quite different - yet I say unto thee - it is different than thou hast fancied it.

No man maketh "The Call" - it is of God The Father - and He hast sent forth a Fiat this day that ye awaken---

For the day of awakening is now come -- And as the coming forth of the morning Sun - so shall the Sons of God awaken and come forth for the hour hast struck and all the Angelic Host sing forth their praise. Hallelujah - Hallelujah - it is come - IT IS COME -- When they awaken their song shall reverberate thruout the Earth - and there shall be a quickening - and man shall be stirred - and moved -- He shall become moved by the Song of the Mighty Host - and they shall join the Glad

Anthem - and they shall sing forth their Song which shall echo thruout the lands of all the Earth ---

So be it a Glad Day!

I have spoken - and I am not finished--

So be it I shall speak again of Love --

Thine Tongue Shall Not Belie Thine Deeds

Sori Sori:

Hast it not been said - that there shall be a Great Host come to thine assistance? And it is so -- So be it the time is come when the gates swing wide - that they might receive them which are prepared ---

Let it be understood that they bid thee enter in-- Yet it is given unto thee to prepare thineself for to enter in -- While it is said: "Come ye - enter in" - it is said: "Thou shall come clean of hands and pure of Spirit".

Let not thine heart be black -- Pure shall be thine heart - pure thine motives - sure thine foot -- And thine tongue shall not belie thine deeds for I say: Ye shall let thine motives be pure - and ye shall be as one contrite of Spirit - and clean of hands -- Let not thine garments be stained -- Let thine hands be swift to take up the Shield and the Armor of God - and be ye as one prepared to go the last mile -- For I say unto thee - the way is prepared before thee - and there are the ones which have gone before thee which reach out unto thee - that ye might not fall.

Obey ye The Law - and make strait the Way of The Lord - for He hast prepared for thee a place - and ye shall enter therein as one prepared ---

Let it be said this day - they which enter therein shall rejoice forevermore ---

Let it be said: That they which enter therein shall be as ones lifted up - and they shall no more enter into bondage - no more shall they go into darkness - no more shall they go into the darkness of the pit ---

No more shall they have their memory blanked from them -- No more shall they be born of woman ---

No more shall they know sorrow -- So be it I am come that they be lifted up --Let it Be --

The Mirror

Hast it not been said that - "Every tongue shall confess - every knee shall bend" - and is it not so ---

For they shall stand before the Great Mirror - and they shall see themself as they are -- They shall carry the scales of justice within their own hand - and they shall be as their own judge -- And they shall be as one responsible for that which they have done - and that which they have said - and nothing shall be hidden - all secrets shall be revealed.

And they shall bear witness of that which they have fortuned unto themself - and they shall not deceive themself - for they shall be as one which hast within his own hand the scale of justice - and all things shall be weighed - and balanced - and he shall know himself as he is - and he shall not deceive himself ---

He shall look well into the "Mirror"-- Therein he shall see for himself as he is - and he shall know that which he shall do -- And justice shall be meted unto him - for he shall be his own judge - and he shall be self-responsible - for he shall be as the judge - and no man shall be unto him accuser - he shall stand self-accused – self-judged - for he shall count unto the Law - none other -- And at no time shall, he give to another the part of judge - for he alone shall judge his works - his motives - and his accumulations - his actions - his deeds -- And he shall be his own porter - for he shall bring himself as he is prepared - for is it not said: He holds within his hand his own passport? It is so --

So shall it be --

The One to Come

Hast it not been said - that One shall be sent unto thee - that ye might have great Light - so shall it be-- He shall come and it shall be given unto thee to know Him - for he shall wear upon his brow a mark - and it shall be one which ye shall know -- Ye shall not be deceived by his appearance - for he shall be as one arrayed in garments of men - and he shall be as man -- Yet he shall be unlike man - for he shall be of another Order - he shall in no wise be of the world - for he shall be of another.

He shall bring with him Great Knowledge and power - and he shall be as one humble of heart - and he shall be as a simple man ---

He shall be as one learned of the way of the Initiate - learned in the Laws - and the application thereof -- He shall be given unto few words and great power ---

He shall abide with thee for a time - and he shall give unto thee that which is needful ---

He shall be as one prepared for this part - and ye shall be as one prepared to receive him - and of him -- So be it and Selah --

The Responsibility

Hast it not been said many times - that thou art as one responsible for that which ye do with "The Word" of God -- It is given unto thee for thine own sake - for thine own well-being/ for thine own upliftment/ thine own preparation - and at no time shall ye be excused from the law when thou dost desecrate the Word - And it behooves thee to weary not of it -- It behooves thee to ponder well the Word - for it is given unto thee in such manner for a purpose - and that purpose is beyond thine imaging -- Yet it is said: All things shall be revealed unto thee - all mystery shall be revealed - and it shall be as thou art prepared -- So let it profit thee to ponder well the Word - as it is given unto thee -- So be it I have spoken of The Word and the preparation thereof - and the responsibility it carries -- I say unto thee - it behooves thee to consider well thine responsibility -- When thou hast received "The Word" thou hast been given the Great Responsibility of receiving it - yet ye shall consider well that which ye do with it -- Hold it dear unto thine heart - consider well its preparation - and its action -- Let it suffice thee that it is the Word of God -- Hold it sacred - and be ye as one prepared to receive it -- For this is it given unto thee - that ye be prepared to receive the Greater Part -- So be and Selah --

The Law

Be ye as one which hast received The Word - and ye shall be as one responsible for that which ye do with it ---

Ye shall hold it sacred - and give it not unto the profane or unjust - for they shall likewise be responsible - and when they have desecrated it - it is therefore their condemnation - yet thou hast had part in their condemnation ---

When they ask of thee - give unto them that which they ask - and it shall be with wisdom - for many things shall be given unto thee - that they could not bear--

Let thine preachments cease - let thine example be unto them the worth of thine learning -- Let thine light so shine that they might see it and be drawn unto it ---

Let them come asking of thee Light - then give unto them "The Word - adding no preachments - no opinions - just give unto them "The Word" - and then ye shall have no responsibility for their actions/ deeds or words ---

While it is given unto man to bear false witness against the prophets and to slander the Messengers of God - it is given unto them to desecrate "The Word" -- Yet he is no less responsible for his actions - for the LAW shall not become invalid -- It shall remain valid - for it is The Word - and The Word shall not pass away or become void ---

Let thine mouth be sealed - and let no condemnation pass from thine lips - and let the Word become thee -- Let thine Light guide them -- "Let thine Words be Mine Words - let thine hands be Mine Hands - let thine feet be Mine feet" - sayeth the Lord thy God ---

Let it be - for this hast He given unto Me the Authority to speak unto thee ---

I say unto each and every one which hast been given The Word - they shall ponder My Word - and be as one thotful of The Law - and none shall escape IT ---

I speak that none come under condemnation ---

So let it be according unto the Law.

The One to Come

Sori Sori - Hast it not been said - that one shall come unto thee - which is prepared to be Great assistance unto thee?

He shall be Great Light - and he shall know that which he is about and he shall walk upright - knowing where he goes - and that which he is given to do -- He shall do his part with Grace and ease -- He shall be as one illumined - and he shall be as One Sent -- So shall it be -- It shall be as the Word manifest --

So be it and Selah --

One Shall be Sent

Hast it not been said - that One shall be sent - it is so -- And it shall be given unto thee to Know Him - for he hast been no stranger unto thee - He hast walked with thee and counselled thee - yet ye know him not to be that which he is -- He hast awaited the hour - and the time is now come when he shall come - and he shall counsel thee in many things - and he shall be unto thee Great help -- It shall profit thee to follow his guidance/ his counsel - for he hast the wisdom and the Knowledge - for this is he sent - let it be for the good of all ---

So be it that he shall bear thee a gift - and ye shall accept it - and ye shall be blest to accept it - for it shall profit thee much ---

Hast it not been foretold of His coming?

I say unto thee - He comes as One Sent -- So be it and Selah --

I am -- He Hast Sent Me

Therefore I say unto thee - many come saying: I am he - yet he beareth not the Name of I AM -- I AM HE - which hast Sent ME -- I AM HE - LO - I AM HE ---

Be ye as one acceptable unto the LIGHT Which I AM---

I AM ONE with Mine Father - I AM ONE with Mine Beloved Sananda - for We art not divided against Ourself ---

I AM HE Which speaks with the Power given unto Me by The Father God -- All Might is He - All Wise is He - And He hast invested within Me the Authority to use HIS NAME - I AM ---

I AM -- He - hast Sent Me forth as a living Witness that HE IS ---

So be it I bear testimony of HIM - for All that HE IS I AM ---

I AM the Manifestation of The Word Sent forth from His Mouth - before the Earth wast formed - yea - before the Heavens were formed - for WE Created the Heavens - and supported them by The Word ---

Hear ye Mine Words - ponder long that which I say unto thee -- Know ye that there is a LAW GOVERNING ALL THINGS - and I AM ONE WITH THAT LAW ---

I AM - THE LAW - - - I AM - HE - - -

Blest art they which heareth that which I say -

I AM H E ---

So be it I have spoken - and I shall be heard --

Fear Not the Changes

Let the Hand of God move - stay it not - for it shall be unto all men the renewing - and the end of the old -- The old shall pass away - the new shall be unto thee the beginning of a new day - and ye shall stand free even as the Son of God is free ---

I say - rebel not for the changes which are to come - be ye as one prepared to meet them - giving thanks for the new day ---

I say unto thee: The day for which thou hast waited - approaches swiftly - and it is given unto Me to say unto thee - fear not - for it is the finish of the old - the beginning of the new - and at no time shall ye fear that which is to come upon thee -- For it is said: "There is a law governing all things" - and it is so - no man escapes it ---

While it is said: Ye shall be unto thineself true and prepare thineself for to receive thine freedom - yet unto them which have not prepared themself I say: Thou hast been given the law - the day - the time - and thou hast squandered it in riotous living -- Now ye shall learn well thine lesson - and that is thine fortune -- All that is required of thee is obedience unto the law -- And I am mindful of them which have made a mockery of The Word -- I am concerned for their sake - for I say - it is for their sake - that We put forth the effort - that they be brot out of bondage ---

The sick needeth the physician!

Wherein is it said - that they have betrayed themself - their trust?

I say unto them: WE - of the Mighty Council - work without ceasing that all might be well with thee ---

Think ye that We are not aware of thine askings - I say We know thine every thot -- Too - We know that which prompts them ---

Let it be said: Let all thine thots be prompted by LOVE - and it shall be profitable unto thee ---

Let it be said: That We Know thee by thine Light ---

I am come that it be increased -- So be it I am come thru and by the consent of The Mighty Council --

Self-Responsibility

Sori Sori

Hast it not been given unto man to have the Word placed with their hands -- Hast it not been given unto thee from the beginning - and it hast been desecrated - desecrated I say! ---

I come that they might now know that which they do -- I come that they be prepared for that which shall be given unto them to do - and they shall bear the burden of their own fortune - none shall carry it for them ---

I say unto them: Desecrate NOT - THE WORD OF GOD - for greater sin hath no man! --

Neither by action or implication of word/ deed - shall ye desecrate the WORD ---

Be ye thotful of thine speech - be ye thotful of thine actions - and be responsible for them - for it is for this that I speak - that ye become responsible -- This is the day when ye shall become responsible for thine actions -- Ye shall not pass thine responsibility unto another - for it is given unto thee to be responsible for that which ye do - that which ye think -- For know ye that thine record shall be kept intact - and ye shall read and respond there to ---

It is given unto man to be as the ones thotless of the WORD - and the Servitors - the ones which minister unto them -- They think themself self-sufficient - yet it is said they walk not alone - they are NOT alone.

They ask for help - yet they accept it not as it is offered - they accept not that which should profit them ---

They cry out for release from bondage - knowing not they have bound themself -- By their own fortune have they bound themself - for they have given the dragon power over them ---

They serve him willingly - questioning not his authority -- Yet they shall now begin their questioning of him ---

They shall have proof - he is THE TRAITOR ---

They shall have proof he hast misled them - they then shall cry out, then they shall no more serve him willingly and faithfully ---

He - the dragon shall be disarmed - and he shall lose his power - for he hast only the power given unto him by them which serve him -- So be it that they shall turn from him - and ask for Light - and they shall be given as they are prepared to receive --

So be it and Selah --

They Shall Stand Witness

Sori Sori -- Hear ye that which I say unto thee - and they shall bear witness of Mine Saying -- Let it be Mine Testimony unto them -- And they shall stand witness before The Throne of The Most High Living God - and they shall remember that which I now say unto thee ---

Let it be recorded as I say it - for all to see and to know -- For I say unto thee: That which is done secretly shall be done openly -- And I have given unto thee the authority and the power to speak in Mine Name -- And I have seen thine record - I know thee and I have seen fit to use thine hand as Mine Hand - and I now say unto thee: Take up the Cross - and follow Him which hast called thee "Beloved" - and He shall bring thee into the Holy of Holies -- He shall bear witness of thee - for He hast stood Sponsor for thee -- He hast given unto thee a gift - and thou hast proven thyself worthy -- So shall it be multiplied - and it shall be for the good of All mankind -- So be it I now pronounce thee Mine Servant - on whose head I lay Mine Hand in Holy Benediction - and I pronounce thee worthy of that which I have for thee -- I say unto thee: Be ye as one prepared for yet greater things -- For it is now come when all things shall be made clear unto thee -- Receive of Me Mine Benediction - and rest in the knowing that I am with thee -- So be it I say unto thee in the Name of The Father Son and Mighty Council - partake of Mine Cup - and be ye as one forever blest -- Lift up thine eyes and give thanks this day is come -- So be it ye shall walk knowingly before men ---

Let it be as The Father hast Willed.

So be it and Selah --

Sanat Kumara hast spoken ---

Book Number Two

Sori Sori

Hast it not been said - that ye shall receive as thou art prepared - so shall it be -- Thou art now prepared to give unto them this Mine Word and as they art prepared - so shall they receive it -- When they have received it - then I shall touch them - and they shall be quickened - and they shall know ---

Ye shall now give unto them this part of this book -- It shall be divided here - and this shall be the second part ---

It shall begin with this page - and they which hast followed the other parts - shall be blest to receive this part -- And they which have been blest to receive unto themself this part - shall be given that for which they have waited - they shall find their waiting hast profited them ---

Blest art thou - O Mine Beloved - for I have given unto thee Mine Benediction - Mine Blessing - and ye shall now go forth as One qualified to say unto them - that which I give unto thee to say -- Ye shall be Mine Handmaiden - and I shall uphold thee in thine labors - and strengthen thee in the time of weakness -- So be it I am the One

Sent for this part -- It is Mine part to prepare thee for thine next part -- So be it I Am The Most Worthy Grand Master of The Inner Temple.

Blest shall ye be --

So be it and Selah --

* * * * * * *

Sori Sori

While it is now come that this part be prepared for them - let it be as it is given unto thee -- Let it be given unto them without change - and in its purity -- For it shall be received as I give it unto thee - and no man shall add to - or take away -- So be it I say unto thee - NO MAN shall add to or take away - and let no one place upon it a price - neither set his seal upon it -- It shall not be pilfered - and no man shall deny the authority thereof -- For I come with the consent of The Mighty Council and The One which hast given unto Me Mine Inheritance - The Allwise, All Powerful Father the Solen Aum Solen -- Therein is Mine Authority. So be it I say unto thee - woe unto any man which denies Mine Authority - for I am not an imposter - I Am Sent that The Father's Will be done - So let it be ---

I now place Mine Hand upon thine - and I command thee to write that which I say unto thee - for this have I prepared thee ---

There are many now which are prepared to receive the Rites of The Order of Melchezedek - and none are without a part -- None shall be overlooked which are so prepared - for there are many which walk within thine midst which have been prepared - and they too - shall become known unto thee - they too shall come to know thee - and there shall be an assembly - a coming together - and there shall be an Elder present - and He shall instruct thee in the Order of Melchezedek -- He shall be as One which hast been prepared for His part -- He comes with the Power and Authority invested within Him of The Mighty Council. He hast within His hand the Rod of Power - and He Knows well His part -- And He hast within His hand His Passport into the place wherein. I Am -- He hast long served the Light - He hast long awaited the day when He might go forth as One prepared for this part ---

The time is now come when it is expedient to send Him forth - for the time is now come when We find it expedient to give unto thee the part which is for them which await this part ---

It is said: As They are prepared - so shall they receive - it is so ---

Yet I say - the half is not told - for Greater things are in store for them which are now ready to receive -- Let them come - let them partake of the Rites - and let them know that which is their Right ---

So be it I shall speak at length on the Rites of Melchezedek ---

So be it at a later time --

Ye Shall Accept Mine Assistance

Hear ye this say that which I say unto thee - for it is the time of accounting - the time of sifting and sorting -- And the ones which are so prepared - shall be brot out of bondage - and the ones which have not prepared themself - shall be put into a place wherein they shall wait and it is said - their waiting shall be long and hard ---

Now there are none so sad as the ones which betray themself -- It hast been said many times - yet they which betray themself - are the ones which have denied the Word - and put their fingers in their own ears - that they might not hear ---

Yet it is said - that their waiting shall be long and hard -- Let it suffice that it be hard and long - for no man knoweth the duration - neither the torment -- While it is said - they have danced to the "piper's tune" - I say they have given no thot of that which is before them - that which they shall become - that which they have fortuned unto themselves. Yet it is said: Ye shall ponder well that which I say unto thee - for there is but little time in which thou hast to set strait that which thou hast made crooked -- So be it that I am come this day - that ye have assistance ---

And it behooves thee to accept it in the Name of The Father which hast Sent Me ---

I say ye shall accept Mine Assistance in the Name of The Father Which hast Sent Me -- For I come in His Name ---

Let it be for thine own sake that I speak unto thee - take it unto thineself - and be it as ye will -- For none shall put into thine mouth words which thou wilt not speak -- I say - none shall force upon thee that which thou art not prepared to receive ---

Hear ye that which I say unto thee - and give unto Me credit for being that which I am - and I shall touch thee - and I shall give unto thee that which I have received for thee - so be it - it shall profit thee - Let it be for the good of all - that ye receive Me and of Me -- So be it as The Father hast Willed it ---

The Day of Accounting

Hear ye this day - that which I say unto thee: Thine time hast come when ye shall account for thineself - for it is now the day of accounting when ye shall be called to account ---

Yea unto the last one ---

And it behooves thee to hear that which I say - for I am come that ye be sobered - that ye give some heed unto that which We of The Mighty Council sayeth ---

We are aware of thine plight - of thine sore - and We come unto thee in Great Compassion - that it be healed -- We come not to comfort thee - We come that the sore be healed and be no more -- It is now time when ye shall see the cause of the sore - and that ye be rid of it forever. Let it be for the good of all - that it be cleansed out - and therein is wisdom ---

It is said - that the way is hard - and ye weary of it - yet it is given unto Me to know the end - and therefore I say unto thee - cleanse out the old and be ye made whole -- I say unto thee: The end justifies the means - and it is Mine part to say unto thee: I Am the Most Worthy Grand Master of The Inner Temple - therefore I am prepared to do Mine Part -- I ask of thee: Canst thou say as much for thineself - canst thou go all the way - I ask of thee - wherefrom comest thine strength - thine assistance? ---

Ponder well Mine questions!

For I am thotful of thee - I weary not of Mine part -- I ask of thee: Be ye alert -cast off thine slothfulness - and bless thineself in the doing.

Be ye up and about thine preparation - and I shall remember thee in the days of thine affliction --

There is No Death - Its True Meaning

Now it is said - that the time swiftly comes - when there shall be Great Light flood the Earth - and none which are unprepared shall stand the strength thereof ---

I say unto thee: Hear ye and be ye as one prepared - for woe unto him which remaineth in darkness -- Woe unto him which finds himself unprepared - for he shall remain in darkness ---

He shall seek the Light - and it shall profit him---

Let it be said - that WE of the Mighty Council draw nigh unto thee that ye be as one prepared ---

I speak unto thee which read - which see - which hear these Mine Words -- For I speak unto thee - that ye prepare thineself for that which shall come to pass -- For swift shall be the change -- and let it profit thee-- No place have We spoken unto thee as the "Change" being "Death" - for I say unto thee - there is no death -- That which thou hast called death - is but the taking off of the pore - and taking up another form - tho lighter of substance -- Thou hast not known the true meaning of "Death" -- Let Us speak of Life - ETERNAL LIFE - for there is but the Eternal Life - and for this do We say unto thee: Come ye forth - and be ye as one prepared for that which shall come about by natural law - And thou shall stand as one shorn of all thine possessions - all thine vain glory - and ye shall be as one prepared to face thineself -- For ye shall be as one on whose shoulders rests thine own judgment ---

Thine own fortune shall be thine -- Thine own burden shall be thine. Thine own shame shall be thine ---

It is said: "Cleanse thineself of all thine guilt - let peace be established within thee - let there be no malice - no hatred within thee". Come ye unto the fount -- Wash thineself - and be ye as one prepared to go into the Holy of Holies - wherein there is Only LOVE ---

So be it I say unto thee - all thine words/ deeds shall be prompted by Love - and ye shalt be thine own porter --

So be it and Selah --

I Give No Magical Formulas

Hast thou not been given the law? Hast thou been as one obedient unto it? Hast thou put on the whole Armor of God?

Hast thou been as one obedient unto the call? -- I ask thee - that ye might take an accounting of thineself - that ye might be as one prepared. I say unto thee: Look well unto thine preparation - for it behooves Me to ask of thee many things -- Discount them not - for it is thine part to remember that which I say unto thee ---

I give unto thee - not great and magical formulas - for which men ask -- I give unto thee the law by which ye live - by which ye shall be unbound -- And it is said: By no other way do ye enter into the place wherein I abide - for the law shall not become invalid - or nullified - therefore I say unto thee - seek no other way -- For it shall be given unto thee - to <u>bring</u> thineself - by obedience unto the law - the application thereof ---

It is said - that ye shall be "brot" into the place wherein I am - yet it is by thine light that thou art found - and by thine preparation - So shall be the light - let it so shine - and ye shall be given in like measure -- It is said: Empty out the dross - and thine cup shall be filled to overflowing - so be it and Selah ---

Hold firm unto the Light - and heed that which is said unto thee -- Make it thine own - and be ye obedient unto thine Calling -- Turn not away - for it is given unto man to be impatient - and willful - and I say unto thee - there is no tomorrow -- THIS DAY is the time - and it shall not always afford unto thee time - for "time" shall pass - and thine fortune spent - thine victory lost - and what hast thou profited?

I speak unto thee in language simple - and in a fashion thou canst comprehend -- For I am about that which I am given to do - and by any method it shall be done - for I am not to be sent away empty handed - for I know what I am about - and it is for that - that I have given unto thee this part ---

Do with it as ye will - yet ye shall say not: It hast NOT been said unto thee ---

For I have spoken -- I have placed it within thine own hands - now ye shall bear the responsibility of thine own actions -- Let it be accorded unto thee -

As The Father Wills it --

The Lord God is Come

Mighty - O Mighty is the Power which The Lord God holds within His Hand -- And Great is His Light - and It shall be known by man - for he shall see and know that HE is Come ---

I say He is come -- Holy - Holy is HIS NAME -- Praise ye The Father Solen Aum Solen - for He hast sent Him - the One known as Sananda -- Bless Him - for He is come this day that there be LIGHT -- For It shall go forth as a great onrush of Power - and It shall consume the darkness -- And not a place shall there be wherein they shall hide - for the Light shall flood the Earth - and great shall be Its power --For The Lord God shall stand as a Great Beacon of Light - a tower set upon the Mountain ---

And He shall speak forth The Word - and it shall become manifest - and nought shall stay the power of The Word -- For out of His Mouth shall go forth such Power - that man can not stand against -- I say - the unholy shall flee unto the hills - they shall cry for the stones to cover them - they shall torment themselves - they shall fall within their tracks for fear ---

They shall fear the Light which He brings for they shall know their end is come -- I say - woe unto them which are found wanting ---

Too - I say - blest are they which are found prepared - they shall see the Glory of The Lord --

So be it and Selah --

Be Alert and Obedient

Let this be a part which shall be added unto the first Book of the Kumara - and it shall be for the good of all -- At no time shall We of The Mighty Council - ask of thee more than thou canst do -- At no time shall We ask anything of thee - save for thine own sake ---

At no time shall We give more than is lawful for thee to do -- Now for that matter - that which We give unto thee is for thine own preparation -- For thine own sake do We give unto thee a part -- It is lawful that We ask of thee obedience unto the law - and it is expedient that ye be alert and obedient - for it behooves thee to know the law - and abide thereby -- And at no time shall ye be held responsible for the failure of another - yet ye shall mind thine own preparation - and ye shall attend unto thine own -- And forget not <u>this</u> is the day of preparation - it shall be shortened - so it is becoming unto thee to walk ye as one sober - and as a Son of God -- Falter not - fear not - and wait upon The Lord thy God ---

The Holy Rites of the Order of Melchezedek

Be ye one which hast heard the Word - and be ye as one prepared - for I shall speak - and it shall profit thee to hear that which I say - for it shall be for the good of all that I speak ---

Let them which are so prepared - hear that which I say ---

By Mine own hand shall I anoint them which hear - and prepare themself for greater things -- I say - I shall anoint them - and they shall be blest - of Me and by Me - for I am come that they might know that which is in store for them ---

I say they shall be anointed - <u>then</u> they shall be given in greater capacity ---

Yet the unjust shall not receive of the Rights of the anointing ---

Neither shall they see from afar - for they shall not plunder the secrets of The Holy Rites of this Order -- They shall neither see - or hear that which is done - for I say it shall be hidden up from the unjust, the imprudent ---

They shall first prepare themself - then they shall be given in wisdom - and with the love which We share ---

So be it that the Mysteries of the Order of Melchezedek - shall neither be written or spoken in their presence - for they shall be barred from the Assembly wherein The WORD is spoken - wherein it is practiced ---

Yet they shall see the light from the Holy Ground upon which these Rites are performed ---

I say they shall be as ones which see the light - yet the Source they shall not see or know ---

For there are traitors within thine midst - and they would but pick thine pockets - and call thee foolish ---

Think ye that it is becoming unto Us to betray Ourself - and to misuse the energy which is Ours ---

I say unto thee: We are not in any wise foolish - We know them which are prepared to receive of the Mysteries ---

Let it be said: Never hast the Mysteries of The Order of Melchezedek been written - they come thru and by direct revelation - given unto the just and the prudent ---

Forget not that there is a Great responsibility placed upon thee - when thou hast received the Sacred Rites of The Order -- For it is said: "There are none so sad as the one which hast betrayed himself or his trust" - so be it - and it is given unto Me to Know ---

I speak from out the Inner Temple - wherein there is no mystery - yet it is necessary to hide from the unjust - unworthy - that which We Know ---

We speak with wisdom and compassion that they be prepared - yet they weary of their preparation - for they are weak of character - they are want for strength of character - frail of spirit -- For they are as ones blown about by the foul winds - which toss them about -- They are not firm in their knowing - for they ask of man his opinion - and it is freely given - and therein is no light ---

It is said: Keep thine own counsel - heed the Word of God - seek the Light - obey the law - and be ye as one found worthy - and ye shall receive in Great measure - so let it be -- According unto thine preparation shall it be --

I Am The Most Worthy Grand Master of The Inner Temple ---

I have said: I Am HE - I AM HE Which is Sent for this part -- And it is Mine part to appraise thee of the condition of men - men in bondage.

And at no time hast it been given unto him - the "Man" - to be in greater danger - <u>danger</u>! I say ---

Yet he hast not been given unto revelation - he hast not been given unto asking of The Father - for revelation ---

He hast been as one drunken - he hast squandered his substance - he hast given unto himself the bitter cup -- Now it runneth over ---

He shall cry out for help - for his "innards" shall sting - burn of his own bitterness - his own cup shall be bitter - and he shall be as one which hast prepared it ---

Lo - I say unto thee: Their bellies shall swell and burst - and they shall cry out for release - For I say that which they have prepared for themself - shall fill their bellies - and torment them exceedingly---

While it is now come that they shall know by which they are tormented - I say they shall be as ones responsible for their torment -- For is it not said: As ye prepare thineself - so shall ye receive - IT IS SO! - So shall it be - for it is the Law ---

I speak unto them in terms which they might understand - for it is given that there be no misunderstanding -- It is given that they might not be confused - by the terminology -- The words which I choose are Mine - yet the law changes not ---

I speak unto men - I speak unto them which weary of their lot - that they might know by which they are bound ---

I say they have fortuned unto themself all their misery - all their torment ---

Let them turn unto the Light - seek relief of The Father - the Giver of Life - and then they shall be relieved -- Yet there is a "Price" - that of The "Wholly Sacrifice" - the "Holy Ordinance" -- And it shall be their right to partake of the "Holy Rites" of The Order of Melchezedek when they have made the sacrifice ---

Let it be said: First the Sacrifice of Self - then the "Holy Rites" of The Order of Melchezedek shall be administered upon them ---

I say: "Then - the Holy Rites of Melchezedek shall be administered upon them" -- For this do I now speak -- So let it be as THE FATHER hast Willed it---

Thine is a Sad Lot

Hear ye - all which read these Mine Words - for I speak unto THEE - I say unto thee: Be ye aware of The Mighty Council - be ye aware of The <u>Word</u> -- And be ye as one prepared this day - for a part which shall be given unto thee -- It is given unto Me to speak of "The Council" - and to say unto thee - there is more yet to be said ---

Yet ye shall first prepare thineself to hear - for there are things thou couldst not bear -- It is given unto Me to hear thee deny the Word - to question the Word - and to pilfer the Word ---

Yet I say unto thee - make it <u>thine</u> <u>own</u> - and bless thineself in the doing ---

Hear ye that which I say - and take it unto thineself - for I speak unto thee - as well as thine brother - and thine neighbor ---

Yet there is not one which hast the power or the authority which is invested within Me - for I come of Mine Father's Will - and I Am One of The Council -- Therefore I know that which I am about -- And I say unto thee: Be ye as one which can say as much for thineself -- For I say unto thee - little dost thou know of that which goes on about thee - for thine is a sad lot -- I say: Thine lot is a sad one indeed - for thou dost not see that which is before thee - thou hast not heard that which hast been said ---

Yet it is said - ye shall seek the Light - and ye shall be quickened - and ye shall see and hear -- And I shall pour out Mine Spirit upon thee. So be it as The Father Wills it ---

So let it be -- For this do I speak unto THEE --

Mine Hand Maiden

Sori Sori -- While it is given unto thee to be Mine Hand Maiden - I say unto thee: Be ye as the one which hast gone the long way -- Thou hast taken up the garment of flesh for their sake - and it shall be for their sake that ye shall be unto them Sibor -- For I say unto thee - thine work hast but begun - for it is but little that hast been accomplished this day. Yet the time comes swiftly - when ye shall arise as on wings of light - and ye shall be as one prepared to give unto them in greater measure.- For ye shall stand with Me upon the Mountain top - and ye shall know as I Know - and no man shall deny thine right -- For none shall take from thee thine Inheritance - it is thine by Divine Right - and it is by the Right of thine Inheritance that ye shall receive as I have received. So be it and Selah --

Thou Art in Need

Sori Sori -- I say unto thee - thine hand shall be Mine hand - and ye shall record Mine Word - for all which seek the Light -- None shall be denied - and It shall not be hidden from them ---

It shall be given freely - and they which shall receive - shall give freely - for they shall know the law: It is more blessed to give than to receive - so let it be ---

I am the One sent for this part - and it shall bear Mine Name - and the Authority which is Mine - for I say unto them: I AM SENT OF MINE FATHER - that I might be as One which hast the Power and Authority - to speak in His Name - for He hast given Me full Authority to use His Name -- And for that I say unto thee: Go ye forth in MINE NAME - and say unto them: It is nigh time when ye shall awaken - for time shall be no more - and ye shall be as one wanting ---

I say: Ye shall speak unto them that which thou hast been given -- Say it as it is given unto thee - for not one thing shall be taken away or added to -- For it is given unto Me to know thine need - and thou hast need of Me - and that which I say unto thee -- I say: Thou knowest not thine need - yet ye shall come into the knowledge of thine need -- Ye shall see thine want - and ye shall likewise ask that ye be given as thou hast need -- For it shall be given unto thee to know thou <u>art</u> <u>in</u> <u>need</u> -- Yet it is given unto thee to want many "things" which are not needful. And these are but thine legirons - these are but thine undoing -- While I say unto thee: Seek ye the Light - and It shall not be withheld ---

Will it not be given unto thee as thou need - as thou art prepared to receive. So shall it be --

We See -- We Know

Hold out thine hand - and I shall touch thee -- Accept ye that which I say unto thee - and be ye as one prepared for to receive of Me in greater measure ---

Let it profit thee to receive of Me - for I give not unto the unjust - unto them which would betray Mine trust ---

I say - I am not so foolish as to trust the unjust - for I know them -- I speak that ye prepare thineself that I might touch thee - that I might give unto thee in great measure -- So be it that I know thine capacity - and it shall be as thou art prepared -- I say unto thee - increase thine capacity - walk ye knowingly -- Be ye alert - and know ye that ye art not alone - for I say - thou art never alone - Never! - I say NEVER! ---

Be ye as one alert unto that which goes on about thee - and be ye unafraid - for I say - ye have nothing to fear save thine own darkness which blinds thee ---

I say unto thee - let the darkness blind thee no more - for a Mighty Host hast assembled that ye have Light -- And none are hidden - for each unto his place - each is known - not one is lost from sight - for We have the Greater Vision - We are not bound in darkness ---

WE SEE - WE KNOW -- So be it - nothing is hidden from Us -- We are as Ones alert unto that which goes on - and We are come that All might see as We SEE ---

So let it be - as The Father Wills it --

Ye Shall Know the Value of Mine Gifts

Wait upon the Lord - and be ye quick to respond unto Him - for He calls unto thee from the High Place in which He is -- He hast no other thot than to serve The Father's Will - for He knows well THE WILL of The Father Which hast sent Me ---

So be it I am One with HIM THE LORD GOD - The King of Kings, The Host of Hosts - for He is Lord of All - Our All - and He is The Lord God -- Rest in the knowing that HE IS -- And none shall take from Him His High Estate - for He hast come unto thee as such - and as such man crucified Him - and as such they know Him not - for they but knew that He was "man" – they knew Him not to be The Son of God The Father - Sent - that they be lifted up ---

They were too - in darkness -- They too - were a sad lot - yet they rejected Him as THE ONE SENT ---

I say unto thee this day - I am too - Sent of The Father - that ye be brot out of bondage - that ye too might be free - even as We are free.

Now ye shall do as ye will - for none shall bring thee against thine will - for it is thine to choose - which way ye shall go -- Prepare thineself to go the Royal Road - and it shall profit thee - for ye shall as one lifted up - and ye shall know no more sorrow - no more suffering - no more waiting ---

So be it I have said - I Am Sent - I AM SENT --

And I come even as The Sananda -- I come with the "Rod of Brass". I come with Authority - and Power - for I bring unto thee a Host Which shall sustain thee in thine ascent -- I come bearing Gifts -- Ye have but to accept them in the Name of The Father which hast Sent ME ---

So be it - the gifts which I bear shall be becoming unto thee - for I give not the priceless Pearls - which would be unto <u>thee</u> unbecoming. Ye shall be as one prepared to receive Mine Gifts -- Ye shall Know the Price - the Value - and ye shall therefore treasure that which I now withhold from the unjust - imprudent - until such time that they learn that which is just and prudent - and that which is needful ---

I say it is necessary that they examine well themself - and they shall be aware of their needs - and therefore they shall ask for LIGHT - and It shall not be denied them ---

Let it suffice - that I shall hear them and answer them -- There shall be sent one unto them - to give unto them as they are prepared to receive.

So be it I Am One Sent ---

So be it I await thine Call --

His Hands Shall Be Clean

Hold high thine head - bow down unto no man - give no man thine will, plunder not the sayings of the Sages -- For thine own sayings shall be thine - and it is given unto fools to plunder the sayings of the Sages ---

I say unto thee: Walk YE in the Light - and be ye as one illumined. Give of thineself that all men be lifted up - forch not thine sayings upon any man - Let him which asketh of thee - see thine light that he might know thine strength - and the measure of thine love -- Such would be Mine Word unto thee this day ---

Say unto them which asketh of thee: "The Lord thy God hast commanded of thee thine sacrifice - and it shall be demanded of thee ere ye pass within the Holy of Holies"- I say - ye shall give unto them THE WORD - yet ye shall first accept it as thine own -- For I say unto thee: Let it be thine - Engrave IT upon thine heart - that It might not be lost - such is Mine Word this day---

Let it be understood - that he which asks shall be heard - and given as his needs be - as he is prepared to receive ---

Hast it not been as of old - there hast been denials - and betrayals - so shall there be -- Yet there shall stand before thee One Mighty and Just - and He shall be as the One which is Sent -- and He shall be as One favored of God The Father - and His raiment shall to be spotless - and His hands shall be clean - of all blemish -- For He shall have upon His hands no blood - no stain - for He hast been as One Sent -- And for this He shall not take upon Himself the stains of flesh - for rebellion shall be no part of Him -- He shall know no rebellion - and He shall be One with The Father Which hast sent Him ---

Hallowed be His Name -- So be it that I have spoken - and it shall be as I have spoken - so be it ---

I Am The Grand Master of The Inner Temple --

All is One
(Let it be a good account)

Let it be understood that there are many which have gone the Royal Road - yet they have been as ones prepared for their Royal Raiment -- They left the grosser/ denser garments of flesh within the realms below, they were as ones prepared to step forth into their Christ Body - of Light Substance - and which is their own body of Light Substance -- And for this do they have the power and the authority to control the lesser substance (the denser substance) -- They are free to go and come at will yet they lower their LIGHT that they might come into the denser matter, the denser world - and for that are they prepared - that there be greater understanding in the world of men ---

I say - they come as ones prepared that man might partake of their Light - and that they might have the same joy of serving the Earth and Her Sons - as they have known ---

Therefore it is said: Come - and be ye made whole - be ye as one freed from bondage -- Yet in thine freedom ye shall ask for all mankind bound in darkness -- For when thou hast tasted of such joy - ye shall <u>ask</u> for all mankind - that they too might partake of thine joy ---

Let it be remembered that all are One - all are brothers - and each unto his own -- And not one can be lifted up - without the blessing of the WHOLE - for all are One ---

It wast said by The Son of God - Sent of Him: "If I BE LIFTED UP I draw all men unto ME"---

So shall it be - for All are One ---

So be it - All shall be as One united - and they shall come to know their Oneness - and <u>then</u> the Angels shall sing together - and they shall know that they are of One Body ---

Therein is joy untold - and the Earth and the fullness thereof shall be as One - lifted up and transformed - and <u>IT</u> shall be as the Sun unto planets yet unformed -- Such is Mine Word unto them which hast ears to hear -- I say - ponder long on thine <u>own</u> preparation - for the day comes swiftly - when ye shall be as one called to account for thineself so let it be a Good account ---

Concealed Identity

Lo I say unto thee: There are many within thine midst - which are of the Inner Circle - and they which ye know not of ---

I say - they are within flesh as man - they walk as ones incognito - and they give no sign - no identification -- Yet I say unto thee - the Seal is upon them - and they know that they are sealed -- Yet too - I say - the Seal shall be broken - and they shall be revealed for that which they are -- They are as the Ones walking in flesh - yet they shall be as ones free of flesh - and they shall become as ones free of flesh -- And they shall wear the Royal Robe - neither spun or fabricated -- They shall wear the Royal Helmet - and the Mark of Royalty shall adorn their Helmet -- So be it that these which now walk in the shadows - shall be brot into the Light - and they shall be known - Yea by their Light shall they be known ---

For this is it said: Let thine eyes be opened - and let thine eyes behold the Glory of God -- For I say - He hast given unto thee eyes for to see - and ears for to hear - and ye shall be touched - and ye shall be quickened - and ye shall know thou hast been touched -- So be it ye shall be glad ---

While I say unto thee - many walk as under a mask - for is it not a mask which hides the "man" -- This is the Word I would give unto thee this day: - Be ye as one alert - and seek THE LIGHT and It shall not be hidden -- And ye shall see beneath the "Mask" - and ye shall know them and they shall be as ones Revealed unto thee -- So be it that they shall pass - and they shall come - and they shall come asking/ seeking the Light ---

Yet too - I say - amongst them shall be the traitor - and he shall reveal himself - and I say - he shall be the <u>sad</u> <u>one</u> - for he shall be unto himself traitor - and there are none so sad ---

I tell thee of a surety - there SHALL be One amongst them which shall be the traitor - it is ever thus - so be it I know whereof I speak -- Fear him not - for he shall reveal himself unto thee -- I know him - and for this do I warn thee ---

So be it I am aware of them - each of them -- I know their every thot - I know their motives - their hearts -- Too - I say - some have hearts of stone - some have hearts of blackness - some have hearts filled with Love one for another - and none deceive Me ---

So be it I come that all be revealed - for I am within the place where All things are known ---

I Am The Most Worthy Grand Master of The Inner Temple --

The Announcement: The New Post for Thedra

Sori Sori

Let thine hand be Mine hand - and swift to do Mine Work - for I too - shall give unto thee a Part - and ye shall be as one blest - as one prepared for that part ---

Ye shall stand Sentinel upon Mine Holy Mountain - and ye shall receive them which come out of the shadows-- Ye shall stand watch - and ye shall know them which come - for they shall bear the Seal which hast been given unto them ---

They shall be liken unto them which pass within the gate of the Great Portal of the _____ (?).

They shall bring with them nothing save their credentials - their passport -- I say unto thee - they shall identify themself - and ye shall know them by their identification -- And it shall be as the part which shall be new unto thee - yet thou hast been as one prepared for this part/ this post ---

When it is come that the veil shall be removed - ye shall see that which hast been accomplished -- And it shall be as the fortune which thou hast accumulated for thineself -- Let it be said: Thou hast prepared thineself for this part - by the assistance of The Mighty Council - The OVER-ALL COUNCIL ---

So be it ye shall wear the Robe of Authority - and ye shall hold within thine hand the Rod which shall be made BRASS -- So be it I speak unto thee on behalf of The Mighty Council - and it shall be thine part to accept it - in the Name of The Council ---

It is said - that this part is <u>not</u> new unto thee - for it is said - long hast thou been prepared -- Yet thine time is not yet come when ye shall come into the fullness of this knowledge - for thine time is not yet fulfilled ---

I say: Thine work - thine mission shall be finished - done - then ye shall be given the full knowledge of thine new part -- And without any delay ye shall step forth in command - ye shall stand sentinel - and ye shall know the fullness of thine work - which hast been assigned unto thee - thru and by The Mighty Council ---

I say - the Shoe is yet large - yet ye shall grow into the shoes -- Be ye as the <u>foot</u> of The One Which hast Sent ME - that I might give unto thee this announcement - for I AM HE - which makes the announcements ---

I Am HE -- Sent Am I - that ye might have this Part --

The Mighty Judgment Seat

I say unto thee this day: See ye the hand of God MOVE -- It moveth in ways ye know not of - I say: SEE YE THE HAND OF GOD MOVE - for IT moveth in ways ye know not of!! ---

Let IT move - and let It bring forth the Light! Let it be said that no man - shall stay THE HAND OF GOD - IT shall set the porters aside - and It shall pass thru the Gates unstaid - and It shall be as the Mighty Judgment set over a people - and It shall be the Arm of THE LAW ---

IT shall be the Balance - The Scales of Justice - and man shall stand upon the scale and be found wanting---

I say - the Scales shall not balance in his favor - for he hast been found wanting - It is said: He hast betrayed himself ---

I say unto thee this day - man hast betrayed himself - and he shall be found wanting ---

I speak out this day - for the law - hast been given unto him - and he hast rebelled against it - he hast been as one which hast committed crimes against himself - his fellow man - and against the "Holy Ghost". He hast betrayed himself - and it is said: "There is none so sad - as he which betrays himself or his trust". He hast this day - stood on trial - he hast this day stood as one before the Bar of Justice ---

And - I say unto thee: He hast condemned himself - for he hast signed his own warrant - his own "death warrant" ---

I say unto thee in all humility - in great compassion - this is the Day of Condemnation - this is the day which is to be known as Black _____ and it is a grievous thing - for long shall ye remember this day - and poor shall they be which partakes of the Judgment---

Peace - Peace - Peace be unto thee - for I say: Ye shall keep thine peace -- Be ye still - be ye thotful of the signs of the TIMES - and know ye that the "End Time" is come ---

So be it I am come also -- So be it that I say unto thee - Peace - Peace - Peace -- Yet they shall not find peace - for peace is not within them -- Let it be said - that they shall tear the flesh of their brother -

and they shall rend their father and mother - they defile their sisters: ---

So be it I say unto thee: The half hast not been seen ---

Stand Up and Be Counted

Let thine heart be filled with love and compassion this day -- Let Peace be established within thee -- For I hear them cry - peace - peace – peace, yet there is no peace within them ---

It hast been said that there shall be trying times and it is so -- While it is given unto 'them' to run amuck - I say unto thee: Hold ye firm - keep thine feet firmly planted upon the Rock - Which shall be unto thee thine sure foundation - and it shall not fail thee ---

Bless them which are the forerunners of Peace - for they shall be as the ones Sent - that they might partake in the Work at hand - that they might help establish a New Order - and that they might be within the place wherein they are prepared for yet greater things ---

Let thine hearts be filled with Love and Compassion for them – and give thanks that <u>they</u> are come - for theirs is no small part ---

So be it that I say unto them: "There is a Greater part for thee - yet ye shall be as one prepared to receive it" - for this is the Classroom - the School of Gods - wherein ye learn thine lessons - thine part - wherein thou art prepared for thine next part ---

Ye shall stand up this day and be counted ---

Whom servest thou?

Answer ye Me - Whom servest thou?

This is the day in which ye answer ---

Call unto The Light - and ye shall be heard ---

YE SHALL SEEK THE LIGHT - Walk ye in IT - and be ye as one prepared for Greater things -- So let it be - as The Father hast Willed it.

I Am The Most Worthy Grand Master of The Inner Temple -

Bells of Freedom

Hold ye high the torch of "Freedom" -- Let freedom ring out -- Let this day bring forth the freedom for which the Great Ones have died/ given their lives ---

Let the freedom bell ring out - let them hear the "Bells of Freedom" ring out - thruout the lands ---

Let no man bind his fellow-man in bondage -- Let no man take his brother bondage -- Let no man be unto his brother the "overseer" - the "turnkey" - for I say freedom <u>shall</u> ring forth -- For man shall learn well his lesson - they shall learn to love each other - they shall learn that suffering will bind them together in the common bond - there is the lesson to be learned ---

I say: Man shall learn love for each other -- They shall remember their suffering - and they shall be as ones prepared for their next place of abode -- They shall come to know that there is no death - that Life is eternal - that they shall account for all their misspent energy - and they shall atone - they shall atone for all their misspent energy -- They shall be weighed in the balance - and they shall be their own judge - and none shall escape - for the law of balance is JUST - and it is Justice that shall reign ---

I say: Justice shall reign Supreme -- So be it and Selah ---

I have spoken -- Consider well that which I have said - for I am not given unto idle sayings ---

Amen - So be it -

Today's Blessing

This would I say unto thee - be ye as one blest this day - ye shall see that which hast been hidden from thee---

Ye shall know that which hast not been revealed unto thee ---

Unto them which read that which I say unto thee - I would say: As they prepare themself - so shall they receive ---

Now it is said - that the ones which receive ME and of ME shall be as the ones prepared -- I say: It is given unto Me to speak out - and therein is wisdom - for I give of Mineself that man be lifted up - and therein is Mine Love - for them ---

I give of Mineself unto <u>All</u> which are so prepared to receive of Mine Love - for it is given unto Me to be the manifestation of LOVE ---

I am not a far off false god - neither do I make false claims -- I am as The One Which sits above thee - yet thou art no less for thine <u>beneathness</u> -- I am no greater for Mine <u>aboveness</u> -- For I am given this station from the beginning - and thou hast chosen thine way - and the ways have gone separately - yet they shall meet at the appointed time -- And ye shall do well to hasten unto the place wherein I sit - for I say: Mine position is not a lesser one - it is given unto Me to be one of the OVER ALL COUNCIL - THE MIGHTY COUNCIL ---

And therefore I speak knowingly -- I am not to be classified - neither am I to be cast out ---

I say unto thee: I am come that '<u>Ye</u>' be made to see and hear - to know that thou art of the same Source - from - and of the same Source. So be it that ye shall accept Mine WORD - Mine assistance - Mine Love - or - ye shall reject as thou will -- So be it - it shall profit thee to accept it -- Ponder <u>well </u>that which I say unto thee - and it shall profit thee ---

I am come that ye be lifted up -

Man is Dependent Upon the Forces of Light

Hear ye - O man of Earth! Hear ye Me - for I stand upon the High Holy Mount- and I gaze afar - and I see thee as ones bound in darkness! And it is given unto Me to see the pity of thine plight ---

Yet it behooves thee to be up and about thine deliverance -- Knowest thou that ye stand not alone - for no man stands alone - he is dependent upon the Forces of Light -- And them which put their trust in the arm of flesh shall perish -- Them which are given unto seeking the Light - shall be found - and they shall be enlightened - for they shall be given as they are prepared to receive -- I say: They shall first seek THE LIGHT - and they shall be blest -- They shall bless themself - for wherein is it said: By their own light shall they be found ---

Now man's days upon the Earth are numbered - and they shall be few - for it is given unto him to be given a new place of abode -- He shall have a new place wherein he shall abide - and let it be according unto his preparation - for it is the law: As he prepares himself - so shall he receive ---

Now it is given unto Me to say unto thee: No more shall the ones which are fortuned the new part - which is the taking off the old garment of flesh - inhabit the Earth -- They shall be removed ---

No longer shall the Earthbound sit at the table of the ones yet unbound - for they shall be removed - and they shall no longer ride the back of the ones which know not ---

For it is said: There shall be a division - the sheep shall be separated from the goats - the wheat from the tares - and there shall be a gathering up -- The tares shall be plucked from the thrashing floor and burned - and no more shall the seed thereof fall upon fertile soil - to bring forth forbidden harvest – I say: The seed shall no more fall upon fertile soil, they shall be gathered up and burned -- No longer shall they be blown about by the foul winds that blow them about -- No more shall they be sown in the wheat - for the wheat shall be as the harvest clean - pure - unadulterated -- It shall be put into its proper place - wherein there is neither moth or rust -- So be it that the seed of the new harvest shall be "Special" - it shall be separated and selected with care - preserved and protected - and no man shall be able to adulterate or poison the seed - for the new harvest ---

Therein I have spoken unto thee a parable - and ye shall do with it as ye will ---

Yet ye shall find great revelation therein -- I say: Ponder well Mine Saying - and I shall reveal Greater things unto thee -- Be ye wise - and see that which I have hidden from the foolish - which would belittle thee - and which would belittle Mine Word ---

I say unto thee: There are none so foolish as he which thinks himself wise - none so sad as he which betrays himself ---

Hold Ye the Lamp

Hold high the Lamp - for it shall light the way for them which follow after thee -- It is now come when ye shall gather them together - and ye shall give unto them which shall satisfy them ---

They have not found satisfaction - they have not found peace -- They have not found the Love which they seek - for love is not within them ---

They shall turn their minds unto things which they have not known for new things shall be shown unto them -- They shall turn from the war - one against the other - they shall find the futility of their wars - they shall be as ones desolate from their futility and foolishness ---

They shall see the futility of all their peace - pacts - all their mumblings - all their speakings -- For the hatred beneath the covering of their hypocrisy shall bring forth new signs of their hypocrisy -- The fires which smolder beneath the cover shall break out anew - and ye shall see the futility of the "Oil" which hast been poured on the troubled waters ---

For it shall be as the Oil added unto the fire -- For their hypocrisy shall be brot to light - and they shall see it - and know that it is for their own good that they have cried Peace - Peace -- Yet they have much to gain - by laying aside <u>All</u> their plans - and seeking THE LIGHT - for IT shall be their Shield and their Buckler -- They shall do well to listen unto what THE SPIRIT sayeth - they shall do well to listen unto that which WE OF THE MIGHTY COUNCIL sayeth - for We are not afar. WE know that which goes on behind closed doors - for We are not bound by flesh - neither are We amongst the dead -- I say - We are amongst the enlightened - the ennobled -- We are the Founders and Builders of Universes - and We hold within Our hand the Power and the Authority to command ---

I say unto THEE - O Man: Hear ye that which WE say unto thee - for the time SWIFTLY comes unto the end -- I say - ye shall choose well this day - for thine choice it is ---

Which way goest thou?

CHOOSE YE WHICH WAY!

So be it - I Am One MIGHTY and STRONG and I Am no fool -- MISTAKE ME NOT ---

All Else Shall Fail

Look ye well unto the Light - for all else shall fail thee -- All else shall be as ashes within thine hands---

I say unto thee: Look ye well unto the Light - for the Light shall not fail ---

I say unto thee: O - frail art thou - O man - and thine, labor hast been spent vainly - for thou hast groveled for a pittance - and wherein hast thou profited?

"Wherein hast thou profited? Answer Me O man!

Wherein hast thou profited? ---

I say unto thee - O rebellious man: Thou hast sold thine inheritance for a pittance - thou hast been as the foolish virgins ---

I tell thee of a surety: The Son of God is Come - yet He finds thee eating - drinking - and making merry---

I tell thee: Thou hast been found unworthy to unlatch His sandals. Thou knowest not the Lord thy God - for He hast not revealed Himself unto the unjust - and the bigot -- He shall lift up the foolish and the meek - the down trodden - the weary and oppressed -- And He shall pluck out from amongst them - the ones which are of a mind to receive Him and of Him -- He shall give unto the just - the Royal Raiment - which they shall wear with dignity - and they shall stand as ones purified and justified - and they shall no more know oppression and sorrow ---

While I say - the oppressor and the unjust - the unholy - shall weep and wail - they shall cry out for mercy - yet I say: Justice shall reign Supreme ---

For they shall atone for all their deeds -- And when they have made atonement - they too shall come unto Him as ones prepared - and He shall receive them unto Himself -- So be it by His Grace that they shall enter into the place of His Abode - for none come save thru Him ---

None come any other way -- So be it I have spoken--

So Be it as The Father hast Willed it --

He is the Eternal Father

This day - let it be understood - that there is but ONE GOD - SOLEN AUM SOLEN - and HE is The Eternal Father - The ONE Which hast brot thee forth in the beginning -- And HE hast the Will to bring thee back unto thine rightful estate -- And for thine rebellion - hast thou waited - bound in darkness -- Bound in flesh art thou - born of woman art thou ---

Thine memory blanked from thee - thine wandering hast been long and pitiful - for thou hast suffered much ---

Yet it is said: Thine wanderings shall end - thine memory returned unto thee - and ye shall be given thine inheritance in full ---

Yet it is said: Thou shall be as one prepared to receive - it is so ---

While it is given unto Me to be as One free of all bondage - as One free of all creeds - all dogmas - all that which binds thee - I tell thee of a surety - thine inheritance is a princely fortune which awaits thee - ye have but to prepare thineself for to receive it - ye have but to claim it- to the Name of The Father - Son and Holy Council - The Mighty Host and it shall be given unto thee ---

Yet ye shall purify thineself and stand as one blameless - spotless - and ye shall be as one prepared---

While it is said: Prepare thineself - I say it is for thine own sake that we say: "Prepare" -- Yet thou hast sickened of the Word - and thou hast cast aside the WORD and rejected IT ---

Yet - I say unto thee: It shall be unto thee thine salvation - and thine freedom ---

While there are many which come unto thine assistance - I say: Ye shall first assist thineself - and ye shall accept the "WORD" and apply IT unto thineself - and WE shall find thee by thine light ---

Let it be seen from afar - and we shall give unto thee that which is kept for thee ---

Hold ye high the Lamp - let not thine foot slip - for the way is steep and there are many pitfalls -- While I say unto thee: There are many pitfalls - I too say: Many there are which shall assist thee in thine climb. Take the hand of One which hast been sent to assist - fear not - for One hast come into thine midst - that ye might be lifted up -- Yet ye shall not place thine trust in the arm of flesh - for He is not of flesh -

He is more than flesh - for flesh is flesh -- SPIRIT is Spirit - and Spirit is Greater than flesh - and animates flesh - on this I give Mine Word -- So let it suffice thee - that there are Ones sent - that know thee and wherein thou art - they know where to find thee - they know thine needs - even before thou hast the need -- Ye have but to see thine need and reach out thine hand in love and acceptance -- Wherein is it said - that all in thine needs shall be supplied - so shall it be ---

I Am One Sent -- Let it be as the fulfilling of the law --

Ye Shall Go Forth as One in White Linen

Shall they not be given in Greater capacity - shall they not be given as they are prepared -- Is it not said: "Cast from thee thine legirons - cut them away" for ye bring them not with thee - ye bring nothing save thine self - yet it shall be required of thee - for ye shall sacrifice self – self-will - and it shall be a joyful sacrifice ---

For the Love which we give unto thee - shall be unto thee thine strength - and ye shall go forth as one arrayed in White Linen - and it shall be spotless - and it shall be given unto thee to stand firm - knowing well from whence cometh thine strength - and at no time shall ye deny thine Source ---

I say: Behold ye the Hand of God move - SEE IT MOVE - Know that It moves swiftly and surely - and at no time shall ye be misled -- Hear ye Mine Words - and give ye heed unto that which I say unto thee. I say - bless thineself that ye hear Me - for I shall give unto thee greater comprehension - and ye shall be glad ---

Let thine time be Mine time - and I shall speak unto thee - that ye might have Greater Comprehension - so let it be ---

I have spoken and thou hast heard Me --

GRACE

Hast it not been said - that there shall be Great conflict - great stress - and is it not come - is it not Come! ---

I say it is so - I say: It is come - and it is the day for which thou hast waited -- This is the day of The Lord - the day of Salvation - and it is too - the day of great stress ---

And there are ones now prepared to be lifted up - to be brot out of bondage -- Too - there are ones which rebel against the Light - which rebel against THE LAW - which rebel against The Father - Son - and Mighty Host-- Yet these shall be sorted out - removed into a far place and they shall be no more seen by man -- They shall no more be within the place wherein the remnant shall abide ---

For it is said: The "remnant" shall inherit the Earth - and they shall be as ones which shall stand steadfast - and they shall be as ones which have been true unto themself -- They shall be as ones chosen - for they shall be as ones "Prepared" -- These shall be as ones which have heard The WORD - and prepared themself for to receive The Greater Part - So shall it be.

While I say unto thee: The two - shall be separated - the 'sheep from the goat' - I say the 'wheat from the tare' - and it shall be according unto their "Preparation" - is it not said aforetime -- Many times it is said. So be it ---

Yet they know not that I speak unto them! They turn aside - and say unto themself: "Why - I am one of the Chosen am I not -- I am a member of this church - this organization - I pay my due - I give my pittance -

and I sacrifice my time -- I buy fine raiment to adorn myself - that they might know to which I belong -- I go to the meetings wherein the best people go -- I search the Scriptures for verification of my beliefs -- I give unto the Charities of my money - I pay my bills ---

I am not a coward. I stand up and speak my mind -- I rebel against the poor of spirit - for they should be like unto me - they should do as I do - they should take my word as truth - and me as their example"---

Yea - I see - and hear the bigots" the liars - the whoremongers declare their intention - and their desires -- I see their deeds as black - there is no light within them - for they are as the hypocrites -- They blaspheme the Name of The Lord --

They transgress the law -- They make of themself liars -- They are as infidels - they are as the whores - bastards art they - for they call themself "Christian" ---

LO - I say unto them - they are traitors - and <u>anti</u>-<u>Christs</u> ---

I say - they are anti-CHRISTS!

I know them by their works - for there is no light within them to be seen -- They are not of the Light -- Behold them in their darkness - behold them in their dis-Grace - for they are not Graceful -- And Grace shall not be extended unto them - until they have cleansed themself - and purified themself - <u>then</u> they shall receive the Grace of The Lord God -- And He stands ready to give unto them - as they are prepared to receive - so be it and Selah ---

I am The Most Worthy Grand Master - and I have spoken unto them which are of a mind to hear -- And unto them which hear - I say: Turn from thine own way - and follow ye the Light - for it shall profit thee - --

Amen - and Selah ---

Measure for Measure

Let it be understood that I - The Most Worthy Grand Master - hold within Mine hand the Key unto the Inner Temple - for I Know the WORD - I Know the Power of the WORD -- For Mine Father hast given unto Me the Power and the Authority - to speak the Word - as HE spoke It in the beginning -- For HE gave unto Me the WORD - and I hold within Mine hand the POWER OF THE WORD - as The Father spoke It in the beginning ---

Yet I say unto thee: None amongst thee knows the "WORD" - the Power of The WORD ---

Yet it is said - that one amongst thee shall be given the power of the Word - and It shall go forth as a rod of iron - and It shall be as a Mighty Power in the land -- It shall break down the barriers -- The waters shall spill over the lands - and the parched Earth shall be watered - and the land shall drink up the water - and the land shall bring forth fruit of a new variety ---

And the ones which have been athirst shall be as ones filled -- No more shall their tongues be parched - no more shall their bellies be empty - no more shall they cry - as ones bleeding from the lash of the oppressor - no more shall they fall from the blow of the oppressor -- So be it I speak out against the oppressor - for I say: The law is just - and the word Justice shall be the watchword - for Justice shall be brot about - for I say: The Law is Just - and it shall be as the law requires - "Por of por" – "ounce for ounce" - "Measure for measure" - and none escape the law - "As ye sow - so do ye reap" - let it be a profitable harvest ---

Mine Word I have made known unto thee ---

So let it profit thee to hear that which I have said --

The Lord God is Come

Lord of Lords - Host of Hosts is He - The Lord thy God -- Come unto thee is He - that there be Light -- The Lord God is come - He walks amongst thee as one of thee -- Yet He is not <u>bound</u> in flesh - He is free and He knows no bondage - no bounds ---

I say unto thee: The Light Knows the darkness - yet the darkness knows not the Light - for the darkness hast no comprehension of the Light ---

The Light is comprehension - therefore - there is no darkness - no unknowing - no fumbling - no stumbling - all is <u>Order</u> - perfect order with the Lord God - the Lord of Hosts - The Same. Yesterday - Today and forever ---

He hast not forsaken thee o man - He hast awaited the time when thou art prepared to receive Him and of Him ---

He wearies not of His waiting - yet it hast been said: He wearies of thine rebellion - and willfulness -- He hast been as One in Council on thine behalf -- He hast asked that action now be taken - and We of The Council - have responded unto "His Command" - for We respect "His" Command -- We know the value of cooperation - of obedience - for the law - for the WORD - for I say unto thee: The WORD is GOD - was GOD - and IT is ALL POWER ---

Wherein is it said - that God The Father spoke The WORD - and It went forth to do His Will -- Is it not said - that HE IS THE WILL - I say: None other hast He -- So be it there is little comprehension of that which hast been recorded for them in ages past ---

They have placed upon it their interpretation - and they have been laboring under the veil yet seeking not of the Light ---

They seek of man -- While it is said: "they place their own interpretation upon that which hast been given unto them" - I say unto thee: Change not that which I give unto thee --

Let the burden of change rest upon their shoulders -- Let it suffice thee that I know that which I say unto thee - and I shall give unto the greater comprehension - and ye shall grow in Grace - and knowledge ---

So be it I shall do Mine Part - ye shall do thine---

For this do I say unto thee: "Obey the law - apply it - and walk ye in the Light"

So be it I AM The Most Worthy Grand Master --

List' Ye Man of Earth

List' ye man of Earth - I speak unto thee - as One which knows - I Know of which I speak ---

When man hast spent his energy - in ways which are unrighteous - and opposed unto the Light - he shall be brot to account ---

He shall stand as one shorn of all his vain glory - of all his self-esteem - his self-praise - and he shall know that he hast squandered his inheritance ---

Ponder well Mine Word - and hear ye that which I say - for it is given unto Me to see thee giving and taking the compliment - asking favors - and recognition of man - putting thine fingers into the till of them which are trusting -- They are as the traitors - they betray their trust -- I see them swearing allegiance unto the dragon - serving him with all their might -- They ask of <u>him</u> no proof ---

They bow down unto him in wonderment - for he performs for them great wonders - that he might hold them fast - that he might bewilder them ---

It is said: Ask of no man signs and wonders - for they do give unto thee of their magic - and of their trickery - their sorcery -- They trick thee - I say - and for that they pick thine pockets ---

I say: Ye fool - thou hast been tricked - thou shall be deluded - and disillusioned - for they shall be revealed for which they are ---

Now let it be understood - that I seek of thee nought - save obedience unto the law -- It is for thy sake that <u>We</u> of the Mighty

Council counsel thee thusly - that ye might know them for that which they are -- Too - I say: The Ones Sent that ye be lifted up - ask nothing in return for their labor - for Theirs is a sacrificial labor - a labor of Love -- Yet - let it be said: He which takes from the laborer his bread - is a foolish man - for it is more blessed to give than to receive -- So be it that I Know - I KNOW - for I give unto thee that ye be lifted up - yet what hast thou given unto Me? Hast thou asked of Me - Hast thou given unto Me credit for being that which I Am ---

I say unto thee: Ye shall awaken o man - and ye shall be as one glad for the assistance now offered unto thee so generously - and lovingly.

Yet it is said - that many shall turn away - as the foolish they shall be confronted with their foolishness - so be it ---

I have spoken - think ye well of Mine Words ere ye cast them aside.

In Mine Father's House

Hear ye O man - hast it not been said that "In Mine Father's House are many mansions" ---

It is so - so let it be -- For this do I say unto thee: There are many parts - many places - many stations - yet none surpass the Station which we of The Mighty Council hold - for WE - the over all Council - hold within our hand the Secret of the Universe - Yea the Galaxies yet unformed ---

For it is given unto Us to be Co-Creators with The Father which hast given unto Us the Power of THE WORD - for WE have the

POWER OF THE WORD -- We Know that which hast been given unto Us - and for that we are prepared to counsel thee wisely -- We have been within this place long - and we are efficient in Our Part - We know it well - and therefore we are apt in Our Part -- We counsel thee with Great Wisdom - and it is for this that we say unto thee: As thou art prepared, so shall ye receive -- So be it that we Know thy capacity - let it increase, prepare thineself for Greater Revelation - a Greater Part - greater heights - greater Glory -- While it is given unto thee to weary of the WORD - tire of thine preparation - I say unto thee: Be ye up and about <u>thine</u> <u>own</u> <u>preparation</u> - let "them" be - let "them" find their way let "them" come - and ask - and they shall not be turned away ---

Let "them" knock - and it shall be opened unto them ---

I say unto THEE: Watch! Look! Listen! - and fret not for the ones which reject thee -- Hast the Prophets no respect within their own homeland - I say unto thee none - save that of the Servants of God - they shall recognize each other - and pay respect unto each other -- Yet each shall do his part - his part being different from another - shall be no cause for controversy - and mistaken identity - I say they shall know each other -- So be it and Selah---

Nothing is Hidden from the Council

Hast it not been said - that there is A Mighty Host to assist thee in thy ascent - and it is so -- For this do I say unto thee: The Host stands ready to assist thee - and it shall be unto thee sufficient - for as thou are prepared - so shall They give unto thee -- Mighty is Their Wisdom - for

They Know thine every need - nothing is hidden from them - Nothing! I SAY NOTHING!!

Wherein is it said - that ye shall first obey the law - and seek the Light - and ye shall be as one prepared to receive greater Light -- Ye shall stand as one prepared - ye shall be as one humble of heart - and ye shall walk as one sober - fearing not -- Ye shall be as one which hast thine hand upon the plowshare - and ye shall prove thineself -- Ye shall not defile thine - self by that which ye say - ye shall not give unto thineself the bitter cup ---

Ye shall stand erect - and bow down unto no man -- Call no man father - yet all men shall be as brother -- Yet remember that all are not of the same Order -- Yet ye shall be as one which hast thine hand outstretched - that they might receive the love and light which emanates from thee -- It is said: Let thine light so shine that all might see it - and walk by it - and therein is the Light - for by the Light ye shall be sustained -- And ye shall be upheld by the Power of God - and ye shall know from whence cometh thine help --

So be it I speak unto thee that ye be blest this day ---

* * * * * * *

Sori Sori

Hast it not been said - that "Greater things shall ye do" - it is so -- And now cometh the time when ye shall go forth in the Light - and ye shall be as one prepared - for it is the time of fulfillment - and ye shall walk in the Light and not weary -- Ye shall be as one filled with power, strength - and in Light - ye shall be as one fortuned thine inheritance in full -- Ye shall not want - neither shall ye need - for all things shall be made known unto thee - for there shall be no secrets from thee - there shall be nothing hidden from thee ---

Ye shall know as I know - and ye shall be as, one found trustworth. Ye shall stand on the right hand of God - and ye shall receive from Him thine enua - and it shall be as thine inheritance in full -- He shall place upon thine brow the sign which shall signify thine station - and it shall not be hidden up ---

So be it I speak unto thee thusly that ye might know that I Am with thee -- I Am with thee unto the end - so let it suffice thee -- When I speak unto thee it is given unto Me to know that which I say - for I am not given unto speculation or idle sayings - I speak for the good of all. So let it be --

I Am The Most Worthy Grand Master -

The Nameless One

Who hast the Key - unto the Inner Temple shall be admitted -- He who hast the "Word" shall enter in - for it is given unto Me to know him - for he shall be as one prepared ---

He shall be as one prepared -- Know ye that which I say unto thee? Know ye that which hast been given unto thee? I say unto thee: thou hast been given the Key - ye shall use it - and ye shall be as one prepared. So be it that ye shall be the one to admit thine own self - for it is by thine own effort that ye turn the Key - for it fits thine hand - it is placed within thine own hand - and none other shall open the door for thee - I say ye shall turn the Key - for by thine own effort it shall be opened unto thee - the Key which opens up the door unto the Inner Temple - and therein ye shall receive of Me that which I have kept for thee ---

Now ye shall appraise that which I have given unto thee - and then look again - and ponder well upon it - and ye shall give consideration unto it - and ye shall be as one prepared to receive a Greater part -- Think ye <u>well</u> of Mine Sayings - and ye shall be as one wise to accept them for that which they are ---

I now stand aside for another - which shall give unto thee a part - Hear Him out and ye shall be blest to hear Him -- So be it I am with Him - for He is come that ye be blest of Him and by Him --

I speak unto thee that ye be blest of Me - and by Me -- This is Mine time - when I shall give unto thee this word ---

It is said: that one shall come unto thee - and he shall give unto thee a part - and it shall be for the good of all - it shall be so -- May I say unto thee: I am thine Sibor ---

I say unto thee: I am no stranger unto thee - yet thou hast not heard Mine Name - neither Mine whereabouts are known unto thee -- Yet I say: Ye shall come to know Me - and ye shall call Me by Name - and ye shall be as the one which knows the meaning thereof -- While I say I am One sent of the Council - I say: I am come of Mine own will -- I ask that I might serve in this capacity ---

Yet it hast not been revealed unto thee what manner of assistance I shall give -- It shall be shown - and ye shall know for a surety that I am HE which is Sent --Ye shall first find Me as One trust worthy - and as One apt in Mine part ---

I speak unto thee Mine Sister - that ye might know that I am now prepared to give unto thee a part hitherto unrevealed -- So be it I shall for the present be known as The Nameless One - so let it suffice --

The One to Come

Sori Sori -- I speak unto thee this day - and I say that this One hast within His hand the power and the fortune to be unto thee great assistance and much light---

He - hast the Authority to be as the Sibor - as the One Sent - for He hast proven Himself trustworth -- He hast been true unto Himself - He hast been as One which hast gone the Royal Road ---

Let that which is given unto thee be of Great Light -- Let it be unto thee thine talisman - and ask of Him nothing more - for He shall know thine needs - He shall be as One which shall act upon the need -- And He shall endure much - for thine sake - for He shall come unto thee as One which hast the Love - Patience and Wisdom which is given unto the Initiate -- I tell thee: Ye shall accept Him as a Brother - and ye shall accept that which He hast for thee --

So be it and Selah --

Self-Examination

Hast thine time been spent in seeking the Light -- Hast thine days been spent in thanksgiving -- Hast thine ways been the way of The Lord?

I ask thee: Hast thine way been the Way of The Lord? ---

I say unto thee: Free thineself of all thine legirons - and stand as one free -- Be ye no longer bound by thine own legirons - which thou hast forged for thineself ---

Ask of no man his assistance - I say: Cut them away thine own self and wait for no man to give unto thee assistance ---

Hast it not been said: Ye shall break all that binds thee -- Forsake all and follow ye where The Lord thy God leads - for He shall lead thee into the path of righteousness -- and no more shall ye turn back - for woe unto the man which puts his hand to the plow and turns back -- I say: He shall go strait forward - and he shall not turn to the right nor to the left -- I speak unto thee in parables which is appropriate -- I say unto thee: The time is come when ye shall stand as one accountable for thine own self - for friends shall forsake thee and ridicule thee - and they shall despise thee --

For the sake of the Truth shall ye suffer affliction and sorrow -- Ye shall bear no malice within thine heart - ye shall not judge thine persecutors - for ye shall be without blame -- Ye shall pray for them which persecute thee and ye shall bless them which give unto thee their hand in fellowship -- I say: Ye shall walk with them which are of like mind - yet ye shall neither eat nor drink with them which defile the Word of God - for they are not of the Light ---

I say: Let thine own light so shine that they might see it and be drawn unto it ---

So be it and Selah -

I Am with thee - So be it and Selah --

Death?

Hasten ye to make ready - O man - for the day cometh when thine name shall be called - and ye shall answer without hesitation - and not one shall stay thine flight - for it is the law - when the Angel of "death" summons thee - ye shall answer ---

Yet it is said: "There is no death" - "death" (as ye see it) -- For it is not death which ye see - it is the taking off of the old pore - the old garment of flesh -- While ye see not with mortal eye the putting on of the new garment - the garment - or light body - the Garment of Light.

I say unto thee: The body of Light is beyond the sight of mortal eye. While it is no less for thine blindness - I say it is more brilliant than the noon day Sun ---

Wherein is it said: "Ye go from glory unto glory"-- While the body of Light grows in brilliance in its swiftness in its flight - for when it is released from the pore - or - the pore is released from it - it is not so brilliant - for it still remaineth within the darkness - the density of thine atmosphere ---

Yet it ascendeth beyond that density within due season -- It is for this that it is said: "Swiftly - shall ye go - swiftly shall ye arise - for none shall stay thine flight" ---

Wherein is it said: Cut away all thine bounds - put from thee all thine petty ways - all thine possessions - and free thineself ---

Wherein hast thou been bound? - I say: Ye shall free thineself of all thine ties -- "Let thine time be Mine thine"- sayeth the Lord thy God - "for I am with thee" ---

I say unto thee: Thou shall know that there is no death - there is only the change - rejoice for the change -- And I say unto thee: Ye go forward into the Light - ever brighter - ever more glorious - and ye shall bless thineself - ye shall free thineself and stand ready - for at any moment the summons may come -- I say: Ye shall make thineself ready, prepare thineself - for greater things are in store for thee -- I bid thee - be ye sober - consider well that which I have said - treat Mine Words not lightly - for I Am "Sober"- I am not want to speak lightly - I am not given unto idle talk - be ye as one blest and I shall bless thee.

O - man - thou hast been bound long in bondage - I speak unto thee that ye might be unbound ---

Come - Come - and be ye blest -- Arise with Me and know ye that ye are never alone --

The Wheat & The Tares

Hast it not been said - that there shall be a great gathering in - is it not so - So let it be - for the harvest is ready - and the time is come - and there shall be a great and mighty harvest - for it is given unto Me to see the yield - and to know the wheat from the tares -- And it is said: There shall be a sifting and a sorting - and well shall it be - for I declare unto thee: Each shall be put into the proper place - each unto his own ---

And at no time shall there be any mixture of the wheat and the tares.

When the tares are sorted - they shall be put in the place wherein the tares go - the wheat into its place -- And the tares shall no more be planted with the wheat ---

When it is come that the two be separated - they shall no more be put together - for the time is now come when they shall be known for that which they are - they shall be recognized for that which they are. And no more shall the tares fall upon fertile soil - they shall fall no more upon the fertile Earth - for the Earth shall no more bring forth the tares and the wheat together ---

Now I have spoken unto thee a parable - ye shall do well to ponder upon it ---

Think ye well of Mine Parable - for I have given unto thee a truth in parable ---

While it shall be revealed unto them which seek the light - it shall be a hidden thing unto the unjust - it shall be as a closed book ---

So be it I have spoken and thou hast heard Me --

I am Sent of Him

Wherein is it said - that there are many which are prepared to receive their inheritance in full --

I say unto thee:

There are many - prepared this day - and yet - they are now in flesh. These have atoned - and these have paid the price - these have paid the forfeit - they have made the sacrifice ---

These have gone the last mile - for they have given of themself that all might be blest - that <u>All</u> mankind be blest ---

Now - I say unto them: Come Home - Come Home - and find rest.

Yet - they shall yet give more - for unto them which have - more is required -- Unto them is given the greater - and they know the joy of freedom - they know the peace which comes with such freedom - and they choose to assist the ones in bondage - I say: They choose to assist them which are yet in bondage -- While the bound may be unaware of the assistance - I tell thee of a surety - ye have assistance from these which have won their freedom – thru and by the same law which is given unto thee --

Place thine hand in Mine - and I shall give unto thee food and drink, I shall clothe thee in raiment whiter than snow ---

Place thine hand in Mine - and I shall bring thee out of the place wherein thou hast labored in vain ---

I say: I shall do this - and more - for I am not limited -- I say: Mine Father hast given unto Me unlimited power - and I know how to use it wisely ---

So be it I Am One with Him -- I Am Sent of Him - that ye be blest. So shall it be when thou hast accepted ME for that which I AM --

Strange & New Things

Hast it not been said - "Greater things than these ye shall do" - it is so - so let it be ---

I say it is so - and it behooves Me to give unto thee this Word: There are now those within flesh which shall do the Work which shall be new unto the men of Earth -- While the ones which shall do the 'strange and new' things shall be as ones sent to bring these things about - to bring in the New Order -- And they shall belong to the New Order - and for this shall they be given assistance by the Mighty Council - for they shall be as ones chosen for the 'New Part' that the 'Strange and new' things be accomplished ---

These strange and new - things shall be as they have not seen - or beheld -- They shall wonder - and be as ones astounded at the wonderment of it ---

They shall be as ones confounded and they shall marvel - for they know not that which they shall see ---

It shall be brot about thru and by the ones which have been prepared. They which have been given instruction from and thru the Council -- They shall be dedicated and alert - they shall know well - their part - and they shall not fail -- I speak unto thee that ye might be prepared for thine new part - for I say it is now time to give unto thee in greater measure - so let it be for the good of all ---

I Am with thee that it be so - So let it be --

The Dragon Spins His Web

Let it be said this day - that many shall turn their face - that they see not that which is about them - they shall be found eating and drinking while they are wont to see that which goes on about them -- They shall be caught up in their common pleasures - their lethargy - and they shall find themself entrapt ---

I say - they shall find themself entrapt – for the dragon spins his web with precision -- He hast a mind and a will to entrap them ---

Let it be said: They have been warned - and warned again -- So be it they put their fingers in their ears that they hear not ---

I say unto them: Hear ye - O Nations of the Earth - Hear ye Me - for I speak as the voice in the wilderness - I cry aloud that ye hear - the dragon lies in wait to devour thee - while ye serve him diligently -- Thou hast served him with <u>All</u> thine strength - <u>All</u> thine might - and I say: He shall lead thee down into the pit - he shall devour thee – SWALLOW THEE UP -- Ye fools- poor of spirit art thou - for thou hast not the mind to see him for that which he is -- He hast spun his web meticulous and artfully - he hast lain his plans carefully and bidden thee enter in - he hast conspired against thee - O foolish ones! - I say: HE HAST CONSPIRED AGAINST THEE!! ---

Now ye follow him down to the pit ---

Ye shall be eternally ashamed! Ye shall live to know thine shame - for I say ye come under condemnation - for ye have been warned - ye have been given the law -- Ye have closed thineself out - ye have pilfered the Words of the Prophets - and ye have not put them into thine own pocket -- Thou hast mouthed them - and it hast been as vulgarity in our sight - for these Words have not been becoming unto thee -- For thou O whore - cannot put on the garb of the Saint and deceive Us the Mighty Council -- I say: Ye come under condemnation!

When thou hast spent thine energy serving the dragon - thou shall repent and be as one spent ---

Then --- ye shall cry out in thine pity - for mercy -- Yet I say unto thee: Ye shall atone - and no hand of mercy shall be extended until thine atonement is made - to the last moment -- To the end - shall ye finish thine atonement ---

So be it I have spoken out - and I say unto thee Mine Beloved - ye shall give unto them that which I have shown unto thee ---

Ye shall place it with this Mine Word - that they might have it ---

So be it I shall see that which they do with it--

A Revelation in Spirit

The scene opens as I sat alone in peace - on the grass of a great city park --

A man approached with a woman companion - - they seated themself so close to me - I wondered what their motive--

He lay on his back - one foot on the ground - the other across the upraised knee - beating a steady tattoo against my temple - until the skin was raw -- I wondered at this provocative act -- What did he expect of me?

I arose to face him silently - to study him -- I saw an unholy face - and wicked eyes -- His thots: "Oh no - you do not escape from me!"

In his hand he held a hypodermic needle -- I instantly know the meaning of the intrusion --

I thot: "Oh NO! Not that! I should rather drink the cup of hemlock". For I knew if I fell his victim - my mind should be taken from me - and I would become his pawn --

A battle of might - against might ensued -- I fled - he in pursuit.

When I reached the street - it was blocked by a great procession --

As far as the eye could see - came multitudinous teams of Clydsdale and Percheron horses - drawing huge flattop wagons - the width of the street --

Multitudes sitting atop the wagons - as if glued in their seats - staring strait ahead with blank eyes - faces expressionless - so unaware of the movement beneath or above them --

The wagons - and horses - and street were moved by some power beneath - as if on a conveyor belt --

The horses' <u>feet</u> moved in perpetual motion - while they appeared to be going nowhere --

Above the whole scene - far overhead - was a red steel dome with many beams - which I particularly noticed --

I looked about anxiously - seeking one who might understand - and give me assistance in the fight against the evil one - and give me safety.-

I saw one Elderly - white haired - be-whiskered man standing by a lead horse - his hand on the rein --

I thot: "Here is one of responsibility - a foreman - more alert - Elder" --

I told him my story - he stared at me - unmoved --

I flung myself against his chest weeping - imploring his help - his understanding of the great danger -- For proof I extended my hand with the "two" needles which I still clutched in my hand -- These I had taken from the evil one by great force --

The Elder/ Forman - said curtly: "Climb aboard - I will give you safety" --

I took a place on the far side of the great wagon - hoping to put as much distance between myself and the evil one as possible --

After a very short while - a young woman messenger of the Elder - came and said to me: "He said - you cannot go on - you have to get off here - NOW --

One woman who sat with a male companion - facing East (different from all the others) - said - in a sympathetic voice: "I should not want you to get off <u>here</u>! It is 3 o'clock in the morning - and we are coming into Toronto -- There is great wickedness and much crime --

3 o'clock in the morning? - Toronto? - I asked --

"Yes - we crossed the Lake in the night" was her reply--

* * * * * * *

My Lord - I need Thy help -- How can I put this great drama into few words without help from the Council? Help I ask -- I implore Thee - use these hands to Thy Glory -- For their sake I ask it -- I Am Thedra

Let it suffice - that which is written -- So be it I shall speak unto thee in language <u>they</u> can comprehend --

* * * * * * *

My Lord:

How can such a great drama be brot to life in so few words? The letter is dead - and loses the Spirit -- Many shall put their own interpretation upon it --

Thedra

I shall give life unto the letter --

I shall place Mine hand upon them which seek Me out - and I shall sober them -- I shall bring forth Servants to be thine allies -- I shall ferret out the wicked - and they shall be known - and the traitors shall be as the traitor -- Yet thine reward shall not be less for thine persecution ---

I say: They have surrendered up their will unto the oppressor - and yet he pursues the just and the unjust -- Yet the just shall find refuge in Me - while the unjust shall not come nigh unto Me - they shall go into their temples and synagogues - to find them empty - cold - and no comfort shall they find therein ---

They shall cry for relief - for they shall weary of their trials - and they shall see the futility of man's way ---

They shall not find peace in their temples and synagogues - for I shall not be included amongst them - for they have closed Me out - they have no room for Me - The Lord of Lords - The Host of Hosts --

The Victory

Bring unto Me thine hands and thine talents - and I shall bind up thine talents and multiply them tenfold - and I shall make thine hands Mine hands - and I shall give unto thee strength - and ye shall go forth in the presence of thine enemies - and ye shall walk amongst them victoriously - and they shall not touch thee - and I shall give unto thee the rod and the staff - which shall overcome all the foes - and all the darkness ---

I say unto thee: Ye shall cross over Victoriously and ye shall have no fear - yet ye shall be as the Victor - and ye shall hear the shouts - Hail! Hail! Unto the Victor - for thou hast fought a good fight - and thou hast overcome the last enemy --

So be it and Selah --

... Then Ye Shall Stand Blameless

Law is law - and no law shall be broken or transgressed without consequences -- I say unto thee: Heed ye the law - transgress not - be ye as one responsible for thine own self - and ye shall stand blameless of all guilt - without guilt -- Ye shall be free of all guilt - all condemnation -- And it shall be as thine own part to free thineself of all guilt - for none shall take the blame from thine own shoulders - neither shall ye place it upon another ---

I say: Ye shall carry thine own "Cross" with dignity - and responsibility -- Ye shall be self-responsible - let no man put the blame of his shortcomings upon his brother - for I say - it is his alone - for he hast been his own fortune - he hast brot upon himself his own "misfortune" -- I say: He hast created his own fortune - it is his and he alone is responsible - so shall it be ---

Let it be said: There is the dispensation which is given unto the Messenger Sent of God The Father - which is persecuted for His Sake for He hast atoned aforehand - therefore he stands perfect in sight of the Law - for he hast done his part - and he stands free of guilt ---

I say unto thee: Stand ye up and be ye counted - answer with surety when thine name is called - step forth as one unafraid - for I say unto thee: There is nothing to fear -- Know ye that ye are not alone -- I say: Ye are not alone ---

I Am with thee ---

Ye Have Squandered Thine Time

Hast it not been said - that it shall behoove thee to give heed unto that which is given unto thee - of and by the Mighty Council ---

It is said: Ye shall do well to heed the Word - for It is for thine sake that it is given -- Pay ye heed - and forget not We speak no idle Words. We ask nothing of thee except obedience unto the LAW ---

Yet thou O man - art prone to be willful and wasteful - wanton in thine ways -- Thou hast squandered thine time and energy - and turned away thine face ---

Thou hast walked as one drunken - reeling to and fro - wavering in thine beliefs and opinions - bound by thine dogmas and creeds -- Pity is thine lot -- And at no time have I said ye shall pay homage unto Me for I say: Seek ye the Light - seek first the Light - and ye shall have assistance -- Ye shall find - and there shall be given unto thee strength and peace - and no man shall take from thee thine peace ---

I say - ye shall find peace when thou hast complied with the Law - for it shall be unto thee thine justification -- Ye shall walk as one sober as one which hast a Crown upon thine head - and it shall tilt not -- Be ye as one come out from among them which walk the way of unholiness - Walk ye in righteousness - and ye shall be as one blameless - for ye shall be justified - and peace shall be established within thee ---

Let it be - for I shall give unto thee in greater measure - and ye shall be glad for thine preparation -- So be it I know well thine capacity ---

I say - I shall increase thine capacity when thou hast given thineself in holy surrender - as a holy sacrifice --

So be it - I AM -

This Day Ye Shall Choose

While it is given unto men to go into bondage - into darkness - it is given unto them the choice - it is given unto them the choice which way they go ----

They choose their way -- Too it is said: "THIS DAY - ye shall choose" -- Ye shall have thine choice which way - choose ye wisely - for this is THE DAY for which ye have waited ---

The Day of Salvation ---

I say unto thee: Accept <u>this</u> day - wait no longer - for great and miraculous things - great manifestations - for it is come when ye shall step forth from the pore - the chemical body - as one which hast been bound by thine own limitation -- And ye shall be as thou art now - when thou hast not freed thineself of all thine notions/ preconceived ideas/ dogmas/ creeds and prejudices - ye shall have them still ---

While I say unto thee: "Hear ye Me" - thou hast closed thine ears - thine eyes - unto the Wonders of Heaven - I say - put aside all that which hast bound thee - and greater wonders shall ye see - greater things than thou hast dreamed of ---

I say ye shall arise - and ye shall be as one free - ye shall hear and see - and know that there is NO death - for death shall be no part of thee. I say: Putting off the old - taking up the new - shall be as the part for which thou hast been prepared -- Ye shall walk in the Light - ye shall be as the Light - free to go and to come -- Ye shall walk and weary not - ye shall be as free - and therein is the Truth -- "FREEDOM" -

freedom from flesh - from all that hast bound thee! Thine legirons shall no longer hold thee bound - no longer shall ye drag them with thee - no longer shall ye be attracted unto them - for hast thou not been attached unto them? Hast thou not asked for them - hast thou not sought of men, the opinions of men - hast thou not asked of men "forgiveness of sin"? Hast thou not asked of men <u>their</u> blessing - seeking of them freedom from guilt? Hast thou not been bound by thine guilt/ hatred/ opinions / beliefs/ and thine own hatred/ thine own puny plunder ---

I say thou hast plundered the sayings of the Prophets - that ye might justify thine errant ways -- Thou hast pilfered them - that ye might find justification of thine hatred/ prejudices and superstitions ---

Now I say unto thee: Ye shall be responsible for thine own self - thine own ways/ deeds/ actions - and ye shall put aside all thine pettiness - and ye shall free thineself - and <u>then</u> ye shall be given the Cup of Living Water -- Ye shall no longer serve the forces of darkness And ye shall <u>then</u> say: "Yea - Lord - I come unto Thee as Thine Servant, prepared for that which is to be done -- Yea - Lord - use me for the Good of <u>All</u>" - and it shall be done ---

So let it be - for this day ye shall choose the way ye shall go --

New Habitation / Attention / Consciousness

Wherein is it said - that there is a place prepared for the ones which shall put off the old - and take up the new habitation -- I say the habitation is prepared - and it shall be as thou hast prepared thineself for to receive - for it shall be becoming unto thee - and it shall not be strange unto thee -- Ye shall be as one returned unto thine abiding place for it is said - that Spirit is not bound by flesh -- Spirit is free - and it is given unto thee to go into the place wherein the Spirit dwells -- It is said - all is Consciousness - and that which ye place thine attention upon - that ye are conscious of - that which ye become conscious of - ye become one with - and it is so ---

Yet I say: Ye are not as one conscious of the fullness of the Father's House - for therein are many Mansions -- Yet there is a place provided for His Children in each and every one - and He hast prepared for thee as thou art prepared to receive -- It is given unto the Sons of God to be as Ones above the Sons of Man - for they are as ones yet unawakened they are as yet asleep - and they have not as yet been reborn -- They are as yet in darkness - and know not the fullness of their inheritance ---

They are as yet not -- They are as the embryo - and not as matured. While I say the day of maturity cometh swiftly - they shall awaken! They shall know ---

Yet it is said: Arise this day - come forth and claim thine inheritance. For this hast the Word gone forth: Arise ye Sons of God - come forth and receive thine inheritance in full -- Be ye blest to hear - and to awaken --

So be it and Selah --

Consider Well

Wherein is it said: There shall be a Host to come to thine assistance. I say it is so ---

While it is given unto thee to know not the magnitude of their Light, neither the power they have -- I say: It is no less for thine unknowing - it is no less for thine unknowing -- For it is The Mighty Council which is the "Hand of God made manifest" -- For this hast He The Father - set the Host - The Council over His Creation - and He hast given unto IT the Power and Authority which is His -- And at no time shall we - of the Council - take from Him the Honor and the Glory - for We know from whence cometh the Power - and unto Whom the Credit ---

Consider well that which I have said - and it shall profit thee - I say: "Consider well that which I say unto thee - for greater things I have to say" -- So be it ye shall be as one prepared to receive of Me the greater part--

* * * * * * *

Sanat Kumara speaking:

Hail! Hail! unto thee - Sons of God!

Hail! Oh mighty Victor

Hail! O - Sons returned --

Put on thine Royal Raiment and receive thine Inheritance in full.

Be ye as ones blest THIS DAY --

Say I unto thee:

"Be ye as Ones blest This Day"

So let it Be --

Joy or Sorrow?

Hast it not been said: There shall be much sorrow - and great weeping. Is it not come?

I say - it is come -- Be ye as one prepared - for there shall be yet greater - for the end is not come ---

Wherein is it said - that there shall be a great laughter -- I say - it is so - and let it be well with thee ---

For this is it said: "PREPARE thineself for that which is to come"

NOW - I say unto thee: Hasten ye and make ready thineself - that ye might not be one amongst the weepers ---

I tell thee of a surety - ye shall see the works of thine hands before thee ---

Ye shall see the meditations of thine heart before thee ---

Ye shall see that which ye have done before thee---

Ye shall see the words of thine mouth made manifest before thee.

So let it bring unto thee joy and laughter ---

When thou hast accepted Mine hand/ Mine Word - I shall take thee into a Greater place - a place wherein ye might have the Greater Vision, the Greater power - Greater comprehension - and ye shall know ---

Ye shall be as one illuminated ---

Seek ye first the Light - and it shall not be hidden from thee ---

I come that ye be blest - so be it ye shall accept Mine Blessing - Mine Assistance -

Hast Thou?

Hast it not been said many times - there shall be a great uprising within the lands - and is it not come - is it not known unto thee - knowest thou the cause? Hast thou been without blame? Wherein hast thou been without blame? ----

Consider well thine part -- Hast thou given thot of thine part - hast thou given thot of thine guilt?

Hast thou been without guilt? Hast thou been blameless?

Hast thou been as an emissary of Light - hast thou given comfort to the sick and dying - hast thou fed the hungry - hast thou given sup to the thirsty?

Hast thou given shelter to the homeless - hast thou clothed the naked?

Hast thou loved the loveless - the lost - hast thou found them and given comfort? I ask of thee ---

Consider well Mine Words - Answer ye Me - and be ye as one mindful of thine part in the unrest - in the turmoil -- Be ye as one blameless - and know ye well that thou hast done that which is required of thee - before thou hast answered Me ---

> I say - ye shall not deceive thineself--
>
> Be ye as one responsible for thine own
>
> part - and ask of no man the right to
>
> go into his pocket - for it is given
>
> unto man to pick the pocket of his
>
> fellowman -- Hear ye me - and count
>
> well thine blessings -- Trespass not
>
> upon the brother ---

Ask of no man his favor – yet ye shall go with him the last mile - that he might be lifted up --

They Desecrate the Word

Go ye into the places set aside for the Lord thy God - see that which they do - list unto their speech – see them as they are -- Know ye that there is yet much to be said - much yet to be learned - much yet to be accomplished - ere the victory won ---

I say: They parrot the Sayings of the Prophets -- They parrot the Words of the Lord thy God ----

They but make a mockery of His Words -- They make of themself liars - and they desecrate the "Word" --

I say: "They" desecrate THE WORD ---

Let them come before The Living God in humility and submission with a contrite heart - and they shall be as fit subjects to receive of Him His Blessing ---

They ask of Him His blessing- While they are filled with prejudice/ hatred/ malice-and I say unto them: "CLEAN IT OUT - and come as ones fit to receive of Him -- For the new wine is not put into old bottles I say: Cleanse thineself - and He shall touch thee -- Ask not of Him - until thou hast first made clean thine own altar -- Prepare before Him thineself -and present thineself as a fit subject to stand in His Presence, For I say unto thee - thine own offal hast been a stench unto Him -- Thine words of mockery hast been known unto Him -- He hast seen thine going and coming -- Thine sayings hast defiled thine lips - and desecrated thine house - I say unto thee ---

Hear ye that which I say unto thee - prepare first thineself - and thine own household ---

Yet if thine household shall turn thee out - seek first them which hath cleansed themself - then ye shall grow in strength and Grace ---

Come ye out from amongst the hypocrites and infidels - be ye no part of them ---

Stand blameless before them -- Prattle not of thine righteousness -- So let thine own light shine that it be seen by all -- Praise ye The Name of Solen Aum Solen --

Condemnation

Harken o man -- I speak unto thee as I have not spoken before - yet I say unto thee: There is yet time to turn unto the Light - and seek thine freedom -- Ye shall first seek the Light - and all things shall be revealed unto thee ---

Ye shall redeem thineself - for thou hast transgressed the law - thou hast blasphemed against the Name of The Father - thou hast forfeited a King's ransom ---

Yet thou hast not humbled thineself before The Lord thy God - thou hast been as one proud and haughty in thine bigotry and foolishness -- Thou hast paid the piper - and thou hast paid a price - dearly hast thou paid ---

Ye shall give unto The Father all the credit and the Glory for thine favors - the Mercy shown thee - for by His Grace thou art spared this day ---

Yet it is said: "He shall not always strive with man of Earth" -- It is said: "The hour swiftly cometh when the gates shall be closed - and ye shall stand face to face with thine foolishness -- Ye shall cry out for Mercy" - and it is so -- For ye shall first come unto the Altar of The Most High Living God as a little child - and ye shall ask of Him Mercy and ye shall give unto Him thine heart - thine hand - and ye shall not deprive Him that which He hast given unto thee ---

He asks nothing more than that which is His ---

He The God of All - The "ALL" The "ONE" The Merciful Father - Holy is He - All Powerful - Just is He ---

Be ye as one mindful of Him - and He shall remember thee -- So be it and Selah ---

I say unto thee: Be ye mindful of thine Source --

Be Ye Self Responsible

Mine hand I shall extend unto all - yet ye shall accept it or reject it as thou will - and ye shall choose this day ---

For none shall be unto thee thine porter -- Ye shall be as one responsible for thineself - and thine own "salvation" -- It is said: The law is given unto thee - the prophets have given of themself that ye might have the Word -- Yet <u>this</u> day - I speak unto thee a new commandment - "Prepare thine own self" - and it is Mine part THIS DAY - to give unto thee this part in a new language - strange -- Ye say it is in the language of man - not that of the mystic - not that of the poet, that of the unknowing - that each and every one <u>might</u> <u>know</u> ---

I say - I complicate not the Word which I give unto thee -- I have spoken for the benefit of ALL - and I have spoken fearlessly - for I know whereof I speak -- Be ye slow to utter aught of chastisement -- Be ye slow to add to or take away -- For I say unto thee - I have given these parts with great thought and preparation ---

I am not apt at mistakes - I know full well that which I say and do and all for a purpose -- Wisely have I given unto thee these words ---

Now ye shall be as one responsible for that which ye do with them.

And it shall be either unto thine glory or thine fall -- Let it be unto thee Glory - for I say: "Ye shall be responsible for that which ye do with these MINE WORDS ---

Be ye as one SELF RESPONSIBLE -- It is for thine sake that I have entrusted thee with them --

Thou Hast Not Remembered

Hast it not been long since thou went out from thine abiding place.

Hast it not been long since thou made the Covenant with The Father. Hast it not been long since thou took upon thineself mortal flesh ---I say unto thee - it hast been long ---

Thou hast forgotten the time when thou sat with Me in the place wherein I am ---

Thou hast not remembered thine abiding place ---

Thou hast not remembered that which thou hast said -- While thou hast been bound by flesh - thou hast come under the law of flesh -- Thou hast been as the fortune of flesh -- Flesh hast weighed heavily upon thee - as a black cape -- Thou hast wearied of it - thou hast cried for Mercy and surcease from thine toil - the persecution - anguish - and darkness ---

Thine hands hast bled at the plow ---

Thine feet hast blistered from the hot sands - and frozen from the cold ---

Thou hast been born of woman many times - and thrice hast thou been torn by the lions ---

I say: Thrice torn by the lions -- And now it is come when ye shall stand victorious as one returned unto thine abiding place ---

I say: Ye shall be as one returned unto the place of thine going out.

No more born of woman -

No more torn of flesh -

No more pain -

No more suffering -

No more want -

No more cries -

No more shall ye play the scene so familiar unto man of Earth -- For the time comes swiftly when thine name shall be called - and ye shall answer - and account for thineself -- And let it be a Good account.

So be it --

Behold Thee - The Dawn

Sori Sori

Sayeth The Lord thy God unto thee ---

Mine time is come - and I shall speak unto thee in like manner unto My Beloved Brother Sanat Kumara ---

Sore is the foot of one Sent -- Sore is the foot of the prophets -- Sore is the hand of the plowman -- Sore is the hand of the spearman ---

For they go forth into the jungle -- They go forth into the deserts --

They go forth into the valleys and they spare not themself ---

I say: Sore is the foot of one Sent - for he spares not himself ---

Sore is the hand of the plowman - he spares not himself ---

Sore is the foot of the one who goes forth - for he gives of his strength that others be given strength and light - that his fellowman might be free -- He thinks not of himself - he behaves himself selflessly. He cares for others while his blisters blister still -- He wearies not of his labors - he knows it not to be vainly spent -- He is want that All be healed -- He hast devoted himself that there be light in the dark places.

Yet I say:

Many pass thee by - unsung - unknown - and they leave no card - no place can their mark be found -- Yet they have placed their hand to the plow - and they look not backward ---

Behold thee - the dawn -- Behold thee the Sunrise - so surely doth it come! So Surely!

SO TRULY doth the LIGHT come.

So patiently are they which wait --

The 'Unspoken Word'

Now I say unto thee: This is the first of Mine new part - and it shall be for the Good of All mankind that I speak ---

Now it shall be given unto them in the same manner as the other parts -- Yet it is now come when the ones which have followed the Others unto this point - shall be led forth as ones illumined ---

These I shall touch - and they shall know that they have been touched ---

I speak of the ones which have accepted - and applied the Word unto themself - the ones which have written the Word upon their heart.

I say: These shall know that they have not followed in vain -- I am not of a mind to forsake them which follow - where I lead them ---

They shall find Me trust worthy - and I shall not fail them --

They shall apply themself wholeheartedly - and I shall reveal many things unto them--

There is a great many things I have to say unto them - neither pen nor tongue can convey -- Yet I say: I shall quicken them - and they shall know - and it shall convey the truth of the Unspoken Word ---

I say: That which cannot be written - neither spoken - shall be revealed unto the trust worthy - and they shall then know - The Truth - And NO man shall pilfer the "Unspoken Word" which is neither spoken nor written ----

They know not a method by which to pilfer it!

I say: I guard well Mine tongue - and Mine hand is swift to do the Will of Mine Father which hast Sent Me --

So be it - and Selah --

Word from the "Great and Mighty Council"

Sori Sori -- Hear ye this day Mine pronouncement ---

I say unto thee: Thou art Mine Hand made manifest for this part - which I have chosen to give unto thee in this manner -- For the Good of All do I give this unto thee - that all mankind be blest -- So let it bless thee to receive of Me - for I have laid Mine Hand upon thee - and I have said unto thee that which is sufficient ---

Yet - there is more to be said - and let it be said - for it shall profit the ones yet unborn ---

I speak unto thee - that they might have the knowledge of this form of communication - and that which I say unto them ---

Let them know that they are not alone - that there is a Council - which far excels theirs - even unto their highest ---

I say: None excel The "Great And Mighty" Over All Council ---

Wherein is it said - that theirs is a poor counterfeit of the Over-All Council - So it is ---

Now ye shall add this part unto all the other parts - including that of Mine Beloved Brother Sananda's - and it shall be given with this in parts - and as they are prepared to receive ---

Let it be said - that the power of speech is a gift unto man -- And it wast given unto him to utter sound - that he might become as the fortune of The Father - that he might come to know each other - that they might have the power of communication - that they might speak forth words whereby they might create from the Elements that which they might have need of ---

Yet they have not been given unto conservation of the energy or the power of speech - They know not the power - the gift which is so precious - hast been defiled - and the Word hast been desecrated ---

Therefore they babble on in their unknowing and foolishness - creating for themself great turmoil and unrest ---

They have as yet not learned the wisdom of silence---

I say - thy BABBLE as foolish children - of their power and wisdom. They prattle and they strut/ boast of their power - yet they use it in the way which brings them great stress and sorrow ---

I say: It is their own sorrow - their own stress-- Yet it becomes part of the whole - and it becomes as the Great black dragon - which is the "Great and hungry beast" lying in wait to devour them -- They feed him, keep him alive by their own creation - for this is his meat ---

He hast none other - for man hast created him - the black dragon -- He lives! He thrives on their food which they so generously provide him -- They support him as they would that they be supported - for he wants for nothing ---

I say unto thee: -

When man hast learned the lesson of the creative power of the spoken Word - <u>his</u> <u>own</u> <u>word</u> - he shall be no part of the dragon - and have no responsibility of his support - for they shall withdraw their support - and he shall no more have power over them ---

Man hast created the dragon - and now he hast become their enemy and he shall be unto them their own downfall -- I say unto thee O - man of Earth - thou hast sown unto the wind - now ye shall reap the whirlwind - and ye shall be as one which sees the fortune which thou hast stored up ---

Hast thou not been responsible for thine own sowing?

Hast thou not been told: "As thou sowest - so dost thou reap"? It is so.

Let it be a bountiful harvest unto The Father - for ye shall father thine own children -- That which thou hast brot forth thou shall own -- And be ye as one aware of thine own creation -- For this have I spoken unto thee thusly --

Sanat Kumara's Benediction

Before Thee Almighty Father - I speak in Holy Order - unto these Thine Children -- For their sake I speak unto them in their language - simple and plain – that they might have comprehension of the things they need know ---

For this do I speak forth these simple Words in Holy Benediction - that they be as ones prepared to receive the fullness of their Estate - the fullness of Thine Love - Thine Light -- Father Solen Aum Solen - take these Thine Children unto Thineself - as the ones returned - as the ones which have prepared themself ---

Let them stand as ones arrayed in fine linen - as ones of Pure Light Substance - as ones which have upon their heads the Crown of Royalty, the Victory won - and may it Be - So let it Be --

Great Is!

Great is the joy of them which enter in -- Great is the joy of them which are prepared to enter in --

Great is the joy of them which come into the Presence of The Lord. Great is the joy of them which hast won their Victory --

Great is the joy of them which hast been brot back from their sojourn --

Great shall be their joy ---

Let the freedom bells ring out: FREE - FREE -

Free Am I -- I Am Free - I Am Free - Let it Be---

ASK that ye be free - work that ye be free - sing freedom's Song - let nothing stay thine lips -- Make thine Voice heard throughout the land -- Let it be heard - let it ring out that All might know that freedom is theirs ---

They need not impose laws that bind their fellowman -- They need not make laws to secure their freedom---

I say they are free -- Let the freedom of which I speak be a Reality within the world of man -- Hear ye O man - accept thine Sonship -- Be ye as a Son -- Let not thine ways of darkness bind thee longer ---

List to Me - hear ye Me - and give unto Me thine hand -- I shall give unto thee assistance - and ye shall come to know the meaning of FREEDOM ---

Be aware of the assistance which I can and shall give -- Yet remember ye well - I give not unto the unjust -- Cry not for assistance while thou set foot against the righteous -- I say: No assistance cometh from the Great and Mighty Council - while thou dost sit in judgment against the helpless - and the righteous ---

Ye shall first settle thine own account - and come as one clean - spotless - before the Throne of God.- Then - Nothing shall be denied thee ---

So be it I have spoken - line Word hast gone out - and it shall be given unto all which ask/ which seek the Light -- Therefore - I say unto thee: Prepare thineself for the fullness of thine Inheritance --

They Speak Without Words

Sori Sori

Ye shall be as Mine Hand made manifest unto them which have come unto this part - with understanding and patience ---

I say - patience and understanding -- While many have wearied of the Word - "Prepare"- I say unto thee: Thine preparation hast brot thee thus far - and it shall be by thine preparation that it shall bring thee all the way ---

It shall be unto thee thine salvation -- Yet "they" weary of their preparation and forsake not their ways - and their opinions -- Their fortunes shall be theirs still - and they shall pursue their own course -- Yet they cometh unto the end of their way - then their cries shall be heard - and no more shall they be seen in their familiar places -- Yet they shall not be hidden from Us - The Mighty Council ---

They shall be as one in bondage still - and they shall cry without tears - speak without words - and they shall lament their fate ---

Yet it is said: "As ye are prepared so shall ye receive" ---

Have they prepared for the Greater part?

I say unto them: "This thou hast fortuned unto thineself - thou hast turned a deaf ear to the "WORD" - Thou hast profaned the Name of God - Thou hast denied THE WORD -- Thou hast blasphemed the WORD - and adulterated It -- Thou hast partaken of the food of the dragon -- Thou hast drunken from His cup --

Yea - thou hast forfeited a princely fortune -- And now ye stand naked - in want - as one impoverished - and nought hast thou to comfort thee ---

I say: NAUGHT hast thou to comfort thee ---

Yet - the law hast been given unto thee -- O foolish man - hast thou not been given the WORD - hast thou not seen the Word - hast thou not heard? -- Hast thou not laughed at the ones which give unto thee the Word? ---

I say unto thee: Thou hast not heeded the Word -- Thinkest ye to transgress the law without the last penny paid in full -- I say: The last penny shall be paid - the account shall be balanced - and then ye shall ask for the Light - and It shall be shown unto thee --

Blest are they which are shown --

Blest: Are They....

Sori Sori

Long - Long - hast thou waited this day - when ye shall return unto thine rightful place of abode ---

I say unto thee: Ye shall return - and there shall be many to receive thee ---

It shall be as thou hast not been away - for they shall remember thee.

They shall be as ones which have watched over thee in thine wandering - and in the days of thine unknowing---

I say: Ye shall return Victorious - and Great shall be the joy ---

Blest are they which return --

Blest are they which wait --

Blest are they which are prepared this day - for they shall return Victorious --

Blest are they which hear the Word --

Blest are they which heed the Word - for they shall apply It unto themself - and they shall be prepared --

For that is it given –

So be it and Selah --

The Plan Shall Not Be Aborted

Behold this day the Hand of The Lord move -- See It move - for I - Sanat Kumara sayeth unto thee: The Hand of God moveth - and at no time shall It be staid---

At no time shall It be staid ---

Let It move and know ye that there is a Plan - and that Plan shall not be aborted -- For like unto the Plan shall The Hand Move ---

It shall fulfill the Plan - and not a plan goes for nought ---

I tell thee - not a plan goes for nought ---

Be ye as ones brot out from amongst the unbelievers - the infidels and the harlot ---

Speak ye the Word -- Stand ye steadfast - and be ye as ones prepared for yet greater revelations -- For I shall lead thee into greater plans - greater heights -- And I shall give unto thee as thou art prepared to receive -- So let it be as ye are prepared -- So be it I speak unto thee present here - now --

Ashelea -

(Go forth as ones prepared)

A New Order - Upon the Earth

By Mine own Hand - shall this Word be recorded -- For I have set Mine Hand unto the task of bringing forth a New Order - upon the Earth - and at no time shall I know defeat ---

I shall bring forth a New Order - for I am given the Power and the Authority of Mine Father which hast Sent Me ---

I come with the "Rod of Iron" -- I come with the Force and Sanction of the "Mighty Over-All Council"---

I come as One prepared for that which shall be accomplished ---

I am not dependent on 'one' man - for I shall bring forth ones which are prepared -- such as Mine Hand made manifest - and I shall give unto the meek and lowly the power to speak - and they shall stand as one arrayed in Splendor - for I say unto them: Take upon thine shoulders the Cloak of Power -- The Robe of Authority they shall wear with honor and dignity - and no "man" shall cut them off or turn them out ---

For I shall set aside a place for them which have persecuted the "Prophets" and ridiculed the "Saints"-- They shall have their place - yet it shall be without honor ---

For they have defiled the Word - and made a mockery of The Word of God - Hear ye Me - for I stand upon the High Holy Mt of Zion - and I proclaim unto thee The Word of God -- And it is given unto Me to know It - and the Power thereof ---

I say unto thee: Ye shall stand firm -- Look neither to the left - nor the right -- Place thine hand to the plow - look not backward ---

Bless thine life - and Great shall it be! ---

Bless them which labor with thee -- Bless them which ask for Light, Bless thineself --

So be it I bless thee --

It Shall Profit Thee

Let the Hand of God move -

See It Move --

Rest ye in the Knowing that He Is God --

Blest is the one which Knows --

Hast it not been shown unto thee -

The power of The Word? --

Hast it not been shown unto thee ---

Oh ye of little Sight - hast thou not

Seen the Hand of God Move?--

Now ye shall see - ye shall Know - for

I have said - it is so -- So shall it be --

Be ye mindful of Mine Word -- Remember them well - and give unto Me Credit for Knowing that which I say unto thee ---

Remember well that which I say unto thee -

And it shall profit thee --

This is the Day

Beloved of Mine Being - this day I say unto thee:

This is the day for which thou hast waited -- Thou shall now place thine hand in Mine - and ye shall put thine hand in Mine

KNOWINGLY -- And ye shall be led into Greater heights - GREATER FIELDS - and ye shall be given in Greater measure -- Ye shall be as one prepared---

Ye shall stand firm as upon THE ROCK - for I say unto thee: Ye shall not fail -- I AM WITH THEE --

So be it I Am The Most Worthy Grand Master -

Mysterious Ways?

Be ye as ones prepared for a great part - for as the winds doth blow - and the storms doth come - and the rivers doth rise - and the snow doth come -- So doth the Sun shine - and so doth the roses bloom - and so doth the Hand of God move in mysterious ways ---

I say: Mysterious ways? - yet do I not know the movement thereof?

I say unto thee: I know the movement of the Hand of God - and too I see the handwriting on the wall --

I Know the meaning thereof ---

Let it be said that one shall stand before thee and declare the Word and He shall be as One which hast been given the fullness of Its meaning - for He shall be as One quickened -- And yet he shall be as One despised and shunned by men -- He shall be as One which Knows the meaning of suffering and sorrow - for this hast been His lot ---

I say - this hast been His lot ---

Ye shall be as ones prepared for He shall show thee many things.

So be it and Selah -

The Will of The Father - The Council

Hast it not been said - that all things belong to The Lord thy God? -- Hast it not been said that "He and The Father are One"----

I say unto thee: Thou hast nought - save that which is His ---

Thou standeth impoverished without substance - save by His Grace, For He is the Grace - and WILL of The Father made manifest -- He hast no other Will - save that of "The Father" which hast Sent Him forth.

Let thine Will be His - and it shall be done - as it is prophesied for thee - according to the plan-- For He Knows the plan - and He is apt with the plan -- He given of Himself that it be according to "The Plan" which has been from the beginning ---

I say: It is given unto The Mighty Over-All Council to be ONE with THE WILL of The Father - and It shall be done -- Be ye one with it - and ye shall not fail - for it - The Council Knows NO FAILURE - neither does It know any barriers ---

Let it be said: All barriers shall be removed ---

All barriers - shall be removed --

And the WILL of The Father shall be done ---

So be it I have spoken -- So be it ye shall hear that which I have said unto thee by this means ---

Little By Little

Let this be recorded within these pages - for them which shall read -- There is nothing hidden from the Over-All Mighty Council -- And it is known that which shall be accomplished in a short while - And it shall be for the benefit of All - not one - but All -- It is given unto Me to Know the design of the Plan ---

Little by little - is it unfolded -- Now ye shall be as one prepared to go forth as the Emissary -- For it is now come when the Word shall be carried into the places wherein there is little Light -- Ye shall be as one which hast upon thine shoulders the Cloak of Authority - and ye shall speak the Word -- Ye shall be as One Sent - for from this Temple shall The Word be sent forth -- And It shall fall on fertile soil - and not a plan shall go astray ---

So be it I have spoken and thou hast heard Me ---

I Come Gently

Born on winds of love - I speak unto thee -- Born on winds of love - I touch thee as a gentle breeze -- I speak unto thee in voice smooth and sweet -- I speak softly yet firmly --

I speak wisely -

I speak knowingly -

I speak as One with Authority -

I come as One with thee -

I come as One at all time present -

I AM with thee - for I am not afar off -

I come gently -- I come as a friend – as a Counselor - as a Brother.

I come as One prepared to lead thee – as One prepared to give unto thee that which I - have for thee ---

At no time shall I be out of hearing -- Call and I shall hear thee - and I shall extend Mine hand unto thee in loving assistance -- So be it and Selah –

Look Not Back - Look Forward

Hasten ye to say that which I give unto thee to say -- See that which I give unto thee to see -- Be ye as ones alert - for the Hand writes and passes on - and is no more seen ---

I say: The Hand writes and passes on - and is no more seen -- So be it that I shall give unto thee that which is wise and expedient ---

Ye shall put thine hand to the plow -- Look not back - look forward and be ye as ones watchful -- For I say unto thee: These things are not to be taken lightly - for I say unto thee: Thou hast a calling - and thou shall first be as one called - and therein is the acceptance of the Call.

Then ye shall apply thineself - and ye shall be diligent in all thine service -- Ye shall speak of the work at hand - and of that which hast been given unto thee for thine preparation - and it shall profit thee--

Change is Good

Sori Sori -- Hear thou Me - and remember well that which I say unto thee -- It is now come when there shall be a change - a change which shall be as none before -- For it shall be a greater change - and none shall forbid it - none shall be given the authority to stay the Hand of God ---

It is said - change is good - change is well - So let it be -- And at no time shall it be given unto thee to be put aside or put out - yet it shall be given unto thee -- Let thine time be given over to the work at hand - and it shall be for the good of all - it shall be for the good of All ---

Now ye shall be as one alert - and know ye that thou hast been given the first part - and the second shall be greater -- So be it I am with thee.

For a Surety There Shall Be a Change

Let this be placed within the records which hast been written - as a testimony unto them -- They shall be as ones prepared - and they shall have need of these testimonies ---

To them I say: There shall be a change - and it shall be as strange and new unto them - and they shall be as part of that change -- And they shall be given a new part - and they shall recall Mine Words -- They shall bring forth these Words fresh in their memory - and they shall be glad for their preparation ---

They shall stand steadfast - and they shall weary not of their preparation - for they shall profit there - by ---

When it is come that they are tried - they shall remember that which is said - and they shall be glad for the forewarning -- I tell thee of a surety there shall be a change - and it shall be well with thee - so let it be -- And not a plan goes astray ---

The Covenant

Say I unto thee this day: Wait upon the Lord thy God - and He shall give unto thee that which He hast kept for thee -- For He hast a place - and a part - and at no time shall ye be alone -- Say I unto thee: Wait upon the Lord thy God - and He shall deliver thee out of bondage ---

Wait upon the Lord thy God - and He shall be unto thee that which ye have need of ---

Be ye as ones blest - and I shall give unto thee Mine blessing -- For I say unto thee: Thou hast served well in the place wherein thou art -- Now ye shall be as ones prepared for greater service -- And no man can calculate that service - for no man knoweth the capacity which shall be given unto thee -- For this hast thou been called forth as the ones chosen.

Now ye shall stand steadfast - and ye shall be as ones prepared for yet greater service - for ye shall be called to fulfill thine part -- And long hast it been since thou hast made thine covenant with The Lord thy God -- So shall it be as the fulfilling -- Then ye shall take thine place at His right hand - and He shall pronounce thee - One returned - and He shall say unto thee: Welcome Home Mine Faithful Servant - thou hast kept thine covenant -- Well done --

Hail unto the Victor -- And I shall place upon thine brow - a Bright and Shining Star - which thou shall wear as a Sign unto them thou hast returned the Victor -- So be it I have spoken and thou hast heard Me --
-

SUFFER NO MORE

Suffer no more the darkness of the world -- Suffer no o more the pity of man --

Suffer no more the want of the unknowing --

Suffer no more the fortune of the wayward and the wanton --

Be ye as one brot out of darkness --

Be ye as one delivered from thine unknowing -- Be ye as one obedient unto The Father's Will - The Law Which He hast brot forth in the beginning --

Be ye as one returned unto thine rightful Estate -- So be it I Am with ye that it be -- So let it be --

Be Ye Quick to Give

Be ye as Mine hand made manifest - and record these Words for them which shall read this herein -- And it shall be written in thine own tongue - that they might comprehend that which I say ---

Let it be written thusly:

Be ye as the one filled with LOVE - and love ye one another -- Fear no man - ask of no man more than thou art willing to give -- And be as one quick to give unto him thine cloak -- Ask not of him his cloak - but be ye quick to give thine when he is in need -- Let him have thine part of the bread when he be hungry - and fear not hunger for thineself ---

Yet ye shall not deprive him his - that thine hunger be satisfied ---

Reason not against Mine Sayings - for I know the meaning thereof and for this have I given them unto thee -- So be it - it shall profit thee to remember that which I say unto thee -- Let it be written upon thine heart -- So be it and Selah --

* * * * * * *

Sanat Kumara Speaking:

By Mine hand I shall write the Word - and It shall be followed - and none shall make it void - for IT shall be valid until there is a New Day - a New Dispensation---

It shall profit thee to keep sacred this Word - and give heed - for it shall be thine own passport into the Inner Temple -- LOOK ye well unto thine fortune - for it shall be as the fortune spent - when thou hast disregarded the Law ---

Holy and Pure is The Word -

Adulterate it not -- Bless thineself by the law - protect thineself by the law ---

Hold high thine head - and know ye that thou art blameless before thy God ---

Strut not before man - condemn not the ones which know not ---

Put not thine foot into a hole - for it is given unto thee to know the pitfalls -- I say: Put not thine foot into a hole - while thou art preparing thine own self for thine greater part ---

Let thine hands be free to do the Will of The Father Solen Aum Solen ---

Let thine feet be swift to go where the Council of The Great and Mighty One Sends thee -- Prepare thineself to stand before The Council as one blameless ---

I say unto thee: BE ye as One blameless - by applying the law - for therein is thine Salvation ---

Fortune thineself the Greater part -- Hold fast to Truth and Justice. Uphold Justice - and be ye not slow to defend it -- Yet it is said: Be ye as one blameless -- First consider well thine own house and it shall first be set in order - let it be ---

Hast it not been said that there shall be order - and it is so -- Order is the law - and law is Order -- And let it be as it is so ordered ----

So be it I have spoken and thou hast heard Me --

Behold Thine Fortune

Hast it not been said: All things unto its season - and it is so -- Yet I say unto thee: It is now come when ye shall put thine hand in Mine - and I shall lead thee into greater heights - wherein there are greater glories - greater things than man hast dreamed of -- For I say unto thee: Man hast not glimpsed such glory as I know -- For wherein I am there is no sorrow - no burdens - no limitation - no pity - no darkness - and wherein there is only Light ---

Hast man known such as I speak of? Nay - I say unto thee: Man hast not known such freedom - such joy - such glory -- And for this do I say unto thee: "Come - and behold thine fortune - and be ye as one returned unto thine rightful Estate" ---

I Am thine Sibor and thine Elder Brother -

Sanat Kumara

Obedience Unto the Law

Mine Hand is sure and steady -- Firm is it - and it hast the power and strength to uphold thee ---

I say unto thee: The power which is endowed unto Me of The Father Over All - shall be sufficient unto thee -- For the Mighty Council hast given unto Me the Authority to say unto thee this - and ye shall be blest to receive of ME ---

For I have a part for thee unlike any other part -- Each hast a part for thee - and at no time shall one trespass upon another -- Yet - it shall be asked: Where is The Lord thy God?

I say unto thee - each hast a part for thee - and We are One - One with The Mighty Host - One with The Mighty Council - THE OVER ALL COUNCIL ---

And we are not divided amongst Ourself - We are One of Mind - One of Spirit - One of Body - yet separate as Beings - Sent forth that The Father's Will be done -- Thru Us His Will is MADE MANIFEST and We are the Manifestation of HIS WILL ---

So be it that there shall be established upon the Earth a Council like unto this One ---

And for this art thou now called out from amongst them - these ones which have not answered the Call -- I say: The Call hast gone out - yet many have refused the Call - many have rejected it -- Many have said: "Here I am Lord"- and wearied of their calling - and turned aside ---

I say unto thee: Ye shall put thine hand to the plow - look not backward - go ye forward - and bless thineself -- For I know that which is in store for the Servants of The Most High Living God which wearies not of their Service ---

Serve with thine whole heart - Mind - and Soul - and be ye as ones prepared for the greater part -- So be it and Selah ---

I say: It shall be given unto thee to know that which is meant by obedience unto the Law -- So be it and Selah ---

Hold ye the Lamp high - let not the winds blow thine light -- Let it be as the Light unto them which cometh. Let them be subservient unto the Law -- Command of them obedience unto the Law -- Fortune not unto thineself dis-Grace - for I say unto thee: It is by the Grace of The Lord thy God - that thine fortune is kept for thee ---

Hear ye that which I say unto thee - and be ye as one responsible unto the law -- And Know ye that I Am with thee - I shall sustain thee.-

Peace - Peace - Peace -

The Enemy Shall Flee

For this have I waited - that I might say unto thee this Word -- For I have watched thine going and thy coming - thine wandering -- And thine meditations I have heard - and I have been as One prepared to give of Mineself that ye be prepared for thy return -- Now ye shall arise and come of thine own will - and many shall receive thee as one long away - and great joy shall fill their hearts ---

I say unto thee: Ye shall be as one prepared -- For this have I said unto thee these things - and it shall serve thee well ---

Hast it not been said that there are glories yet unknown by man - so be it -- And not one shall be denied glory - when they are prepared to receive of them ---

They sit in wait - and they ask proof of these glories - and they are wont to give of themself - they are wont to serve The Father which hast given unto them Life -- They sit in wait - asking of Him bread - and what do they give in return? -- I say: They give little thot of Him and His Love for them - they defile the Name of God - Solen Aum Solen. They have been as the wanton ones -- They have been as ones slothful in their ways - and unfaithful - they have desecrated The Word - and brot forth a generation of bastards - which know not their Father -- They have bowed down to the idols - and worshiped at their feet - and they have set up altars unto the force of darkness - and worshiped the one which hast beguiled them ---

I say - they have taught false doctrines - and held the unknowing in bondage ---

And now it is come when the Sons of God shall go forth - arrayed in Armor of Light - Sword unsheathed - and They shall be as a Mighty Army - and the enemy shall flee -- And They shall be as one Man - for under One banner shall They go forth - and no man shall stay Them - for by The Hand of God shall They be sustained -- So be it the enemy shall flee before Them - and be seen no more - for They shall be the Victor! And no more shall the enemy hold sway over a people which hast not the power to overcome -- They shall be given the strength and the power - for this is the day when the oppressed shall raise up - and they shall be as ones which hast suffered much - and they shall come face to face with the enemy -and they shall cry out for Justice - and Justice shall be meted out -- So be it and Selah ---

I have spoken - and thou hast heard Me.

The Awakening of the Child

Hear ye Me this day -- I say unto thee - the time is come when ye shall come forth as one alive - as one awaken - and ye shall stand as one sure upon thine feet-- And thine strength shall be sufficient unto thine weight - for ye shall not fall - neither shall ye faint ---

I say: Thy strength shall be sufficient unto thine weight - and ye shall not fail - so be it and Selah -- Ye shall now say unto them - that which is revealed unto thee - and it shall be for their benefit -- So be it that ye shall foster the Child - and It shall be as One alive - and It shall carry Its own weight -- I say: The Child shall carry Its own weight -- So be at it and Selah --

Mine Testimony unto Them

Be ye as the Hand of Me made manifest - and record this Mine Word - that they might know that which I have said unto thee - for it shall profit them ---

While I say it unto thee - it shall profit All men to hear that which I say - for it is given unto them to be in flesh - as ones bound by flesh.

While I say it is for thee - I say: Ye shall record it that they might have the record of this Word-- Let it be Mine testimony unto them ---

For this is it recorded -- By the time they have found it - I shall have opened up the door unto thee - and ye shall be as one prepared to enter in -- And ye shall be as one prepared - and ye shall be given the part which I have kept for thee - so be it and Selah---

I Am come as a thief in the night - and nought have I found to give unto Me the Glory which is Mine---

Nought have I found which would signal Mine coming---

I said: "Watch - lest ye be caught napping"- and it wast not heard - that which I said ---

For I come as a thief in the night -- I have brot with Me the ones which make up the Mighty Council -- I have come that the sleepers awaken ---

For I say unto thee - the Sons of Israel sleepeth---

I say: The Sons of Israel sleepeth - and for this have I come -- THAT THEY AWAKEN -- Let them awaken! For I say: The time of awakening is come -- And the Day draweth nigh when there shall be great Light within them -- They shall be as ones brot for to do a Mighty Work - and that shall be Mine Work ---

Let it be said - that the Sons of God which have been bound in darkness - shall now awaken and come forth - as the ones which have slept ---

The lost shall be found - and they shall be glad -- They shall rejoice that the time hast come when their sleep is ended ---

O - MIGHTY SONS OF GOD - ARISE! - Come forth this day -- Put on the whole Armor of God The Father - and be ye as ONES AWARE OF THINE OFFICE - of thine Estate -- For this have I waited - and I shall break the Seal - and it shall be a glad day -- So let it be as The Father hast Willed it -

Sananda

Faint Not!

Say unto them: There is little time to prepare for the Great on-rush of waters - for it shall reach them in due season -- And they shall be as one prepared to stand before it - or - they shall fall of their own weight.-

The strength shall be given unto them which walk in the Way set before them ---

There shall be a Great on-rush of Light - and they shall either stand or fall ---

I say: It shall profit them to hear that which is said - for there are many which stand by to succor them ---

FAINT NOT!

Be ye as one firm -- Hold the Light -- Let thine foot slip not ---

Fail Not -- Suffer not defeat!

The One to Come - The Plan

At the place wherein thou art shall come one on whose forehead is written the Word - Light - and He cometh as One Sent -- And He shall bring with Him a gift - and He shall give unto thee a plan - and ye shall accept it - and there shall be a great change within the place wherein thou art ---

Let it be - for it shall be well with thee ---

Hold ye steadfast - and let thine time be Mine time - and I shall speak unto thee further of the plan -- So be it and Selah --

The Adulterated Seed - The Harvest

Hear ye Mine Word - for I would give unto thee a parable---

A man went forth to sow a field -- The field was tilled and the season wast come ---

When he poured out his seed - he found it wast adulterated - for the enemy had placed within the perfect seed the tares -- And he sowed -- Therefore his harvest bore both wheat and tares ---

I say unto thee: Be ye watchful - for there are ones which would put tares within the wheat --

And what should be thine harvest? I say: Be ye watchful - and be ye alert ---

Let not the enemy be as the one which sits at thine board -- Bear well in mind that which I say unto thee ---

Let them come as ones prepared to partake of the feast -- Yet be ye as ones mindful of that which they put within thine cup - for all is not perfect - and bears much watching -- Rest in the knowing --

I Am with thee -

Walk as Ones Sober

Be ye as the Hand of Me - and write that which I say unto them -- There is little time left that they prepare for their next part -- For I say unto them: There shall be a great plan - which is yet to be revealed unto them

-- And it hast not yet appeared - what manner of man they shall become - for as they prepare themself - so do they become ---

It shall behoove them to make ready themself for the next part/ to close the door behind them - and walk as ones sober - and as ones qualified to enter into the place wherein I am -- So let it be as they will it ---

Yet ye shall be no part of their foolishness -- Hold ye the Lamp which is placed within thine hands - and keep ye watch over thine own household -- Place not thine authority within the hands of no other - for I say unto thee: Thine hand is strong and firm - and I am prepared to give unto thee Greater assistance ---

So be it and Selah --

I Am with thee --

As a Wanderer

Blest are they which become Sons of God - for this is a High Estate - Willed unto thee from the beginning ---

I say: Blest is the one which comes into the fullness of his Estate.- So be it I say unto thee: The fullness of his Estate is his return unto his abiding place -- For that which is known as man - hast gone forth as a wanderer in bondage -- And long has he wandered -- Long his journey, sad his wanderings -- So be it he shall return in due season -- Blest shall he be - for he shall be the Victor -- I say:

Blest is the Victor --

Hail unto the Victor --

Beloved - it is Mine time -- I am come into the place wherein I am prepared - and herein I shall abide with

Mine Beloved* -- While it is yet given unto Me to be near unto you, I am at His side -- What joy - what peace - and My Beloved Thedra - you shall be with Us at this place - so beautiful and peaceful ---

I tell you - My time is now come when I am free - and no more suffering -- What suffering the human body can take - yet what freedom.

I now understand the reason for it - for it is like the passing of a fresh breeze over the foulness of a dunghill -- When it is past - and Our Victory won - and it is no more - then we stand in all our strength as the Son of God - arrayed anew in fine Garment and fresh of Spirit -- We remember no more the suffering ---

I tell you Beloved Thedra - My day is now come -- Say unto My Beloved One - and My little babe - that I am with them as one arrayed in new garment - and I am no longer a legiron for her -- At last My time has come -- Say that I am no longer in the sore body - no longer bound by flesh - no longer bound in darkness---

Too - say unto them which stand with her in her hour of sore heart and weariness - that I love them and I shall be unto them that which The Great One hast been unto me - "Comfort"-- I shall give unto them a portion -- And it is now understood what was meant by "No separation" - as the Spirit is never far - never away -- Spirit is Spirit --

The form only falls as the leaf in winter -- I simply take up My new life fresh and new -- No more shall I wander the dark and deep valleys -- I say: The depths of the valleys is measured by man's own mind - for Light is - It penetrates all things and for this is all things created ---

While I am just arrived - and there is great things to see and to do - much to be learned - and found - I am to say to you: Fear not - for I am come with our Beloved Older Brother Sananda - Our Lord and Master, He has brot Me this far - and yet I go on - on - on - where He sees fit to direct Me ---

I love you - and I want them who has given me so much service and care - to know that I am now released from bondage - and I shall return that service from a higher dimension -- A greater Vision I now possess for I see farther and clearer - for Beloved Sananda touched Me and lifted Me up -- When it comes that You shall make this step - fear not for it is but the Greater Step – "To Know is Wisdom" and to "Be is the Reward" -- Be ye as the Victor - and come forth as One Victorious ---

I say unto them - as My Beloved Sananda has said to us: "Come unto Me and rejoice that it is finished"---

Let it come to pass - and let us rejoice that it is passed - and anew We shall sing together as the Sons of God ---

For now let us say: Fortune thineself the Greater part and know there is no death - no clumsy telephone - no long distance between Us, for as I said - I come to you - for this have I waited ---

Let it be the beginning of a new relationship which shall be profitable - So this day I say: Be at peace - and let your hand be Mine for this open letter to them which shall see it and remember Me ---

Let be for all who might be comforted by My humble part -- Be blest and The Lord is with you --

*Sananda

Warning

While it is not yet known unto thee - I shall give unto thee this Word - that ye might know - for it shall profit thee -- There is one amongst thee that hast the fortune of the Porter - and he shall stand at the gate - and he shall be as one wise to see that which shall be done - for he shall be as one prepared to see and comprehend.

I say - that he shall stand porter at the gate - and he shall not be taken by surprise -- For I say - the enemy is abroad in the land - and he hast no scruples - he hast no compassion upon the just -- And it shall be given unto him to know the true from the false ---

Now it shall be said - that he shall sift and sort - the grain from the tares - and he shall know the difference - and it shall profit him much. Hold the Light - and It shall not fail thee --

Hold High the Lamp

Sori Sori

Hold ye the Lamp - speak ye - that which I give unto thee to say - and fortune unto thineself the Greater part - and bless thineself ---

Let them say that which they will - and heed not that which they say - for it shall profit them not -- For I say: they but bring their legirons with them - and they are but bound by them ---

Harken not unto them which source -- I say: harken not unto them which put words into Mine Mouth - for I speak that which is given unto Me by Mine Father and that which shall profit thee ---

While it shall be given unto "them" to bring with them such as they have fortuned unto themself - I say - Ye - shall hold the Lamp - and place thineself not at their mercy - for I say unto thee - it would be but to thine own undoing -- Speak gently and firmly unto them - yet let not them take from thee thine own fortune -- Lose not thine own reward -- And pity are they which forch upon another their own fortune -- Put Not thine hand in theirs - for I shall lead thee thru the mist - and ye shall be as one blest ---

Hast it not been said; "Ye shall not fail"?

Ye shall stand firm - hold high the Lamp which I give unto thee -- Praise ye Solen Aum Solen - and be ye blest - for HE is thine Father Eternal - and HE is thine Source -- So let it be as HE Wills --

Let it Be --

Prove Thineself

Holy - Holy is the Word of God -- And there is none which can make void the Word -- Bind up thine wounds and be thou healed -- Bind up thine Wounds and be ye whole - and ye shall know no more suffering, no more sorrow ---

Hear thou Me - and ye shall be as ones prepared for the Greater part, For I say unto thee: Thou hast kept thine covenant - and thou hast asked for Truth and Light Which shall not fail thee -- It is said: Prove thineself - it hast been done -- Yet too - it is said: Look not unto thine "Laurels" for they shall be as nought -- For it is said too: "Greater things SHALL ye do" it is so -- So let it suffice thee that there is a Host to give unto thee assistance -- So be it as The Father Wills it --

The Light Shall Bear Thee Up

Holy - Holy is The Word -- Sacred is The Word - guard It well -- Be ye as the Lamp - and keep the Lamp burning - for well shall It be kept and the Light seen from afar -- Bear ye in mind that there is naught save the Light which shall bear thee up -- I say: The Light shall bear thee up and ye shall be as one justified and purified ---

Hold high thine head - and know ye that thou art Sent of The Holy One - that ye might be unto Him His Servant - His Hand made manifest. For He hast stretched forth His Hand and thou art there -- And as it is foretold - thou shall be as one brot back -- So be it that there are none which are lost from His sight - for He Knoweth wherein are His Children - and wherein they abide ---

I say: None are lost from His view He Knoweth wherein they are - and He hast given unto them being - and He hast provided for them - that they might return unto Him - so be it and Selah -- For this have I spoken unto thee - that ye might be brot out of bondage -- Know ye that I Am come that ye might have assistance - so let it be --

I AM The Worthy Grand Master of The Inner Temple --

Drag Not Thine Legirons

Let there BE Light - Let there BE Light - and let It shine forth in the world of men -- Let It BE - and for this shall the darkness be dispelled. Let it be dispelled - and at no time shall the darkness consume the Light.

Yet the Light shall consume the darkness ---

Wherein is it said: "and the darkness comprehend - eth not the Light"? ---

Wherein is it said that "Great Light shall flood the Earth" - and it is so - So let IT BE ---

Blest shall be the ones which hold fast unto that which is given unto them - for they shall be as ones which Know the Light ---

Let it be as The Father hast Willed unto thee ---

For He hast asked of thee: Return unto thine abiding place -- Drag not thine legirons - for ye bring them not with thee --

Cut them away --

Cut them loose --

Let them be no more ---

Sing ye songs of freedom -- Be ye as ones free -- Let Freedom Ring. For this have I spoken unto thee thusly.

Let thine heart not be troubled -- Free thineself from all thine fortune which thou hast fortuned unto thineself ---

Praise ye The Lord and let thine Light shine forth this day - and ye shall bless thineself ---

He Shall Awaken

Let it be told - the Glories of Heaven -- Let it be said that there are Glories yet untold - yet unknown - yet unfolded unto man - and man hast not yet found that which is within his grasp -- For he hast not as yet awakened to the fullness of his estate -- So be it he shall awaken and he shall be as one come alive - and he shall walk upright - and he shall be glad for his awakening – He shall be as one responsible for himself - and he shall bring forth great harvest -- He shall glorify The Father which hast sent him forth - so be it and Selah ---

Hail! Hail unto The Victor for he shall overcome --

War Shall Be No Part of Thee

Behold the way of The Lord - It is narrow and strait -- It is

Light and easy unto thy feet ---

Behold the New Day - it is bright and war shall be no part of it ---

For war shall be no part of thee -- And ye shall tread lightly the path prepared before thee -- For it shall be unto thee the way and the Life - the Life set before thee - and the Way prepared before thee -- And at no time shall ye let thine foot slip - for I say: Great is the fall when one slips upon the Path upon which We tread - upon which we have gone.

I say: Slip not - for the Path is strewn with the bones of those which have fallen by the way -- Give unto thineself credit for being a Son of God - and walk ye sober - and give unto Me credit for Knowing thine frailties -- I say: Walk ye with sure steps - waver not --

While it is given unto some to reel and rock to and fro - as one drunken - it is given unto Me to say unto them: Walk ye as one sober - reel not - be ye steady and forget not that I have spoken for thine own benefit --

So be it and Selah --

Resist Not Assistance

Shall ye not see the Word made manifest - shall ye not walk strait ahead into the New Day fearing nothing ---

I say: Walk ye strait ahead - fearing nothing -- Be ye as one upright. Know thineself to be prepared for that which shall come upon thee ---

Know ye that there is a Host to assist thee -- Bless them which stand ready to assist ---

Know ye them - and resist not their assistance - for I say - They are aware of thine needs -- Be ye as ones blest ---

Praise ye The Name of Solen Aum Solen - and be ye BLEST - for None Other Name is so perfect --

None other so Great --

None other so powerful --

None other so Sweet --

Ye Shall Be Given Strength

Behold ye the Hand of God move - Know ye that It moveth - for I say unto thee - It moves with precision and with swiftness -- Hold ye firm and be ye as one prepared to go forth in the days ahead - when great things shall be given unto thee to do -- For I say: It is now come when ye shall show forth great strength and power -- For it shall come to pass that ye shall be tried - and ye shall be given the strength to overcome. So be it and Selah ---

Praise ye The Father Solen Aum Solen - for all thine Gifts and all thine Strength ---

Sing ye the songs of Freedom and deliverance --- So be it that I am come unto thee that ye be prepared for thine next part - let it be ---

For this do I stand ready to assist thee.

So let it be for the Good of All --

Weary Not of Obedience

Sori Sori -- Let thine hand be Mine Hand - and record this Mine Word that they might have it - that they be reminded of their part -- I say: Each shall be reminded of their part - and none shall be as laggardly or as one slothful ---

They shall each have their place and their part -- Yet they shall look well unto the source from whence cometh their help - their strength -- They shall not forget their Benefactors -- They shall not set foot against Mine Messenger -- They shall not set themself up - and forget that which they have been given ---

They shall fortune unto themself the Greater Part - thru humility and action -- They shall act according to the tradition of the "Initiate" - and they shall walk quietly and gently in the House of The Lord-- They shall hold their tongue - and speak only that - which shall profit them - They shall not weary of obedience - and watch well their step - lest they put their foot into a hole ---

For I say: There are many pitfalls - yet they have been marked well. Watch! Look! Listen! Obey! And overcome ---

Be ye as one mindful of that which ye say unto them - yet ye shall hold high the Lamp which I have placed within thine hand -- Hold high the Banner - and be ye as one responsible for that which hast been given unto thee - for it is a Gift of The Father which hast Sent Me -- And I shall be unto thee thine Shield and thine Buckler ---

So be it I have spoken - and I shall speak again of obedience and of discipline --

Cling Unto the Rock

Let this Word go forth from out thine mouth - and let it be according unto the law - and it shall profit thee ---

While they are as yet babes at the breast - they shall not be given the Greater part - for I say unto thee: They cannot assimilate it - and they cannot bear it ---

Render not thineself useless - helpless by their helplessness/ their uselessness -- For I say unto thee: There are ones which are want to put words into Mine mouth - and they are but deluded - and they are not given unto discrimination -- They have not the discernment nor the power of the Word -- I say unto thee: Be ye as one which hast thine calling and fear not - resist not - care not - be ye not part of their unknowing -Hear ye Me - and know ye that I am sure and for that part - I am with thee and ye shall cling unto The Rock upon which ye shall stand firm - Bless thineself and ye shall be blest forever --

No Man Knoweth the Hour

Say unto them: This day begins anew that which wast begun long ago. Now it shall be fulfilled - and each shall have a part in the fulfillment. For long ago thou hast stood upon this Holy spot - and recognized Me as The Lord thy God -- Now once again I say unto thee: I am come as a thief in the night - and no man knoweth the hour of Mine coming - neither of Mine going - for I appraise no man of Mine coming and Mine going -- I say: I come with a loud trump - and with great soundings - yet few there be which heareth - and which have the mind to comprehend Mine Presence -- Yet I say: I am come - and I say unto thee: Behold the Hand of God Move - and Know ye that It Moveth swiftly -- And bear ye in mind - I am about Mine Father's Business - and no man shall stay Mine Hand ---

Let it be said of thee - and ye shall bless thineself -- So let it be --

I Am The Lord thy God --

I Shall Lead Thee Forward

Let thine hearts rejoice this day - and let it be said: This is the New Day and it shall bring forth Great Light -- Let thine feet be swift to do the work given unto thee to do - go where it is given unto thee to go - do that which is given unto thee to do -- Put not thine hands before thine face - neither put thine fingers in thine ears -- For I shall give unto thee the Power to speak for Me - and I have appointed thee Mine Priestess - and I shall not take from thee thine part -- Yet I shall add to - and there shall be Great responsibility given unto thee - and there shall be Great Strength given unto thee - for it shall be for the good of all - let it be.

Now I say unto them: Hold steadfast - hold thineself in readiness for the next part -- Look not back - for I say unto thee: The Greater part is yet before thee -- Speak softly/ gently - and be ye as ones prepared for the days ahead -- Let not thine foot slip - for there are many pitfalls. Learn well thine lessons/ study well that which hast been given unto thee -- Place thine hand in Mine and I shall lead thee forward ---

Yet I say unto thee: Thou shall lift up thine feet and come -- With thine own hand ye shall be brot forward - and none shall bring thee against thine will -- PUT thine hand in Mine - and I shall lead thee - yet thine feet shall not drag - pick them up - walk ye upright and lean on no man - for therein is freedom ---

Bless thineself - and I shall do Mine Part --

The Hand of God Mighty and Strong

Say unto them as I would - that the Way is now prepared before them and they shall walk therein -- And at no time shall they look back -- They shall walk strait ahead with firm step - and they shall reel not -- They shall be as a great and mighty Oak - and bend not by the breeze - for there shall be the breezes - and they shall be as the ones from the east-- They shall blow - and blow ---

Yet thine boughs shall now bend - ye shall stand the storm -- And ye shall bow down unto no man - for I say unto thee: The arm of flesh is weak - and The Hand of God Mighty and Strong -- Be ye aware of The Hand of God ---

See It move and rejoice that this day is come -- So let it bear fruit ---

Let.....

Let this day bring forth Great fruit - and let it be done with dignity and gladness -- Let the way be prepared for them which shall follow after thee -- Let the Way be prepared in silence and with dignity ---

Let thine time be Mine time - let thine hand be Mine hand - let thine voice be Mine Voice - let it be - and there shall be Great things accomplished - and at no time shall I deceive thee ---

Be ye at Peace - and rest assured that I am not afar off - for I am not limited as to distance - time - or space - So be it I say unto thee: Be assured of Mine Presence ---

So be it I Am Sanat Kumara

Behold Ye the Light

Behold ye the Light -- Behold ye The Light!

BEHOLD YE THE LIGHT -

Let thine Light so shine that It might be seen afar -- Let it shine - and seek ye the Light ---

Bless thineself by thine seeking -- I say: Seek ye the Light - and PREPARE thineself for the Greater Part -- Rest not on thine laurels -- Feign not wisdom - for I say unto thee: Thou art not as yet overcome - Be ye as ones prepared to receive that which I have for thee -- So be it I speak into thee of thine preparation for the Greater Part -- Press forward - and be ye as ones steadfast -- Fear not -- Consider well that which I say unto thee - and bless thineself - for this am I speaking -- Behold ye the Light - and resist not The Light ---

Bind not thine feet - for I say unto thee: Walk ye forward and resist not the Light ---

I say unto thee:

BEHOLD THE LIGHT --

SEE THE LIGHT --

I AM THE LIGHT --

I Am He Which is The Most Worthy Grand Master of The Inner Temple –

It Shall Be Said Again and Again

Hear ye Mine Words - let them be written upon thine heart - bear them well in thine mind - heed ye that which I say unto thee -- Bless thineself and abide by the law - and no man shall judge thee ---

No man shall be unto thee judge - for he shall have no power over thee -- Will it not profit thee to hear that which I say unto thee? ---

Hast it not been said before - and shall it not be said again -- It shall be said again and again - until it is inscribed upon thine eternal heart.

Let it be- and then ye shall be as one prepared for the Greater Part. So let it profit thee to hear that which is said unto thee -- Forget not that there are as yet ones to come - and there are ones yet unborn which shall profit by that which I say unto thee -- Be ye aware of this Mine Word - and be ye glad that I have spoken as The Worthy Grand Master for there is but One Worthy Grand Master of The Inner Temple -- So be it I bless thee with Mine Presence -- I bless thee with the Word --

And it shall profit thee to accept it in The Name of The Father Solen Aum Solen --

The Order...

To thee I say Be ye as Mine hand made manifest unto them - and give unto them this Word -- And let it suffice that I am The Lord of Lords - The King of Kings - and it shall profit them to hear that which I say unto them -- Be ye of One mind -- Be ye of One Body - One Order - The Order I have given unto thee - The Order Which I have brot -- And at no time shall ye set thineself up as the high and mighty - for I say: I am The Lord thy God - and I am the First Priest of The Order of Melchezedek - and I am the First and Last - for I am from the beginning unto the end the "First Priest" - for I am the High Priest of the Order of Melchezedek - and it shall behoove thee to wait upon Me the Lord thy God - for I am the One Sent of Mine Father that this be done -- And at no time shall I betray Mineself - neither Mine trust --

Now - I ask as much of thee as I am willing to give - Loyalty unto them which serve thee - loyalty unto Me The Lord thy God - loyalty unto thineself -- THEN ye shall be of service unto All mankind -- So let it profit thee to hear Me --

So be it I have spoken for the Good of All - Mighty is THE WORD and Great the POWER thereof - GREAT THE POWER THEREOF -- Hold ye the Power - for THE POWER OF THE WORD shall Sustain thee - IT SHALL SUSTAIN THEE -- Be ye blest - and heed that which I say unto thee - for I AM THE WORD made Manifest - I AM THE WORD -- I AM THAT I AM ---

BEHOLD YE THE WORD MADE MANIFEST -- BEHOLD YE THE GLORY OF THE LORD THY GOD -

Upon This Rock

Upon this Rock have I built Mine Temple - upon this Rock have I set Mine Seal -- Upon this Rock have I written the Name - and Number -- Upon this Rock have I given instruction -- Upon this Rock have I given The Word ---

I stand before thee as One purified and Glorified - free - and in Mine Holy Estate -- I say unto thee: Carry thine cross with dignity- and be ye as ones swift to do Mine Work - and for that have I called thee forth -- Wait not - for the day of preparation passeth swiftly - and the night cometh - and therein shall be no light to light the way of the laggard -- Be ye as ones which can hold the Light - and swift shall be thine ascent Give unto The Father Solen Aum Solen All the Glory - All the Praise - and sing ye the Song of Praise ---

Rejoice that He hast given unto thee Being - and shown thee Mercy -- So be it I say unto thee: Hold ye firm the Lamp which I place within thine hands - and be ye as one responsible for thine part - and praise The Name of Solen Aum Solen day and night - for He shall send a Host to attend thee -

Be ye as ones forever blest --

I Am Sananda

Sanat Kumara & Sananda are of One Mind - One Will

Let this be recorded and remembered: There is but One Lord God - One Worthy Grand Master - yet we are One -- As One We move -- As One We stand -- As One We Are - for We are not divided against Ourself - Of One Mind are WE - for We are of One WILL -- One Purpose have We - and for this do We speak as One - and for that matter We act as One -- I say unto thee - ye are the Hand of Me - therefore ye are likewise His Hand too - His Hand as well as Mine ---

For hast it not been said: Thou art His Servant -- I ask of thee nought thou wouldst not be asked of Him---

Let it be said - that He and I ARE ONE -- We are of ONE FATHER, ONE PARENT - and We stand as ONE - HOLY KUMARAS - Holy by the Grace of The Father Solen Aum Solen -- So be it that thou art Mine handmaiden - and that makes thee no less His -- For as I lead thee so does He lead thee - for We are of One Mind - One Will - One Purpose, - One Aim - One Cause ---

Be ye blest this day - and I shall give unto thee in greater measure. So be it and Selah --

I Am Sanat Kumara

The Dead

Concerning the dead - these are as the ones in darkness - these are the ones in bondage - these are the ones yet uninitiated into the Realms of Light -- These are as the ones which have not the Light ---

While it is said - Greater Works than these shall ye do - it is true - for great shall be thine service unto the Light - and great shall be thine service unto them which are yet in bondage - yet in darkness - yet in the fog mist -- These shall be found and brot out of bondage - and great shall be their joy ---

Let thine own Light so shine that they might see it from afar - and be drawn unto it -- I say: Great shall be thine Light -- Let them See - let them Come - let them walk by thine Light - let them learn that which shall profit them - for this hast thou gone forth -- Be ye as one prepared for yet Greater Work -- So let it be for the Good of All - so be it, it shall profit thee ---

Hail! Hail unto the King of Glory - for He cometh swiftly -- As the Conqueror He cometh with Sword unsheathed - bearing upon His Head a Crown of Light -- A Breast-plate of Gold and Azure ---

So be it it is I Which cometh --

I Am He -

Fulfillment

Hast it not been said: There shall be a Great onrush of Waters? And it is so - so let it be - and the Spirit shall fill the dead! - for the "dead" shall come forth as ones alive - and they shall no more go into sleep -- I say no more shall the "dead" go into sleep - for they shall arise and walk as ones awake ---

They shall run and not weary - they shall work and not tire - for they shall be as ones delivered out of bondage -- They shall be as ones free - and they shall be as ones prepared for their work ---

Each shall be given as he is prepared -- Each shall receive as he is prepared according unto his talent ---

I say: Each hast been endowed a talent - each hast a talent - and as he hast prepared himself - So shall he receive - so be it the law -- So be it THE LAW - as he prepares himself - so shall he receive - so let it be. I say unto thee: LET IT BE! -- And it is given unto Me to see them hide the talent - and they therefore hide it from themself -- I say: The talent lost - is the talent lost -- They are not aware of their loss - they walk as ones impoverished - as ones poor of spirit - knowing not that they are responsible for their impoverishment - their pity ---

Let them seek the Light - Let them See the Light-- Let them bear the cross -- Let them arise - come forth as ones awaken -- Let them come forth from amongst the dead -- Let them give of themself that they be worthy the gifts so richly bestowed upon the Sons of God ---

I say - Arise! Arise! Come Forth! and be ye as one free -- Let thine own light so shine that it might be seen -- Let it shine forth! -- Put from thee thine puny ways - and come as one responsible - and worthy the gifts of The Father which hast remembered thee - thru His Mercy - since the days of thine going forth --

Let it be as He hast Willed -

Amen - Amen - Amen -

Whiter Than Snow

Mighty is The Word - and Great the Power thereof ---

I say: Ye shall fashion for thineself garments of white - and no blemish shall be found thereon -- For I say unto thee - there shall be no blemishes upon the Royal Raiment - and ye shall stand before The Lord of Lords - Spotless - arrayed in pure linen - and not a spot shall there be upon thine garment -- Therefore it is said: Seek ye first The Light.

Come unto Me and be ye made whole ---

Let it be well with thee -- Let thine Garments be spotless - and let thine Light so shine that All might see it -- So be it and Selah ---

No Rebellion in Mine House

Mine Beloved -- I say unto thee - the time cometh swiftly when they shall cry out for assistance - and it behooves Me to say unto them: Wait no longer - prepare thineself with diligence -- Let thine fortune be as nought - and come forth as ones free - for I say unto thee: I have kept a place and a part for thee - and ye shall prepare thineself to be brot in - and none brings thee against thine will - there is none to bring thee save thineself - and let it be so with thee - for I say - the laggards enter not into Mine abode ---

Too - I say: There is no rebellion in Mine House - for I am Master in Mine House - and the rebellious enter not into communion with Me. Come ye as an empty vessel -- Ask of Me Light - and I shall not deny thee -- Ask of Me anything and it shall be done according unto the law.

Ye shall first seek the Light - and all things shall be added ---

Question not the method by which the addition comes - for it cometh as thou art prepared to receive -- I say: The law is the law - and it is THE LAW - as ye are prepared so shall ye receive - so let it be ---

For it is the law and no man shall make void The Law ---

Peace - Peace - Peace

Hear ye Me and be ye as one prepared to receive of the Greater part -- Hast it not been said - the days of preparation shall be shortened - it is so -- So be it the time draws nigh when no man labors for his bread - and when no man shall bring the labors of his hand to the Altar -- I say the days of his labors shall be shortened - and he shall be as one placed within the proper environment - and wherein he shall be as one with his environment - for he maketh his own environment -- Now I say unto thee - Peace - Peace - Peace be unto thee - and no man shall take from thee thine peace ----

I say unto them which have ears to hear - Peace - Peace - Peace I give unto thee - accept it in the Name of The Father which hast Sent Me - so be it I come in His Name ---

Fortune unto thineself The Greater Fortune - the Greater Part -- For this do I say unto thee Peace - Peace - Peace -- So let it be well with thee -

Sananda

What Symbol - the red buds of the Glads?

Mine Beloved - I ask of thee nothing save obedience - and thou hast complied with that which hast been asked of thee - and at no time shall it be given unto thee to grovel for a pittance -- I say ye shall stand as one which hast gone the last mile with Me - and it shall be a Glad last mile - for I say - Great shall be thine Victory -- Great shall be thine joy and at no time shall ye be as one cast out -- Be ye as one blest this day.

Let it be said that Great revelation shall be unfolded - unveiled - and ye shall know that which I have said unto thee in cryptic form -- So be it

I Am The Lord thy God

Hear Ye Me

Say unto them this day: There is but One Lord God and I Am He - I Am HE! -- I stand upon the High Holy Mountain as One which sees and Knows All that which goes on -- I Know the True from the false. I Know the Way unto Mine Father's House - and I point the Way - and ask that they walk in the Way I point -- I am not an imposter -- I Am He Which is Sent that they have Light - that they be brot out of bondage.

I say: I AM COME that they be freed from bondage -- So Let it Be. For this am I come ---

Hear ye Me -- I Am come that ye be free -- Walk ye in the Way I set before thee ---

Ask of no man thine freedom -- Ask of no man forgiveness for thine sins -- Look unto no man for thine salvation -- Look unto no man for thine atonement ---

Wait not for the morrow -- Fortune thineself this day - for it is the day of preparation -- Prepare thine own self and be ye as prepared to stand before the Throne of The Most High Living God - spotless and as One arrayed in white linen -- Give ye ear unto Mine Words - and be ye accountable for thine own self - and the words which proceed out of thine mouth ---

Hear ye ME - for I have spoken and I Am speaking -

Let it Be -- Let it be well with thee -

Greater Things to Be Revealed

Be ye as ones prepared - for I say unto thee: - Great things are to be revealed unto thee -- Prepare thineself - for it behooves Me to say unto thee "Great things are yet to be revealed unto thee" -- Now ye shall hold thineself in readiness - and ye shall come as an empty vessel - and at no time shall ye deny Me - for I am not to be denied - for I am The Lord thy God -- I have given unto thee a plan - yet thou hast as yet not fully comprehended it - it hast not as yet been fully revealed unto thee - for I say it is not as yet been comprehended that which hast been given ---

Let it be said that as ye prepare thineself for to receive - more is given - Greater revelation is given -- This is the part which thou art prepared to receive -- And I say unto thee - I shall withhold nought when thou hast prepared thineself for to receive that which I have for thee ---

I shall give unto thee as I have received of Mine Father - when thou hast prepared thineself for to receive as I have received - So be it and Selah -- Let it be said that he which puts his hand to the plow and looks back - shall stumble and fall - and great shall be his fall - I say - GREAT SHALL BE HIS FALL ---

So be it I say unto thee: Look - Listen - See and be aware - and I shall lead thee - and at no time shall I forsake thee -- Be ye mindful of that which I say unto thee --

Firm Foundation

Hold ye firm unto that which hast been given unto thee - for I say unto thee - it is the Firm Foundation on which ye build Greater Mansions -- It is the firm foundation on which ye stand - when all others fail - when all others sink beneath thine feet ---

I say: Stand ye firm - steadfast - Waver not - hold high thine head - and falter not ---

For I say unto thee: The time cometh swiftly when ye shall be Glad for thine preparation ---

Ye shall be as ones alert - and hold unto the Light Which We give unto thee -- It is for thine sake that we come -- It is given unto Us to Know thine every need - thine every word - and I say We are not afar off - We know that which thou knowest not -- Yet is it not said: Prepare thineself for the Greater Part - and it shall not be withheld from thee -- Ye shall earn the right to call thineself "Son of God" - So be it - it is The LAW ---

Harken unto that which I say unto thee - and I shall give unto thee in greater capacity --

Make Thine House a Place of Peace

There is but this day - none other dost thou have - none other except THIS DAY - for the day ahead is not come - and there is no promise of the morrow -- Yesterday shall no longer be accessible unto thee - give thine attention unto the time at hand - and let it serve thee well -- Serve it - for there is none other time but the NOW - the present time - which shall be thine ---

And it is thine to do as ye will - yet it shall profit thee to prepare thineself for the work at hand -- Wait not that ye might have another day in which ye prepare thineself - yet ye shall be given as ye prepare thineself -- Wherein is it said: Ye create thine own environment - So be it that it is thine to choose---

Ye shall make of thine household thine resting place - a place of peace and harmony shall be found therein -- Therein is wisdom - for I say unto thee:

Prepare thineself for the Greater Part --

Peace - Peace - Peace -

Ye Earn the Right to Partake of the 'Rites'!!!

Mine Children -- "This day" I say unto thee: It is now come when ye shall be given thine next part - the part which hast been kept for this day -- There is Great things in store for thee - and it behooves thee to put aside all thine smallness - all thine worry - all the trivialities - and ye shall begin thine preparation - for it is no trivial part of which I speak.

Put from thee all selfishness - all puny words and efforts - in which ye struggle for thine next part -- I say - thine next part is now prepared for thee - and ye shall stand as one prepared to receive it -- And ye shall be as ones which have earned the right to partake of the Sacred Rites of The Order of Melchezedek -- I say ye earn the right to partake of the "Rites" of The Order of Melchezedek ---

So let it suffice that I Am The Lord thy God -

Sananda

The Greater Gifts

Mine Children -- There is but the Light of God Which hast brot thee forth -- Be ye as one with It - and enter not into the places of the dead. For I say unto thee - thine feet shall be firmly planted upon the Rock Which I Am -- I Am the Way - the Life -- I say - ye shall wait upon ME The Lord thy God - and I shall give unto thee as thou art prepared to receive ---

Hear ye that which I am saying unto thee - for I say I am sufficient unto thine needs -- Thou needst not give of thine time unto the lesser gifts - for I say unto thee: I bring unto the Greater Gifts than thou hast imaged - than thou hast received --

I say unto thee: I am not amongst the dead - I am of Mine father Sent - and I shall not mislead thee - I shall give unto thee as Mine Father hast given unto Me - when thou hast so prepared thineself to receive as I have ---

So be it that I speak unto thee for thine own sake - and I shall not deny thee thine Gifts which I have kept for thee -- I shall give unto thee Gifts Greater than Gold and Silver - Pearls without price -- Why accept the lesser?

Why tarry thou?

Why be ye as ones cast down?

Why be ye as ones poor of Spirit - when I bid thee come - come up higher - stand upon Mine High Holy Mount with Me and partake of Mine Cup -- Be ye as one with Me - and I shall accept thee as Mine own --

Be ye aware of Me - of Mine Words - and obey Mine Counsel - for I counsel thee wisely and prudently --

I AM The Lord thy God

Sananda

Christ

Let thine hand be Mine Hand and record for them this Mine Word unto them -- Let it be known that I am come even as The Lord of Lords - the Host of Hosts - and We are one of Mind - One of Spirit - One of Purpose. We are not divided against Ourself - for We are as "One" -- As One We stand under One Banner - the banner of The "Christ" -- Thine language is sufficient unto the day - yet ye shall come to know the meaning of "Christ" which is not for the most part understood -- And at no time shall ye use the Word loosely - for I say - ye have not understood the meaning of THE WORD "CHRIST" ---

Blest are they which do understand - for they shall be as One with the Christ - they shall be as ones brot in ---

I say: "Blest are the ones which understand the meaning of the Word CHRIST - for they shall be brot in---

Let it suffice that I am One - and I am not to be put out - I am not to be put into a corner - for I Am He Which is Sent - as Mine: Beloved Brother Sananda - and at no time shall I give unto thee the bitter cup -- I shall not give unto thee more than thou canst bear - for I say unto thee: I am come that ye be strengthened - that ye be lifted up -- I come that ye be brot out of bondage -- I come that ye be made new -- I come that ye be made whole ---

Hear ye ME! And arise!

Come forth and I shall touch thee --

Prepare thineself for the Wedding Feast -

Surrender

Beloved Ones:- This day I would say unto thee: There : is this day - in which thou hast to prepare thineself for to come unto Me -- I say: "Come unto Me" yet none enter herein unprepared -- So let thine preparations be complete - and bring thineself as one prepared - and I say unto thee - thine calling is sure - and thine Victory nigh -- Yet there are many pitfalls - put not thine foot into a hole --

Forget not that which I say unto thee - for the time draws nigh when ye shall stand as ones empty handed - as ones shorn of all thine laurels - and ye shall be as one naked -- Ye shall come as a little child - and ye shall be as ones prepared to partake of Mine Board --

And then ye shall be as ones prepared to go where I go - and ye shall have no limitations - for ye shall be Master of the Elements - the Air - the Waters of the seas - the fire -- And the Earth shall hold no Secrets from thee -- Ye shall go and come at will - and ye shall be as I Am -- Ye shall be as One which hast overcome -- Ye shall be the Victor over All things! ---

So be it that it behooves Me to warn thee - and likewise it behooves thee to be about thine preparation - for it is said: Time is NOW come when ye shall prepare thineself for the "Greater Part" ---

Look not backward -- Walk ye strait ahead -- See that which I bring unto thee -- I hold within Mine Hand the Key unto thine Eternal Victory!

Praise ye The Name of Solen Aum Solen - and be ye glad this day is come --

So be it that I Am

Sananda

The Lord thy God

The New Day

Behold ye the New Day - I say the "New Day" - for it is now come when ye shall come into thine own -- And for this hast thou asked of the Light -- For this hast thou accepted the Light -- For this hast thou wandered - waited - longed - and been as ones unceasingly looking for that which hast been kept for thee --

I say: Great things are in store for thee -- Be ye as ones prepared - for I say: "Great things are in store for thee" - and it is now come when ye shall come into maturity - and receive thine Inheritance in full ---

Ye need not grovel for a pittance - for I say unto thee - thou art Sons of God The Father - Behold ye the Glory of God - The Glory of The Lord thy God - The Glory of His Handiwork - for it is made manifest - for the Sons of God hast wrought a mighty Work -- I say BEHOLD YE that which is made manifest for thine sake -- Be ye as ones Alert - as ones blest -- SEE YE The Hand of God move --

Behold in Me The Light Which I AM --

I Am The Worthy Grand Master of The Inner Temple -

Sananda Prays

Most High Holy Father - Allwise - All Powerful art Thou -- Thou art the Giver and the Taker - Thou art the Sent - Thou art the Sender -- I say unto these Thine Children: "Be ye up and about thine preparation" Let it be - for I say unto them: Thou hast Willed that they return unto Thee -- I say that thou hast Willed it this day -- O Father - that they might hear ME - that they might hear Thy Voice -- Let them be quickened that they might Know Thee as I Know Thee ---

That they put from them all puniness - all rebellion and all doubt.

I say unto them - Arise! - Yet they are not aware of that which I Am. They stand as ones bowed down - with fear - pain - grief - greed – want and poor in Spirit are they ---

I say - they know not that which hast been kept for them -- Let them Arise - and come forth - for this hast Thou Sent Me -- I speak unto Thee that they might Know Thee - that they might know that which I say unto Thee -- Bear them up o Father - have mercy on them - and bring them out of BONDAGE -- Pity art they - pity their plight -- Thou hast not said nay unto them - Thou hast bid them return - Thou hast provided a Way for their return -- Thou hast given unto them Thine Son - as a Token of Thine Love for them --

Let them bear witness of ME The One Sent -- Let them know that I AM HE - I AM Thine Son -

Sananda

Holy - Holy is Thine Name - Solen Aum Solen –

The Cause

Sori Sori -- Hast it not been said that Great changes shall come about – and thru natural cause? ---

I say unto thee it is so - so let it be -- And none shall deny Mine Words - for ye shall see The Hand of God move -- The LAW shall bring forth the results of all the actions which man hast caused to be manifest. Let it be - for it is the fulfilling of the law ---

At no time shall there be given unto thee Greater sorrow than is now come - for this is the "Day of sorrow" - this is the "Day of deliverance" - the "Day of Great Joy" -For unto them which have wasted their Substance it shall be a time of sorrow -- Unto them which have overcome - it shall be a time of rejoicing -- Let them weep - let them rejoice - and it shall be unto them their fortune spent - or their fortune well kept ---

I say it shall profit mankind to awaken unto the part given unto him unto ALL -- And at no time shall the Law become invalid - for the LAW is valid - it is not to be set aside - neither is it to be ignored ---

Let them have "The WORD" and let it profit them - so be it I speak that they might be profited ---

So let them which have ears to hear - hear that which I have spoken and that which I Am speaking -- So be it I say unto them: The Word hast gone out - and It shall be heard thruout the land - so be it and Selah.

I Am

Truth Shall Be Thine Shield

Hold high the Banner of Truth and Light - for Truth shall be thine Shield - and thine Light shall be the Way in which ye go - let it be -- Be ye aware of the Light -- Be ye aware of the Way - and let thine feet be swift to do the Will of God The Father Which hast Sent thee forth.

Let the way be clear before thee - and let it be as the way in which I have gone -- Let it be the in which Sananda hast gone - and at no time shall ye turn thine face from Him - The Light - The Way - for He is The Way - and He hast prepared for thee a place - a part - and it shall be unto thee a place and a part like unto none else -- For He hast gone before thee that ye might follow in His footsteps ---

So let it be as He hast given of Himself -- Let it be given for the Good of All -- Let it BE! Let it BE!! ---

I say LET IT BE - FOR THE GOOD OF ALL --

Sanat Kumara

I am Life

Hear ye Mine Words - and be as ones blest - for I say unto thee: I Am He Which cometh as in the Air - as on the Eth -- As in the Fire - as on the Earth I come -- I Am Come -- I breathe forth the Essence of Life -- I say unto thee - I breathe forth the Essence of Life - for I AM LIFE -- I LIVE -- I AM ---

And I come unto thee as The Immortal Kumara --- I say I come unto thee as The Immortal Kumara – bearing The Light Which I AM.

I bring forth Great Light --

I bear thee up as on The Light --

I bear thee up as on The Light --

For I AM The Light -- I hold thee within Mine Hand -- I say unto thee: - I hold thee within Mine Hand - I bear thee forth as One which hast asked assistance of ME - of The Mighty Council ---

I say - as thou hast asked - so shall ye receive ---

I say unto thee - BEHOLD THE HAND Which bears thee up ---

Behold the Hand - and be ye blest -- Hast it not been said - "There is a Host to assist thee" - so let it be --

For I have come that ye be blest -- So be it that The Mighty Host stands by to assist ---

Hail - Hail unto the Victor Which is Come--

According to Law

Beloved of Mine Being:

This day I would say unto thee: Put thine hand in Mine - and let us explore regions yet unexplored by man -- I say - let us explore regions unexplored by man - for man of Earth is yet bound unto the Earth -- Yet I say unto thee - thou art not of the Earth - thou art of regions beyond the Earth - regions that thou hast forgotten - regions beyond the Galaxy in which the Earth belongs ---

I say unto thee: Thou art not a child of the Earth -- Thou art of the Higher Realm - realms yet unexplored by man of Earth ---

I say - the Earth-man is yet bound unto the Earth as the embryo unto the mother ---

Is it not said that there is Great revelation in store for thee - it is so, so let it be ---

I say unto thee - that it is as yet not known unto man of Earth - that which he shall <u>become</u> -- Too I say - he too shall become of age - and he too shall become mature - and he shall return unto his Source - and be as he wast created to be -- And at no time shall man plunder the "Secrets" of The Most High Living God ---

For I say: He grows - he grows from age to age - from youth to maturity -- And then he becomes as <u>one</u> with his SOURCE – knowingly. And he then Becomes a Son of God ---

Be ye as one which can hear that which I say unto thee ---

Let it be -- For this have I spoken unto thee --

I Am Sananda

Action

Hold out thine hand and I shall touch thee -- Hold up thine head and I shall bless thee -- Lift up thine feet and I shall direct thee in the path of righteousness - and I shall give unto thee of the water of Life -- Ye shall drink of Mine Cup - and ye shall be glad forevermore -- Lift up thine eyes and behold the Glory of The Lord -- Harken ye to that which I say unto thee - and ye shall be blest to see the Glory of The Lord - for I say unto thee - ye shall follow in His Footsteps - and ye shall have no fear ye shall be as ones blest forever - fear not ---

Be ye alert and arise from thine slumbers - and thine name shall be written upon the Eternal record - as having won thine Victory -- I say - Hail - Hail unto the Victor! -- Hail! Hail! Victor! -- Hail! Hail! Unto the Victor -- Be ye as the Victor for He hast overcome -- Let it Be -- For this have I spoken --

Progress

Hast it not been said that Great changes shall come about - is it not so?-

I say unto thee - it is so -- So let it be - for change is well - and for that matter change is progress - let it be ---

Spirit is not stagnant - neither is it static - It is Positive - It is Real - and it is that which brings about change ---

I say - Spirit is the part which animates the physical - and It is the animator - that which brings about the change -- Let it be - and it shall profit thee to go forth as one prepared for that which shall come to pass.

I tell thee - Greater things are in store for thee than thou hast imaged -- Thou hast not heard - neither seen that which awaits thee - so be ye as ones prepared ---

Walk ye as One - walk with Surety - walk ye Upright - let not thine feet drag - place thine hand in Mine -- Put thine hand in MINE and I shall lead thee -- Let thine feet be Mine - let thine hand be Mine - let thine VOICE be Mine - and I shall give unto thee that which I have kept for thee --

So be it I Am

Sanat Kumara

THE PRODIGAL SON

Mine Children -- Hast it not been long since thou went from thine place of abode -- Hast it not been long since thou went into bondage - and hast it not been long thou hast wandered in darkness ---

NOW -- It is come when thou shall return unto thine rightful Estate, Thine abiding place - and ye shall receive that which thou hast forsaken. Thou hast forfeited a princely ransom - when thou went out so long ago.

Be ye as one prepared to enter therein - for this do I now speak unto thee -- Be ye as one which can hear that which I say unto thee -- I am come that ye hear -- So let it be as The Father hast Willed it --

Sanat Kumara

Ye Shall Hunger No More

Mighty O Mighty is the Word of God -- Mighty - is the Hand of God and Great is His Handiwork -- He hast Created all that is Eternal and Everlasting - and at no time shall HIS Work be destroyed - for His Work is Good - and it is well that it endures -- While there shall be change - it is according unto the Law - and the Law shall not become void or set aside - for The Law is the LAW and no man shall set it aside.

While it is given unto Me The Lord thy God - to speak for He Which made the Heavens and the Earth - I say - the Heavens and the Earth shall pass away - While The Word of God shall not pass away - for IT shall endure forever and forever --So be it I say unto thee - It shall endure forevermore -- So let it be - for I have spoken unto thee from out the Eternal Flame - and It shall not die ---

Be ye as one blest - as one prepared to enter into the Holy of Holies. Therein ye shall abide -- So be it I say unto All - Come ye and partake of Mine Board -- Drink ye of Mine Cup - and ye shall hunger no more, neither shall ye thirst -- So be it I proffer thee The Cup - - Come drink and be blest --

Behold!!

Behold - Behold ye! all that is before thee - for The Lord thy God speaketh - saying unto thee:- Behold! All that is before thee!! ---

See that which is made manifest before thee -- Know that it is by The Word that it became manifested ---

I say: By the Word hast All things become manifested ---

Let it be according to the Law - for according to The Law is it done.-

I say: Let it be done according unto the LAW ---

For by the spoken Word shall it be either for weal - or woe ---

Now - ye shall fashion for thineself that which ye will - for as thou create - so shall ye receive -- It is said that "Each shall father his own child - and each shall know his child" - So be it each shall carry the burden of his own creation - and none shall deny it -- So be it each shall be responsible for his own fortune which he hast garnered unto himself. So let it be - for this hast he gone forth into bondage ---

Let him carry his own fortune - his own burden - his own responsibility with dignity - and with reverence unto and for The LAW.

So be it I speak for the Good of All --

I AM Sananda

Responsibility

Be ye as the Keeper of Mine Sobrieties - and as one responsible for that which I give unto thee - and it shall be held sacred -- And at no time shall ye be held accountable for that which they do with that which is given unto them - for it shall be their responsibility - and none shall hold thee accountable ---

Let it be - and give freely - without price - without preachment - without stint - and give unto them that which I give unto thee to say -- Place thine hand in Mine and I shall lead thee into the path of righteousness -and no man shall stay thine progress ---

Bless them which spitefully use thee -- Bless them which revile against thee -- Bless them which close thee out -- Bless them which know not that which they do -- Bless them which cut themselves off - for they know not that which they do ---

Hear ye Me - and it shall be thine own blessing - ye shall be blest thereby - so let it be ---

I Am with thee -

Sananda

The Head of This Council

Let it be said that there is but One Lord God - and He is The Head of This Council - The Over-All Council - The Council Which is over the lesser Ones -- While there are lesser Ones - I say this One of Which I speak is The One over All the lesser Ones -- For mankind shall be served - each according unto his preparation - each according unto his needs ---

I say the Lesser Ones are no less for their part - for They have a part. Yet They serve the ones which know not of The Higher Council - neither have they the mind to comprehend that which This Council have for them - when they are prepared to receive -- So let them be - let them find their way - We of The Council but give unto them the law and point out the pitfalls and the dangers -- We give unto them that which is wise and prudent -- We give not unto the foolish - the Jewels of the First Water - We give not the babe at the breast the meat - that which We give unto "The Man" - one which hast prepared himself for to receive the Greater Part---

I say: The Man which hast become the age of accountability hast prepared himself for his part ---

And at no time do We give unto them more than they car bear ---

I say: Great shall be the onrush of Waters - which shall flow over the land -- And so great shall be the Power thereof - All shall move before It - which are not prepared -- Let It move -- Let It go - Let It flow - for from Its movement shall come great Light -- So let it be - for this hast the Word gone forth this day ---

Be ye as ones blest - for this am I speaking --

I Am Sanat Kumara

The Acceptable Sacrifice

Sori Sori:

Hold high the Lamp which I place within thine hands -- Place upon the Altar thineself - as a living Sacrifice - and it shall be acceptable unto The Father Solen Aum Solen ---

Be ye as one prepared for Greater things shall be revealed unto thee for it is said: There shall be Great Light flood the Earth - and it is so - So be ye one with It - let It go forth that all might see It -- Let It shine forth from the Mountain top -- Let It be seen from the valley - and let them be drawn unto It -- For this have We made known Ourself -- For this have We counseled thee -- For this have We made thee Keeper of Mine Sobrieties -- For this have I touched thee ---

So be it I shall touch them which have prepared themself for to receive -- So let it profit them to be prepared -- So be it I Am The Lord thy God - and I have spoken of "Preparation" -- Yet few have comprehended that which I say -- I say unto them: "prepare thineself" yet they wait - wait - for what do they wait? ---

I have given of MINESELF that they might Know - yet they ask of man- of flesh - of the unknowing ones -- They ask for signs and wonders -- They ask that they touch the wounds in Mine side ---

Yet - - I say unto them: Nay! -- They shall never again put their fingers into Mine wounds - for I shall not bare Mine wounds unto them. I shall not open up Mine Bosom that they put their fingers therein -- For I am not of a mind to let them keep open up Mine wounds ---

No longer shall they display the dirty garments before their ungodly altars for I shall tear down their temples of "Idolatry" - and I shall raise up a New Generation which shall walk in the Way I set before them -- I shall set up Mine Kingdom - and I shall bring forth the Servants of God - and they shall sit upon Mine Right Hand - and they shall inherit The Kingdom of God ---

They shall be the Inheritors of The Kingdom which I shall establish in The Name of The Father Son and Holy Ghost - Which is The Mighty Council - and which is the Will of The Father.-

So be it that I Am He Which is Sent that His Kingdom be established upon the Earth --

So let it be --

For this have I come -

Come as a Little Child

This day I would give unto thee this Word - and for this hast thou come unto this Altar -- I say - ye shall be as ones prepared for that which shall come about by natural law -- Ye shall place thine hand in Mine - and I shall direct thee -- Ye shall put forth the effort to prepare thineself - and at no time shall I lead thee astray -- I say - it is now come when ye shall fashion for thineself greater horizons - and I shall lift thee unto Greater/ Grander heights - heights yet unattained/ heights thou knowest not as yet ---

Ye shall be as ones prepared - for this hast thou come unto this Altar. Hold ye fast and be ye alert - for it is said: The time comes swiftly when ye shall stand as ones naked - shorn of all thine laurels - all thine vain-glory which shall be as nought -- For all thine good works shall not be sufficient unto thine salvation -- Ye shall be as a little child -- Ye shall be as one willing to be led into the path of righteousness - and I shall not deny thee entrance -- So be it I am The Most Worthy Grand Master Of The Inner Temple -

Knowest Thou?

Let it be said this day - that there is but "This day" in which to prepare thineself - for none other dost thou have -- The yesterday past - the morrow shall be the morrow - yet wherein hast thou prepared thineself? Knowest thou what the morrow bringeth? Look not backward - for to look back is to stumble -- I say: Stumble not - put thine foot on firm Ground - and feel that it is firm beneath thine foot -- And I say unto thee: Be ye as one steadfast - hold ye firm - waver not -- Stand ye firm when all about thee seem to waver -- Be ye as the Rock and know ye that there is Safety within the Hand of The Almighty God - The Father Which hast sent thee forth -- I say: Within Him is Safety - and in none other - for He hast set thee apart - and given thee dominion over the lesser of His Creatures -- Yet thou hast not given unto Him credit for thine welfare - for thine safety -- I say - therein is Safety - therein is Peace -- It is said: Let Peace be established within thineself wherein the Spirit abideth - and at no time shall man take from thee thine Peace ---

It is said: Let Peace be established within thee - and no man shall take from thee thine Peace -- Let it be -- For this have I spoken this day.

So be it and Selah -

Eternal Parent

Sarah Speaking:

Blest of Mine. Being: Many - many eons ago - thou hast gone out from Me as a Living Being - as an individual with a Free Will - as a Gift - the Great and Good Gift - given unto thee as thine birthright ---

And it is for this that it is asked of thee - this day -- Let it be given unto thee to Know the value of this "Good and Great Gift"- thine Inheritance ---

Thine Will is that which shall bring thee back into the place of thine abode - from which thou hast gone out ---

I tell thee this day: Thine Will is thine passport into the place of thine abode ---

Thine Will - is sufficient - yet it shall be surrendered up - willing - for WE thine "Eternal Parent" cannot use it - for the most part - when given with reservations/ grudgingly ---

I say unto thee: Give unto Us that which is Ours and WE shall give unto thee that which is thine -- By The GRACE of The Father shall it be given unto thee ---

For He hast provided à Plan by which/ thru which ye return ---

Let it be - Let It Be - LET IT BE - for I say - it is given unto Me to Know – for I am thine Eternal Mother - I have given unto thee manifestation -- Thru Mine womb thou hast come --Thou hast past thru Mine Being - and I have nourished thee at Mine Breast -- I have given unto thee that which hast sustained thee ---

I have watched and cared for thee in thine hours of wandering and waiting -- I have given unto thee that which should profit thee - and at no time have I forsaken thee. I say: Ye shall return unto Me unscathed - unharmed - untarnished - for I have kept thee for this day -- Now it shall be given unto thee to return, even as thou hast gone forth - pure and justified – knowingly - for - thine memory shall be restored unto thee in full measure - and nothing shall be hidden from thee - so let it be ---

And there shall be Great Joy - and Great shall be the Joy - for it shall be as nothing Known - for it shall be the fulfiling of the Law -- It shall be the fulfiling of all that thou hast longed for -- Thine longing shall be no more ---

So be it I am speaking as thine Eternal Parent - and it is said: "The Father and I are One - We are not divided -- "WE" have sent forth the "Word" and thou hast received -- So let it profit them which hear - let it be -- Let it BE as they are prepared to receive - as they are prepared they shall receive - let it BE ---

I Am with thee Evermore - I Am Sarah -

War

Mighty - O Mighty is The Word of God - Mighty is the Manifestation thereof ---

I say unto thee this day: It behooves thee to gather together thineself in preparedness - for there shall be Great need of thee - I say - Great shall be the need -- I say: Prepare thineself for that which shall come upon thee - let it come -- Yet - I have said unto thee: Prepare thineself and it shall come to pass that I shall be unto thee all that ye have need of -- Place thine hand in Mine - and I shall not forsake thee ---

I have said - I know Mine own - and I shall be with thee all that thou need -- Let it be known that I am not afar off - I am prepared to do that which I have said – I am prepared to deliver thee out -- I say I am He which is The Most Worthy Grand Master -- Let it be known that which I have said unto thee - that which I have shown thee - and it shall profit them to heed that which I have given unto thee ---

Prepare thineself – for Great shall be thine revelation -

Hidden Identity

While it is given unto thee to be as ones in flesh - I say unto thee - flesh shall not bind thee - for flesh shall have no power over thee -- <u>Flesh is flesh</u> - and therefore it shall pass and be as the Elements from which it cometh - while Spirit IS SPIRIT - and It shall be as "Spirit" still - untouched - unharmed - and uncontaminated by flesh ---

Yet I say unto thee: The Spirit is that which animates the flesh - and It shall be no less for having flung aside the cloak of flesh -- And the cloak shall not despoil that which hast taken upon itself the cloak -- Yet when I say the Spirit shall be no less for having taken unto itself the cloak of flesh - I too say: Let not the garment which men wear deceive thee - for many a martyr weareth the pauper's cloak - many a pauper weareth that of a king - and not one recognizes the other ---

Let the garments not deceive thee - for I say unto thee: The Master of the house sets the table before thee - and therein sits One which hast worn the Robe of Royalty - and hast walked with the High and Mighty - yet I say unto thee - there is no sign of the unknown - no laurel wreath to be seen no sign that man might read - and no place shall ye find a place where there are the words of the pore - which shall tell the history of this One of which I speak - for history hast not recorded that which shall be revealed unto thee ---

I say - history is mute - while I say - The Council shall speak out that it might be Known - so let it be Known ---

For this have I spoken thusly.

The Perils Shall Not Touch Thee

Hast it not been said - there shall be changes? And there shall be great changes - there shall be changes such as thou hast not imaged! For this do I come unto thee that ye be prepared - let it be -- Give thineself in Holy Surrender unto the Will of The Father Which hast sent thee forth and at no time shall ye fail ---

Let it be said - that many shall go and come - many shall fall be the way - yet ye shall fail not - neither shall ye fall - ye shall stand firm as the Rock -- Let thine feet be firmly planted upon the "Rock" - and nothing shall be unto thee a peril - for the perils shall not touch thee -- So be it I say unto thee: "The Perils shall not touch thee" -- I have said: Place thine hand in Mine and I shall lead thee out and it is so - So let it Be --

I Am Sanat Kumara

The Witness

I Am The Most Worthy Grand Master - Sent forth from out The Father's Bosom Am I -- I am of Him Sent that I bear Witness of Him -- I come as One of the Eloheim - AS ONE OF THE ELOHEIM ---

I Am the One Which hast been the Guardian of the planet Earth - I have held Her within the palm of Mine Hand -- From Her beginning I have succored Her -- I have given unto Her of Mine Light - that She be brot thru Her peril -- Now again She stands in peril - and once again I stand ready to assist Her - and therefore to give assistance unto the children thereof - I say to assist the Children thereof - for they are in need of Mine assistance -- And I Am Come that they might know that I Am Come to assist --

When it is come that there shall be a Great necessity - they shall prove Me - for I shall show Mine Strength - and they shall know that I Am That Which I AM ---

Be ye as one which knows - and I shall declare unto thee - I shall not deceive thee --

I shall lead thee aright -- So be it and Selah ---

I AM -

Come Ye Out!!

Mine Hand is upon thee and I say unto thee this day: There is not one which hast been as one prepared to go the last mile - for this do I now speak unto thee -- I say: There is but One which hast given unto me credit for being that which I Am -- And there is the One which is prepared to go the last mile - for that One hast been the last mile - and knows Me for that which I Am ---

While it is given unto Me to know the meditations of thine heart - I too know thine frailties - thine weakness -- So too - do I know thine strength - I Am thine strength - yet ye know not for that matter - wherefrom cometh thine strength -- I say - thine strength cometh from the Source - and from The Source THERE IS STRENGTH -- And at no time shall ye be as ones forgetful of the Source -- Thou hast given great power unto the forces of darkness - and added unto -- Wherefore hast it profited thee? Wherefore hast thou been profited? ---

I say: It hast profited thee naught -- Wherein hast thou been lifted up? Wherein hast thou been profited? ---

When it is given unto thee to be called - ye shall give all thineself unto thine calling - and unto thine - self be true - UNTO THINESELF BE TRUE - for the law is the law - and it is exacting - and there is no exception - NO exception ---

I say: Come ye out from amongst them - be ye no part of them which sit in darkness -- Be ye no part of their foolishness - their idolatry, their hypocrisy - their blasphemy -- I say - be NO PART Of them - for they are but hypocrites and blasphemers - they follow Me not --

I say - they follow Me not ---

I come that ye Know Me - and I Am not an idol -- I am not a "poor" priest - I am not an imposter ---

I Am The Lord thy God - and I have spoken - and I am speaking --

So be it I Am speaking for the GOOD of ALL -- Let them which have ears hear that which I say - HEAR - For this have I SPOKEN -

No Hiding Place

I say unto thee this day: It behooves each and every one to heed this Mine Word - for it is designed to be unto thee great strength - Great

Light -- And at no time shall it be unto thee nought -- At no time shall ye hide thineself - for there is no hiding place - there is NO hiding place. For every thot - every word - every act is known - and it behooves Me to say unto thee - there is no hiding place -- For it is known wherein thou art - and wherein thou canst be found -- Let it be said - that as ye are prepared - so shall ye receive -- At no time shall ye be given more than ye can bear ---

Yet I say - ye shall put on the whole Armor of God for it shall suffice thee -- Ye shall stand upon firm ground - and ye shall place thine hand in Mine and I shall lead thee thru the wilderness -- I say - the wilderness shall not hide thee - for I shall lead thee out -- So follow ye where I lead thee - for I know wherein thou hast lost thine way - and I am prepared to lead thee safely out -- Bear ye the Banner of The Christ- lift up thine head - lift up thine feet - and prepare thineself for the Greater Part - for this have I spoken---

I Am The Most Worthy Grand Master of The Inner Temple -

Thou Art Purchased with a Price

Sori Sori -- Behold in Me the Light Which I AM -- Behold in thyself the Light which thou art ---

Behold! The Light! and walk ye in it -- Hold the Lamp which I place within thine hand -- Put thine hand in Mine - and I shall fill to overflowing the Cup - and it shall flow and flow - and it shall suffice that which flows from thine cup -- It shall feed and sustain them which know not the Source -- For I have Sent thee forth as Mine Handmaiden. From the Realms of Light have I sent thee - and I have placed Mine Hand upon thine head in Holy Benediction and pronounced the Word -- I have given unto thee the Authority and the Power to speak out in Mine Name - for I have given unto thee Mine Name - and I have taken unto Mineself the Power and the Authority to give unto thee that which is needful for thine welfare -- I have placed upon thee Mine Seal and I have paid the Price thereof -- Let it suffice that thou art purchased with a price ---

For I say unto thee - I have been unto thee "The Master" --

I have portioned out into thee that which hast been unto thee profitable - and thou hast accepted it in <u>Mine Name</u> - and thou hast been obedient and trustworth - thou hast been watchful - and alert ---

Let it be - for I say unto thee - ye shall keep watch with Me - The Lord thy God ---

So be it and Selah ---

Blest are They

Blest are they which bear Mine Name -- Blest are they which have the Name written upon their forehead - for Mine Seal is upon them -- Blest are they which have Mine Seal upon their forehead -- Blest are they which wear the Cloak which I place upon them - for I say unto thee: I Am The High Priest Which hast the Power and the Authority to give unto them which are prepared - Mine Cloak - and I say it is Mine to give -- So be it I wear it with honor and dignity - and I am not a poor Priest - I Know that which I am about - I Know that which I am to do -

and that which I am to do I shall do - with the Authority which Mine Father hast invested within Me ---

And I say unto thee: Come - follow Me and I shall place upon thine head Mine Hand - and ye shall be blest as thou hast not been blest -- Let it profit thee to follow Me - for I shall lead thee into the place wherein I abide - let it be - LET IT BE ---

And ye shall be forever blest ---

In the Beginning

Mighty! O Mighty is the Word of God -- Behold ye the manifestation thereof - for I say thou are the manifestation of "The Word" - for the Word wast spoken - It wast made flesh - and God breathed into the flesh - and it became a LIVING SOUL -- Therefore thou art the Living SON of God - for He breathed thee forth - and thou went forth A LIVING CREATURE -- Of Him thou hast been endowed Life - Life of His Life - Grace of His Grace ---

And by His Grace shall ye return unto Him as thou went forth - A LIVING BEING -- And not one whit shall be the difference - for from Him thou hast received - and unto Him thou shall return ---

So let it be as He hast Willed it ---

I Am Come that it Be ---

So let it Be ---

The Journey

Be ye as one prepared to go the last mile - for I say unto thee: There is Great things in store for thee - and at no time shall ye be the one unprepared -- For it is given unto all men to have a part - which should be unto them of great value ---

The part which I have given unto thee is not the lesser part - for I have called thee out from amongst them - and I have placed thee in the position wherein thou art - and I have given unto thee that which is sufficient unto thee - that which is at hand - that which is to do - and at no time shall ye be found wanting ---

I say: Ye shall be as the "Rock" -- Ye shall be as one which hast thine hand in Mine - and I shall lead thee - and ye shall stumble not -- While I say unto thee - ye shall stumble not - I too say: Thou shall give unto Me thine hand - and I shall lead thee ---

I shall not deceive thee - neither shall I lead thee astray -- Falter not, bless thineself - and others shall be blest by thine Light -- Walk with surety - and I shall be thine Staff - thine Shield - thine Buckler ---

Let thine hand be Mine - thine mouth be Mine - thine feet Mine - and I shall direct thee into the place wherein I am ---

Lo it is come - and I am glad when it is come that ye hast gone this far with Me -- Come - let Us go -- Come - Let Us finish that which we have been given to do -- So be it I am Come that it be done -

Let it Be -

He - Leadeth Me

Say unto them as I would - there are none sufficient unto themself - for I the Lord thy God - Know their weakness - and I too - Know their strength - I Know their frailties ---

I Know from whence cometh their help - I KNOW their every need, their every want ---

Yet I come not to satisfy their wants - I come that they be lifted up. So let it be -- For this do I say unto them: "As ye prepare thineself - so shall ye receive - so be it the law"---

Holy - is The Word -- And this day I say unto them: Hold out thine hand and I shall fill it - I shall give unto thee according to thine capacity.

I say: According unto thine capacity - I shall give unto thee --

Ye shall be as one which hast the mind to receive of Me - and I shall not withhold from thee Mine Mercy - Mine Grace - Mine Light -- I say: I shall withhold nought from thee - when thou art prepared to receive. So be it I shall give of Mineself that ye be lifted up -

So let it be - for this have I Come -

I Am Sananda

Reason Not Against Me

Holy - Holy! is The Word - and Great the Power thereof - I say: Great the Power thereof -- Hold ye Sacred the Word - and bless thineself - for this is It given -- Hold ye fast unto that which hast been given -- Waver not - put thine foot not in a hole ---

Plant thine feet firmly upon the Rock - and be ye as ones firmly planted -- Hold ye steady - let not thine Lamp flicker before the breeze that blows - let it be steady within thine hand -- Keep thine Covenant thou hast made with Me so long ago -- Be ye as ones self-responsible. Self-responsibility is required of thee - shirk it not -- Be ye as one responsible for thineself -- Hold ye the Lamp which I give unto thee - place it not into the hands of another -- Reason not against Me - for I say unto thee - thou art frail of Spirit -- Reason NOT against ME! for I Know thine frailties - thine weakness ---

Be ye as ones blest to hear that which I say unto thee --

I Am The Lord thy God -

Let it Suffice

Be ye as ones alert - rest in the knowing that I am Come that ye be lifted up -- Let it suffice thee that I have brot forth One amongst thee for Mine Hand maiden-- Let it suffice thee that which I give unto thee - from this Great and Mighty Council - and at no time shall ye deny Me - for I say unto thee: To deny Me is to betray thineself - and at no time shall I betray Mineself -- For I say unto thee: I Am the Lord of Lords - the Host of Hosts - and I come unto thee as such - and I shall not be denied. I say - I shall not be denied -- For this is the day for which thou hast waited - and at no time shall ye be as ones betrayed -- Too - it is said:

Ye shall place thine hand in Mine - and I shall lead thee out of bondage. So let it Be - for this am I Come --

I AM Sananda

Listen!!!

Be ye as one which has Mine Hand upon thee - and make ye ready thineself for to receive that which is kept for thee - for it is said - Greater things are now prepared for thee ---

I say: Wait not for another day - give unto thineself the Greater Part. Fortune unto thineself the Greater Part - for none forch it upon thee - I say: "NONE forch it upon thee"---

Let it be recorded that all might know and see that which I say - for unto them I say: Be ye as one prepared - for it behooves Me to say: "Prepare thineself" Harken unto Me - and I shall be as One Aware of thee -- Take heed and prepare thineself - and at no time shall I turn Mine face from thee -- Yet it is for thine own sake that I speak -- I Am Sanat Kumara

The Living Fire

BEHOLD - I STAND BEFORE THEE AS A LIVİNG LIGHT - AS THE FIRE FROM ON HIGH -- I SPEAK UNTO THEE IN TERMS THOU CANST COMPREHEND - I BEAR MINE BREAST UNTO

THEE - I EXTEND MINE HAND - I SAY UNTO THEE COME! - AND WHAT DO I FIND?

I FIND THEE AS ONES SLEEPING - I FIND THEE AS ONES FILLED WITH DESIRE - FILLED WITH ANXIETY - FEAR! - FEAR!! FEAR!!! - LONGING -- AND I SAY UNTO THEE: THOU KNOWEST NOT THAT WHICH YE FEAR - THOU KNOWEST NOT THAT WHICH YE SEEK - FOR I SEE THEE SEEKING IN THE LOW PLACES FOR ME - AND THOU ART BORN OF FEAR. THOU ART WONT TO KNOW ME - FOR I SAY: THOU ART AHUNGER AND ATHIRST -- KNOW YE THAT I AM THY SHIELD AND THINE BUCKLER?

KNOW YE NOT THAT I AM HE WHICH IS SENT THAT YE MIGHT BE SATISFIED - THAT YE BE LIFTED UP - THAT YE BE BROT OUT OF BONDAGE?

HEAR YE THEN - THAT WHICH I SAY UNTO THEE -- HEAR YE!! I SAY - THAT WHICH I SAY UNTO THEE: COME - FOLLOW YE ME - BE YE AS ONE PREPARED TO GO WHERE I GO - FOR I GO UNTO MINE FATHER WHICH HAST SENT ME.

I SAY: BEHOLD IN ME THE LIGHT WHICH I AM ---

I AM HE WHICH COMETH AS A THIEF IN THE NIGHT -- I SAY: I COME AS A THIEF IN THE NIGHT -- BEHOLD - I AM COME -- LOOK UP OH YE CHLDREN - LOOK UP! - PICK UP THINE FEET -- LET THERE BE LIGHT! I AM HE -

I AM THE LORD THY GOD – SANANDA

Hear Ye!!

Be ye as Ones prepared for that which shall come about by natural law and therefore it shall come about naturally - and it shall be as the law demands - I say - as the law demands ---

I am come this day - that the law be fulfilled - that ye be prepared - and it behooves Me to say: Prepare thineself - for it is given unto thee to be as ones in bondage - therefore I come that ye be brot out-- Now ye shall go thine way - knowing that I am no less for thine blindness -- That ye see Me not - is no sign I am not - no assurance that I am not ---

I AM COME - yet ye see Me not -- It is said: I reveal Mineself in due season -- I Am Present - I AM PRESENT! Yet - ye see Me not ---

Listen! unto MINE Words - for this am I speaking! I AM COME - yet ye see Me not - hear ye then that which I am saying - and know ye that I am speaking for the Good of All -- So be it I Am now prepared to pour out Mine Spirit upon them which know Me -- So be it I Am Here! --

I AM HERE!

LOOK - LISTEN - SEE

I AM COME --

I Am The Lord of Lords -

The Host of Hosts - The Lord thy God

Sananda

To the Servants

Be ye as the hand of Me - and give unto them this Word - and it shall suffice them - that they are Mine - "MINE WORDS" - that I Am the Author of Mine Words -- THESE ARE MINE WORDS - and I say I AM responsible for them -- At no time do I hold thee responsible for that which I give unto thee to say -- Ye shall say unto them in Mine Name - that I Am the MASTER OF THIS HOUSE - that I Am the Director thereof - and I have given unto thee the Authority by which it shall be cared for - and by which that which I give unto thee shall be used - and cared for -- That which shall be done shall be done in Mine Name - and I say - there shall be no rebellion - no self-pity - no pettiness, no selfishness - no offences - no hatred - no laggards - no parts too small - no parts too great - no task too small/ too great - for all things shall be done in MINE NAME -- I say - there are no lesser tasks, none too large - for I give not unto Mine Servants more than they can bear -- I say I am not a "puny priest" - I Am The Lord thy God - and I Know thine capacity - let it be - and it shall be expanded - and ye shall be as ones prepared for yet greater things ---

So be it I have spoken for the Good of All --

I Am Sananda

The Sore

Be ye as the Voice of Me - and say as I would - that there is but little time in which to make ready thineself - and at no time shall ye be as one rebellious - as one which hast the "Sore"-- I say - the Sore shall be cleansed out - and cut away - and be no more ---

Cut away the "Sore" - and be as ones free from that which hast tormented thee -- Let it not fester and run - let it be cleansed and healed. CLEAN IT OUT! So be it it shall have no power over thee -- Let it be done! And let it be remembered no more ---

I say: LET IT BE DONE! - HEALED - CLEANSED! - Let it be! and I shall be as One which hast Mine Hand upon thee -- So be it and Selah --

I Am Sananda

ALPHA AND OMEGA AM I - THE BEGINNING AND THE END - AND THE WAY BEFORE THEE IS STRAIT - IT IS CLEARLY DEFINED -- MARK YE WELL THE WAY - FOR I SAY YE SHALL GO OUT NO MORE - FOR THINE TIME IS COME WHEN YE SHALL RETURN UNTO MINE HOUSE - TO GO OUT NO MORE ---

YE SHALL BE AS ONE FREE FROM THE WHEEL OF REBIRTH TO GO OUT NO MORE ---

I SAY UNTO THEE: I AM ALPHA AND OMEGA - THINE BEGINNING - THINE END -- THE ENDING SHALL BE THINE BEGINNING - FOR THOU HAST THINE BEGINNING IN ME - THE SOURCE OF THINE BEING ---

HAST IT NOT BEEN SAID - THERE SHALL BE A SEASON OF GOING AND COMING = OF GOING OUT - AND COMING IN.- SO LET IT BE -- FOR THIS AM I SPEAKING - THAT YE BE

PREPARED TO RETURN UNTO THINE ABIDING PLACE -- LET IT BE AS THE FATHER HAST WILLED IT -- I SAY UNTO THEE THIS DAY: YE SHALL HAVE NO FEAR - FOR I - ALPHA AND OMEGA HAST SPOKEN FROM OUT THE FULLNESS OF TIME, NO SPACE - NO TIME LIMITS THE INFINITE ONE WHICH I AM. ALPHA - THE BEGINNING - OMEGA THE END -- AT NO TIME SHALL WE BE SEVERED IN TWAIN - FOR WE ARE ONE -- LET IT BE UNDERSTOOD THAT THE BEGINNING AND THE END ARE ONE -- THERE IS NOTHING BUT I AM - FOR I AM THE ALL AND THERE IS NO DARKNESS IN ME---

I AM THE FULLNESS - I AM THE ALL -- BE YE AS ONE WITH THE ALL - AND FEAR NOT - FOR I AM -

I AM -

Life is Eternal

Be ye as ones prepared to go where I lead thee -- Be ye as ones prepared to do that which I give unto thee to do -- Ask not for a lesser part --

Ask not for a greater part - for I know that which is the part which thou shall do - that which befits thee -- And as there is none small - none greater - there is no small parts -- No part is unnecessary - for all parts shall fit together as a whole -- And at no time shall I give unto thee an accounting of Mine going and coming - for I say unto thee - I come unannounced - "I come as a thief in the night" - Without fanfare I come - without fanfare I shall take Mine leave -- For I am HE which IS - and which shall be Mine own Porter - and I shall do that which I come to do - then I shall depart as I came - and no man shall know the hour of Mine going - neither of Mine coming -- So be it I say: Be ye as ones prepared to go where I go - for I go unto Mine Father which hast sent Me - I and Mine Father are One -- Be ye as one with Me - and I shall lead thee out of bondage --

It is Not Finished

Liken unto that which hast been done shall it be done -- Liken unto that which hast been done shall it be done - and liken unto that which hast been said shall it be said again ---

I say unto thee: Let thine Light so shine that All might see it and be drawn unto it -- Let them come - let them go - and ye shall be as the Rock -- Waver not - hold high the Lamp which I bring -- Fear not - be not tempted - waste not thine energy - pay the price I ask of thee - owe no man a farthing -- Give not thine time unto frivolity - pay ye heed unto that which I give unto thee - ask no favors of any man ---

Rest in the knowing that I am with thee - and I shall give unto thee that which is needful and sufficient - be it so - so let it be --

... Petitions of Fools

Long hast it been said that there shall be great changes - and these changes shall be brot about by law - for the law is exacting - and it shall not be set aside by the petitions of fools which know not the law ---

I say - the law knows no favorites - grants no favors - for it is given unto the law to be exacting - and it plays no favorites -- The law is given unto man as the law - to be unto them their way - their strength - and their power ---

Yet - man hast betrayed himself - and taken within his own hand the law - and he hast been as the fools which have betrayed himself -- I say the "fools" with justice and with knowledge - for I Know them which set themself up - think themself wise - and hold bondage their prey - I say - they hold bondage their prey -- Let it be for their own sake that they turn from their own waywardness - and give unto the law credit - and then they shall apply themself diligently and faithfully -- The way shall be open before them - and they shall see it and know wherein they are staid ---

I say - let them see and know the Way -- They shall hear that which I say - and they shall be as ones true unto themself - and they shall know no more sorrow - no more suffering -- So let them alert themself --

Be ye as one prepared --

So be it I am with thee unto the end --

I - Thedra - in Spirit this morning - was in a country road – unpaved, before a "Great Brick Church" filled with people -- No sound emanated from it - but in front was a small group of people - like unto two dozen or so - "Keeping watch" singing songs - and watching -- We recognized each other -- None appeared to be older than I, few as old as two. A young boy and girl - were very familiar -- I asked them if they were not the children of .... - they just nodded --The boy was of great strength -- I said to the girl: I know him - he is a Son of the Sea - he belongs to the

Ocean -- I asked of her mother - she told me "they" were thinking of sending her to an island (the name I do not recall as I had not heard it before) - when I asked where it was - she said off the coast of California.

While we were there in the road - so suddenly the "Army" came rushing in - battered upon the Church walls in great fury - and we sang louder apparently -- No prayers were said - but we all locked our arms together tightly - and held our ground -- While looking on - the soldiers ask an account of us - but apparently were satisfied and passed us by- unharmed or molested ---

Much more - which cannot be written ---

Fear Not - Forget Not

Sarah speaking:

I am speaking unto thee that ye might be reminded of Me - thine Mother Eternal -- I speak that ye be blest - that ye might have this Word and it is designed to profit thee - Mine Children ---

Fear not - forget not - Know ye that I Am - and be ye as one which hast thine Being in Me - for from Me thou hast Being -- From Me thou hast gone forth - and unto Me thou shall return - for I Am as the Fount from which flows the Water of the Eternal Source -- I put out Mine Hand - and there I find Mine Children close - so close do I hold thee- and for this hast thou been sustained -- I Am the Provender - the Sustainer - and it is for this oneness with ME thou art sustained ---

Forget not that there is nothing between Us - nothing to separate Us and for that are We indivisible - unseparable -- And there is nothing which shall be provided - that which is capable of dividing - or separating Us -- For I Am The Everpresent - I Am The Complement of Solen Aum Solen ---

The Two are One - even as thou art One with Us - for art thou not the Child brot forth as of Our Being -- From Us - hast thou been endowed Being -- There is no other Source - no other Beginning - no other End - for "WE" are the Beginning and the End - wherein thou shall ever Be - worlds without end - so be it and Selah.

Hold forth thine hand - see thine fingers? - even as I extend Mine Hand and find thee at the farthest point of Mine Arm -- I say there thou art - extended out as far as the Creations of Earth -- There thou art - as Children of Mine own Longing - of Mine Own Bosom -- Thou hast wandered long in darkness and forgetfulness -- Now ye shall Awaken. Arise - and come forth - Knowing that I Am - that thou art Eternal Beings - that thou art One with Me --

And ye shall return even as ye went forth from Me - for The Word hast gone forth: "Come Home - Come Home" - and so shall ye hear that Call - and ye shall answer it - and be joyful that it is done - that thou hast finished thine sojourn in flesh -- Shake off thine legirons - the shackles which bind thee -- Come and be ye as one returned unto Me. Let it Be - Let it Be - Let it BE - for therein is Peace Sublime forevermore --

I Am thine Mother Eternal

Mine Father and I are One

Holy - Holy - Holy is The Word -- Most Precious is The Name of Solen Aum Solen -- All Praise unto Him The Giver of All Good Gifts - Praise His Holy Name ---

Hast it not been said: All that He hast is thine? For this is it said: "All that I have is thine" – it is So - so let it Be -- And for this is it given unto Me to be sent that ye might accept thine Inheritance in full -- For it behooves Me to say unto thee: "All that I Am thou art -- Arise! O ye Children! and Come forth as Ones alive - and give unto Me Credit for Being That which I AM" - And ye shall know Me for that which I AM.

I Am Come this day that ye Know Me - and to Know Me is to Know Mine Father Solen Aum Solen --

Let it be said: Mine Father and I art One -- So be it I Am He Which is Sent that ye be brot out of bondage ---

So be it I Am Sananda

The Welcome Home

Hail! Hail! I say Hail unto the Victor -- Hail! Hail! unto the Sons returned unto their rightful Estate -- Hail! O Sons of Is-Real (Israel) - blest art thou --

Hail O Mighty Sons! Be ye ever blest --

I Am Come that ye be blest - Hail unto thee---

I say - ye shall dwell in the House of The Lord forevermore - for thou hast overcome ---

Let it be! I say Hail! unto them which returneth unto their abiding place - for they shall go out no more ---

They shall dwell in the House of The Lord forever –

So shall it BE --

I Am He Which shall receive thee into the Place I have

prepared for thee -- So be it I say Hail unto thee - O Sons of Is-Real.

Welcome Home -

Sori Sori -- Behold ye the Light which I Am - hold ye the Lamp which I give unto thee -- Hold high the Lamp - and It shall blaze - and blaze! that All men might see it ---

Hold ye the Banner which I give unto thee -- Hold high the Banner which I give unto thee - pass it not unto another - fear not - fear NOT! for I say unto thee: Thou art the Foundation upon which I have established Mine House -- I have placed upon thine shoulders the Cloak of Authority - and I shall deal justly with thee - for have I not said - I shall provide that which is necessary for thine need ---

I say: I Am the Provider - I Am the Provender - and I am Come that ye be provided -- So be it I shall place thine feet upon Higher Ground and ye shall stand Sentinel - and ye shall know as I Know ---

So be it I have spoken - and thou hast heard Me - and I Am Glad - be it So - So shall it Be --

Be ye blest as I Am blest -

The Fulfillment

Sarah Speaking:

Mine Beloved Children: Mine longing hast been thine longing - and thine fulfillment shall be Mine - for I say unto thee: Thou shalt be fulfilled - and for this do I speak unto thee now - this day ---

I come unto thee - as thou art waiting not for thine fulfillment -- I accept thee as Mine - Mine own and at no time have I denied thee -- Yet thou hast forgotten Me - in thine dreaming - in thine wandering ---

Long hast thou wandered - long hast thou dreamed - and I say unto thee: Thine dreaming shall end - and ye shall stand in all thine Glory as ones arrayed in fine Raiment - as Children of Glory - for Glorious and most Precious art thou - O Sons of The Most High Eternal God ---

I say thou art Eternal Beings - and at no time shall ye perish ---

I say: Ye art Eternal Beings! and at no time shall ye perish - for I Am with thee as thine Ever Present Protector and thine Comforter -- I hold thee close - I give into thee nourishment - I give unto thee succor and I give unto thee as thou art prepared to receive -- I give unto thee that ye be fulfilled - so let it Be as The Father hast Willed it -- He hast given unto thee of Himself even as I - for are We not One - and art thou not Our Children - therefore One with Us -- Let thine longing be fulfilled in Him/ Us - and no more shall ye be divided - even in thine dreams - for it is now time of thine awakening - and ye shall stand upright - as ones sober - awake - and alert ---

Ye shall walk and weary not - ye shall be as ones Glorified and purified - Holy -- Holy is The Word - and I have spoken and thou hast heard Me -- So be it and Selah ---

I Am Sarah thine Eternal Parent -

Divinity

Sanat Kumara Speaking:

Hear ye Me this day - and know ye that there is but One Lord God. He is the Same yesterday and forever -- He hast the Same Being - the Same Bearing -- The Same Son of God is He - and at no time hast He been else than the Son of The Most High Living God ---

He hast no other Part than that given unto Him in the beginning - for He is no less for having come into flesh - as One of flesh and bone - as man -- And He is no less for having put aside the grosser body of flesh - and no greater for having come/ for having gone and come again---

I say He <u>IS</u> and hast been the Same Lord God that He Is - hast been and always shall Be -- Let it be said that He hast been with thee from the beginning - for He is the Same today as yesterday - and for that have I said: He is the Lord thy God - and The Same yesterday - today and tomorrow ---

Let it be - and I say unto thee: He The Lord thy God shall bless thee with His Presence --

So be it and Selah -

Blest is He

Sori Sori -- Blest is he which awaits The Lord God - Blest is he which waits upon Him ---

Blest is the Servant of The Lord -

Blest is he which gives of himself that others be blest -

Blest is he which gives unto the Lord God credit for Being that which He Is -

Blest is the one which comes unto the Altar of The Most High Living God -

Blest is he which gives unto himself credit for being a Son of God.

Blest is he which Knows himself to be A Son of God -

So be it that I am come that ye Know---

So be it and Selah --

I Am Sanat Kumara

The Prodigal's Return

Holy - Holy Is The Word - and Great the Power thereof -- Hail - O Hail! ye Sons of God -- Hail unto thee O Mighty Sons - Blest shall ye be -- For this do I say unto thee: "Hail! Hail! Welcome - Welcome Home!" for thine return shall be a glad - joyous day when the shouts shall go out: Welcome O Welcome Sons of God! All the Cosmos shall rejoice for the return -- So let it be a time of rejoicing --

I Am Come that it Be -

There is a Plan

Behold ye the Hand of God - See IT move -- See ye that IT Moves -- Hear ye that which I say unto thee -- Know ye that there is a Plan -- Be ye one with It - and at no time shall ye be as ones forsaken - for I say unto thee: Thou art The Sons of God - gone forth into bondage - gone forth as ones in the wilderness - and at no time shall ye be forsaken ---

Yet - I say unto thee: Be ye ever watchful - that ye put not thine foot into a hole - for there are many pitfalls -- The Mountain Top is not as the plain - the plain not as the Mountain top -- I say: Watch ye thine step - hold ye firm unto the Light -- Know ye that there is a plan - and be ye as ones prepared for yet greater things -- Look not unto thine laurels - for I say - they shall be as nought - for greater things shall ye do --

I Am Come that it be so - so let it Be--

I Am Sanat Kumara

The One Sent

Behold! I say Behold! I Am Come - I AM COME! I AM COME ---

Know ye that I AM COME -- I am Come that ye be lifted up - that ye be brot out of bondage - for thou art as ones in bondage -- Now ye shall come into the fullness of thine Heritage - and ye shall be as ones free ---

For this do I come unto thee that it be - so let it be - for I say unto thee: Thou hast long been bound in darkness -- Now ye shall stand as ones alert - as ones prepared to receive as I have received - for I say - ye shall receive of Me as I have received of Mine Father Which hast Sent Me -- So let it Be as He hast Willed it --

I Am the One Sent -

Say unto them: The time swiftly approaches - when they shall see the Hand of God move - when they shall Know that which IT does - that there is "A Plan" - that IT is an intelligent plan - planned by the Great and Mighty Council -- For day and night the Council sits - and IT is prepared for this day - and at no time shall THE PLAN be aborted.

Man's plans shall be as naught - for man's plans go astray - while they know not that the Mighty Council hast prepared a plan which Includes them - yet they know not! They weary of waiting - they fret over little things - they ask not of the Council - they pay little heed unto the Plan set before them -- They put their foot into a hole - then they cry for deliverance-- So be it I see and Know -- I Am He Which sleepeth not -- So be it I speak as One awake -- Let them hear - Let them HEAR! LET THEM KNOW ---

Let it Be as I Know -

For this do I speak out.

Sananda

Mine Hand Hast Written...

Mine Hand hast written in the Book of Life - and it is written that there shall be changes - that change is Good - and it shall be given unto thee to see and know such change as I Know - as I see -- At no time shall it be given unto thee to stay the Hand of God - for It moveth with precision and in Mercy -- And at no time shall be given unto Me to stay The Hand of God -- It is said: "The Plan shall not be aborted"- and It shall come into Its fulfillment as it is said - for it hast been said - and it shall be done ---

For a Mighty Fiat hast gone out = "LET IT BE" - and it shall BE as it is spoken ---

I say - it shall be DONE - "The Plan" shall be done - fulfilled - and it shall be perfect in Its completion - at last It shall be complete -- For this have I spoken ---

I say unto thee: Hail - Hail O Mighty Sons of The Most High Living God - Be ye Blest --

For this have I spoken -

I Am Sanat Kumara

Let it Be ! ! !

Most Holy - Most High art Thou O Father -

Father of Us Which Thou hast Sent forth of Thineself - as Thine Breath made flesh.

I ask for these Thine Children Peace - that they might Know Peace, that they might Know Thee - that they might give of themself that others Know Peace - Peace as they have not known in their wanderings -- I ask that they receive of Thee as I have received of Thee --

And let it be Known unto them that which hast been hidden from them -- I ask that they be made to See - to Know ---

So be it that I Am Thine Son Sananda - Come unto them in Spirit - that they might Know-- So let it Be as Thou hast Willed --

LET IT BE

LET IT BE

LET IT BE

To the Ones Called

Mighty Sons of God - I say - Mighty Sons of God: Be ye as Ones blest for I The Lord thy God hast spoken The Word - and It shall be unto thee thine Shield and thine Buckler - and ye shall be as Ones blest -- Lift up thine eyes - See that which is about thee - and Know that I Am Come that ye be blest -- I say unto thee - Come - Come - and ye shall come as one prepared - and at no time shall ye deny Me -- I say unto thee: Ye shall stand steadfast - and ye shall <u>Know</u> that I AM The Lord thy God -- Ye shall be alert -- Ye shall walk upright - and ye shall do that which I give unto thee to do -- Ye shall be as one which hast Mine Hand upon thee - and be ye as one which hast gone the long way -- I say: Thou hast gone the long way - yet - ye shall be as one which hast come into the age of accountability -- So be it I speak of thine fulfillment -- Let it be understood - that which I say unto thee ---

I say - ye shall now come into thine fulfillment - and ye shall be as ones returned unto thine rightful Estate - so be it and Selah --

I Am Sananda

Obedience

By Mine Hand I shall lead thee -- By Mine OWN HAND I shall lead thee -- At no time shall I deny thee - yet I say: Ye shall be mindful of Me - and ye shall remember that which I have said - and I shall remember thee in the days of stress -- So be it I ask of thee obedience unto the law - and ye shall bless thyself in obedience unto the law -- For this do I say: "Bless thineself - cast out fear - and be ye as ones blest - and at no time shall I give unto thee a stone"---

Hear ye Me and know ye that I Know that which I say - for I am not given unto Idle speakings -- I Am the Lord thy God - I Am One with Mine Father Solen Aum Solen

Return of the Prodigal

Say unto them: Mine Hand is firm - Mine Arm is strong and I am about Mine Father's Business ---

I come that the Children of HIS be brot back from whence they went forth - I say - from WHENCE they went forth -- I place Mine Hand upon thee in Holy Benediction and I put Mine Hand upon thee - as He hast put His upon Me - And I speak The Word as He hast spoken unto Me -- And He hast said unto Me: "Mine Son - go and bring unto Me Mine Own"---

Now I say unto thee: COME unto ME - and I shall make of thee a Keeper of Mine Sobrieties - and I shall give unto thee food which ye know not of - and ye shall eat thereof - and ye shall be nourished and satisfied - and thine longing shall be no more -- Now it is come when thine longings and wanderings shall be no more - for I bid thee place within Mine Hand thine - and I shall lead thee onward - and ye shall be glad forever - more -- So let it be as The Father hast Willed it --

Amen - Selah -

Peace - Peace - Peace -

Direction

Be ye as ones prepared - for ye shall do a Mighty Work -- And I say unto thee: Ye shall be as one which hast Mine Hand upon thee - and ye shall know that I am with thee - and I shall direct thee in all thine ways. I shall give unto thee that which I have kept for thee - and thine time shall be Mine time - and I shall lift thee - and sustain thee all thine days. I say unto thee: Behold the Hand of God move - and ye shall be glad for thine Knowing - for Greater things shall be revealed unto thee -- Hold out thine hand - and I shall fill it - I shall do that which I have said unto thee I shall do -- I shall keep Mine Covenant with thee - and no man shall take from Me the Power to fulfill it - for I say unto thee - I forget not that which is given unto ME -- I say - I forfeit not that which Mine Father hast given unto Me in the beginning –

So be it I Am He which is Sent that there be Light - so let it Be --

I Am Sananda

Solen Aum Solen

Mine Children: I have called thee home - and I say unto thee this day: Thou hast been given a New dispensation - and I have sent forth Mine Sons - as Mine Hands - Mine feet made manifest in flesh that ye be prepared to enter into Mine place of abode ---

I say: "That ye be prepared to enter into Mine place of abode" ---

Now ye shall pick up thine fragments - and return unto ME as One made whole -- As One ye shall return unto ME - for I sent thee forth as One perfect - as One pure -- Now ye shall come as One - as One purified and justified - let it be -- For this have I sent forth Mine Beloved Sons. Now ye shall give unto ME credit for Knowing that I AM thine Eternal Parent - I AM thine Source - I AM The Everlasting - The Eternal Everpresent Father Which hast Sent thee forth - as Mine Own Breath

Which hast taken upon Itself flesh -- I AM HE Which hast breathed forth the Fiat: "Let there Be" - LET THERE BE - and IT BECAME ---

I say - I AM HE Which didst breathe forth the Fiat: "Let There BE Man" - and The Word became manifest - and thou hast been as I commanded -- THOU HAST BEEN AS I COMMANDED - A LIVING ENTITY - separate entities and individual - unlike any other, yet ONE in ME - for I have given of Mineself that ye become -- And as I created thee in Mine house - unto Mine house ye shall return - even as the birds return unto their nesting place ---

I speak unto thee in thine language - simple and clearly - that ye might Know that which I say -- Let there BE understanding ---

I AM thine Eternal Existence

Solen Aum Solen

Crumbs From the Master's Table

Let it be understood that I have set up this Temple - and I dwell therein And I have put forth Mine Hand - and I shall draw unto Mineself Mine Own -- And I shall be the Master therein - and at no time shall I be given the bitter cup -- For the last time I have drunken the bitter cup -- I stand now as One Which hast overcome -- And I say unto thee: Be ye as one which hast overcome - and no more shall ye drink of the bitter cup - for it shall not be given unto thee to sip of it -- Let it be understood that the Cup shall be sweet - and it shall overflow - for I shall fill it and it shall spill over - and they shall lap up that which spills over -- Let it spill - let them lap it up - and they shall be filled from the overflow -

they shall drink from the overflow and be nourished -- I say they shall be nourished from the overflow -- When they have drunken of the overflow - they shall be filled to capacity - for their capacity is not as yet great ---

While I say - they shall drink of the overflow - I say - they shall be filled - for their capacity is not as yet great ---

While it shall be sufficient unto them - I say - as they are prepared, so shall they receive - so let it be - for it is the law ---

Let it be understood that I The Lord thy God

Know their capacity -

Fulfillment

Sarah Speaking: Mine Children: I am speaking unto thee as Mine Own. At no time have I forgotten thee - I Know thine every need - too - I Know thine longings - and for this do I come unto thee this day -- I come - for it is given unto Me to know thine longings - and I come that they be fulfilled - that ye no more be sorely distressed - that ye no more hunger and yearn for thine fulfillment -- For in Me ye shall find fulfillment - for I Am thine Eternal Mother - and I hold thee fast -- I bring unto thee the fulfillment of thineself - yet thineself is not flesh - neither the desires of flesh -- I say - flesh is the lesser part - it is the lesser -- While the fulfillment is not in flesh - it is not to be understood what is meant by "fulfillment" thru flesh* - for flesh hast not the capacity for fulfillment - neither can - nor does it comprehend the meaning of the fulfillment of Spirit -- While Spirit quickens the flesh -

and makes ready for the fulfillment - it remains yet unknown unto thee the meaning of fulfillment ---

Awaken unto Me - and I shall bring unto thee comfort - and ye shall be as one comforted - for I say unto thee - I am the Comforter - for I am thine Mother-- I hold thee close - I succor thee in the time of need. I forget not Mine Own -- I place within thine hand Mine - hold ye fast and be ye as a little child - and I shall come unto thee as One Which hast been thine Comforter - and I shall be evermore with thee - for I forget thee not in thine slumbers - and wanderings ---

I forget <u>thee</u> not - yet too I say: Remember ye Me - and I shall speak unto thee gently and surely -- Put forth thine hand - and know that I am closer than thine hand - for in Me thou hast thine Being -- Nothing is hidden up from Me -- So be it I Am thine Mother Eternal

* Flesh does not or cannot comprehend the meaning of fulfillment - will not until the fulfillment has been consummated - -

That All Men Might Know

Be ye as the Hand of Me and say unto them: I Am The Lord thy God Sent forth from out the realm of Light - that All men might know that there is Light - and that there is a place prepared for them - that there is a Plan - and that plan is now at work -- For We of The Mighty Council sit day and nite that it be consummated - that the Plan be brot to Its fulfillment - and at no time shall it be aborted -- At no time shall it be aborted - for I - the Lord thy God - shall stand Sentinel - and I shall be as One prepared -- that is Mine Part -- And I say unto thee - I am well prepared - for I Am about Mine Father's Business -- For this hast He Sent ME ---

I say - HE - hast Sent Me - that the Plan be fulfilled - and it shall not be aborted -- Fear not - stand ye firm, as The Rook Which I AM - and at no time shall ye be as one cast out -- I say unto thee: Stand firm,- waver not - fear not - and remember* that which I have said** unto thee ---

Be ye as ones blest this day –

* Learn the lessons –

** That which we have been taught -- Yet if we are taught we have learned - if we have not learned we have not heard --

Baloran

I am Baloran: I come with the consent of the Great and Mighty Council under which thou art instructed - under which ye walk as One of the illumined - and I say under - because thou art under the instruction of that Mighty Council of which I speak ---

Mine time hast now come when I shall again speak forth that which I have not said - because the time had not as yet come ---

I have quickened thee unto Me - and I shall use the words familiar unto thee - for I am not for the most part - given unto words -- While they are not Mine - they shall be familiar unto thee - therefore it shall be given unto thee to comprehend them easily ---

"There is a Plan" it hast been said many times - and it is so -- This Plan is Great - Greater than man knows - for it is All Inclusive - not flesh and thine seen world - but the Whole of the Cosmos -- Think ye not to limit it to flesh alone - for it is Greater than the Whole of the manifested world of Man ---

There is a day soon to come - when man shall step forth from his dense world - and view that which hast been about him - and he shall wonder at his blindness -- He shall Know that which he hast not known, he shall be as one awakened from a long sleep -- He shall stretch forth his arms - and embrace the Whole of the Manifestation - and be as the One which stands above and beyond it -- He shall give a glad cry and praise unto the Great and Grand Council for his guidance - his protection - and his learning -- For It hast labored long and weariless for thine deliverance ---

While I have put out Mine Hand and placed it upon thee that ye be quickened unto Me - I shall give unto thee this Word - as thou hast accepted Me -- There are few this day which has been prepared to accept Me - and that which I would say unto them ---

There are few who wait for that which I would say - and the few are as ones which have given Me credit for Knowing that which I say.

While none fully comprehend that which I have said - I shall again open Mine Mouth -- There is but One God - Father of The Cosmos from which thou hast come forth -- There is but One Lord God - Which holds within His Hand The Book of Life -- There is but One Sanat Kumara - and I say unto thee: Thou art as One with Them - for thou hast gone out from Their place of abode -- And it is given unto Me to Know - for I have watched - lo - many eons - and I have gone in and out of the various Galaxies - and I have gone in and out of the many Universes which ye know not of -- For I am not limited unto the pitiful state of travel which Earth men think so powerful -- I say - they have as yet not dared dream of the like which We use - therein is another story -- It is now given unto Me to say - I shall speak with thee at length in the time which is allotted unto thee-- Weary not of waiting - and I shall give unto thee a part which shall be for them which have been given a portion of Mine Word -- I too - speak unto thee for the Good of All ---

Be ye as the One chosen for this part -- Let it be as thou hast chosen. So do I come - let it be as the Council hast given permission -- Be ye at Peace -

I am Baloran

* * * * * * *

Baloran speaking:

While it is said - I shall speak unto thee in this manner - it is not to be misunderstood -- It shall be understood that I am not limited to one or limited by any language or tongue -- I am not responsible for the interpretation placed upon that which I say - and I am not responsible for that which is done with that which I give unto thee -- Yet I am concerned with bringing unto thee enlightenment -- I say now - at this time - when ye have asked for Light - that there shall be given unto thee as the days go by - a bit at a time - and then it shall be compiled into One Volume - and ye shall copy it as ye will -- Ye may edit it or not - but it shall serve its purpose ---

There are many which shall ask concerning Me - and ye shall refer them unto that which has already been given - thru another -- There shall be another such book brot forth by the same hand -- While this shall be different from the other - it too shall serve its purpose ---

There shall be given three parts - first this one and two shall follow and they shall be put together as one -- Now ye shall close the first part with this letter - and I shall add to this in the next few days -- Be ye at peace and weary not --

I am Baloran

* * * * * * *

Baloran Speaking:

I am speaking today on the subject of love - love as ye know it - not as Love which binds All men - all mankind - as the Love which has brot thee forth in the beginning -- Man of Earth knows not the first degree of Love such as I Know - such as has sent thee hence - such as shall bring thee forth - such as freedom -- Freedom is neither understood -- License to act in any manner whatsoever means not freedom – for to have to ask for license - take license - is to be bound by a law -- Wherein is there freedom? Wherein have you found freedom? You know not Love or Freedom -- Now let us consider the love of man -- Has he been unto "himself true"? He has not!

He has misused his energy - he has played a fools game - and "danced to the piper's tune" -- He has misnamed <u>his</u> children - he has called them Christians - when they have been bastards - I say bastards for they are not brot forth in Love -- From the wants of man - the lust of flesh have they come into physical flesh - bound hand and foot by the law of flesh ---

Freedom? Freedom? They know not freedom! I say the shame of it shall be visited upon the third and fourth generation - for they come into flesh for to express that which they know not - and they are bound by concepts unreal - by opinions handed down from generation to generation -- They are taught fear - and there are few among men which know the meaning of Love - for Love does not abound among the children of Earth -- Let it be understood that LOVE is that which frees one from the pettiness of flesh - that which excels all man's joys - all his pleasures - and frees him from all his torment -- LOVE supersedes All manifestation - and It is the foundation of the worlds without end - endless worlds ---

For they are held in motion by this motivating FORCE OF LOVE. Not as man sees/ feels/ understands love - for that which he feels is but the counterfeit ---

When it is said: "Love ye one another" - Love is the Force Which has prompted the command -- For to LOVE is to generate Power which brings back that which has been sent forth - the Light which sustains Life - and keeps the planets in orbit - lifts up the hills - raises up the generations yet unborn - and heals the sick/ the lame/ the blind/ yea - it does all things - even creates worlds - and sends forth the planets spinning within their orbits -- It is the Power which has brot thee forth as individuals - and sustained thee in thy way pertaining unto life ---

Now it is said - that there shall be understanding-- It behooves Me to say at this point - that there is greater things to be learned - to be known - than that which torments the minds of men -- And at no time shall I pay any heed unto men's plea for enlightenment on the lesser parts - for there is a greater Work to be done – I say a Greater Work to be done -- Let Us go forward as One - and let it be for the Good of All. Hasten ye to open up the portals of Heaven -- Come higher and "Let thy feet be swift to do My bidding" sayeth the Lord thy God -- Be ye as one prepared for Greater things - and I shall prompt thee --

I Am Baloran

Flesh Binds Me Not

Behold! Behold! I stand before thee arrayed in Pure Light -- Behold ye Me - I Am the Lord thy God ---

Behold ye ME -- I speak unto thee as man - for I Am man -- I Am that which animates flesh - and flesh hast no power over Me - for I have overcome flesh - and flesh is at Mine command -- I command and flesh obeys - for I Am <u>Master</u> ---

Let it be understood that I Am the Lord thy God come as one amongst thee -- And it is said - I too walk in flesh - while flesh binds Me not -- I Am Free - free of the wants - desires - and longings of the flesh -- I say - the desires of flesh I have not - for I have OVERCOME, I AM FREE -- I bid thee come as One which hast overcome -- Let flesh not bind thee - let it be as the fortune of Me - let it pass from thee as the shadows - for I say - the desires of flesh shall be no more - no more I say - for thine longings shall cease - and they shall no more torment thee - for ye shall know them to be of flesh born - and they shall pass as such - they shall be NO MORE I say! ---

I come that ye might overcome - that ye might be free -- So let it be as The Father hast Willed - for this hast HE Sent Me -- So be it I come as He hast Willed it --

I Am with thee this day -

Sarah speaking: Mine Children - I am thine Mother Eternal -- I Am speaking unto thee this day as Mine Children long away -- Long hast it been since thou hast gone forth as Children of Mine - Of Mine Own longing -- Long have I longed for thine return - for I say - thou art born of Me - born of Mine Own Womb art thou ---

Know ye thou art of Me born - for I have brot thee forth from out of Mine Own Self -- Thou hast gone forth as ones sustained and fed by Mine Body - fed from Mine Own Breast - nourished by - and thru Me for thou art part of Me - and as thou art part of Me - I Am part of thee. I say - thou art not cut off from Me - for thou art as fingers upon Mine Hand - and I cut not Mine fingers off from Me ---

I move them about - and I know each one by Name - and I bring them unto Me as Mine - members of Mine Own Body -- I do know each one as Mine Own - and I weary not of Mine Hand and Mine fingers - for I am not sufficient without each and every one of them -- I am not whole without every one of Mine Children - which I have sent forth -- I say unto thee: Thou art Mine - and I know thee - and ye have no secrets from Me - no secrets hast thou ---

I Am speaking unto thee as One which hast thee within the "Palm of Mine Hand" - and I know thine needs - and I shall sustain and give unto thee as thou art prepared to receive -- I Am thine Comforter and thine Mother -- Be ye as ones blest - for I Am the One Which shall give unto thee succor while thou art away -- Hast it not been sufficient unto thee?

I Am thine Eternal Mother Sarah

Long Have I Waited

Mine Beloved: Let it be said this day - that IAm the Hand of God The Father -- I Am He which is Sent that His Will be done on Earth as it is in the Realm of Light -- I come even as I Am Sent - that it be accomplished as He hast Willed it -- He hast given unto Me the Power and the Authority to do that which I will do - and I am He which hast been sent aforehand that it be done - and at no time shall I betray Mineself or Mine trust -- I say: I Am the One SENT that HIS WILL be done ---

That this day bring the fulfillment of that which wast begun long ago -- Let it be understood that long have I waited for this day - long have I waited! ---

Now I come that Mine waiting end - for there is little time before the waiting shall end ---

While I say - Mine waiting shall end - too I say - thine shall end even as Mine - yea - even as Mine -- What a glad day it shall be ---

Be ye as One blest this day - and I say ye shall be blest as ye have not been blest --

So be it I Am Sananda

The Fulfillment of Time

Be ye as Mine Voice - and say unto them as I would say - that this day is Mine Day - "The Day of The Lord" - for I am come that this Day be the fulfillment - the fulfillment of time - I say "The fulfillment of time" And it behooves Me to say unto thee: It is come when the Mighty Ones walk amongst thee -- These are Come - even as I - that ye be brot out - While there <u>are</u> ones which know not the fullness of their Being - there are ones which <u>do</u> know -- There are ones which have not taken embodiment thru the womb of Earthly flesh -- For I say unto thee: The Heavens shall open up - and her secrets shall be revealed unto them which are prepared to receive -- For this have I said: "Prepare thineself"-- I say: Behold the Hand of God - see It move!! Know It moveth -- And I say It moveth <u>Swiftly</u> -- Put not thine hands before thine face - that ye be blinded - for there are none so blind as them which will not see ---

I say - them which put their hands before their eyes - that they might not see - shall be as the ones which have betrayed themself -- I have made it possible that they see -- I have called out in a loud Voice -- I have said: This day ye shall see and know that ye are not alone – and thou hast stood as graven images -- Thou hast neither heard nor moved. I say - thou hast neither moved or heard that which I have said – At last I shall say: Be ye as ones prepared - and I shall give unto thee as thou hast prepared thineself for to receive --- I say unto thee: I Am the Lord thy God Sent that ye be lifted up --

Behold ye Me - Know ye that I AM COME - and I shall do a Mighty Work - for this am I COME -- I Am Sananda

Holy is the Name Solen Aum Solen

Be ye as Mine Hand made manifest - and say unto them in Mine Name that there is but ONE God - He is The Father - yet in any language HE IS THE FATHER - yet in the place wherein <u>All</u> Things are Known. He is Known as SOLEN AUM SOLEN - and ALL Glory is HIS - ALL Praise is HIS -- At no time is The Name Solen Aum Solen to be belittled or misused - for It belongs unto none Other that THE SOURCE OF BEING -- Let them which will belittle - let <u>them</u> misuse It - yet ye shall not - for unto thee I speak that "YE" might KNOW -- Profane not the Word - use It not for self-gain - for selfish purpose -- Praise ye the Name. Know ye The Name - Know ye the Power of The Name -- Keep It before thee -- Keep It Holy - and be ye as One blest -

I say - bless thineself as ye would that I bless thee -- Hold ye HIGH the Banner which I give unto thee--

Peace - Peace - Peace

I Am Sananda

I am Not Limited

Be ye as one which has Mine Hand upon thee - and Know ye that I Am thine Shield and thine Buckler - that I Am that I Am - that there is but One Lord God - and I AM HE - Sent that there be Light - for this do I come as Sananda this day ---

I Am no less for having taken upon Mineself flesh-- I Am no less for putting aside the flesh -- I Am Master of the Elements - and I take no substance from the Elements - yet I give Substance where Substance is needed---

I see and know the need - for I have the Greater Vision -- I Am not limited by fleshy eyes - eyes of flesh - for they see not -- They see not that which is before them - neither above or below - neither that which is about them -- I say: The eye of flesh sees not! they are blind unto that which is about them - that which is their Substance -- And they know not that they see not - they measure that which they see by the tools which they have fashioned for themself -- They are limited by that which they have done/ thot/ and fashioned - they have not the Greater Vision ---

I say: I - have the Greater Vision - therefore I Am qualified to give unto thee this Word -- "I AM NOT LIMITED" for I Am The Lord thy God Sent that there

Be Light -

Let It Be -

Sananda

IT SHALL QUICKEN THEM

Be ye as One on whose head I place Mine Hand - and I shall pronounce the Word - and ye shall be made whole - for I have said: Ye shall be made Whole - and ye shall stand before the Great and Mighty Council as One made Whole -- And as thine new part shall be given unto thee as the Greater Part - there shall be Great Joy - and it shall be picked up thruout the Cosmos - and a Great stir of Spirit shall be felt - and it shall quicken them which sleepeth - yea - even the dead shall stir - and the dead shall come alive - and be as ones quickened -- I say: Even unto the dead shall be quickened - for the mighty ONRUSH of Spirit shall be so great that they shall be quickened ---

They shall feel it and they shall move ---

I say: Behold ye the Hand of God MOVE -- Glorify His Name - Solen Aum Solen - for this do I now speak - that He be Glorified -- So be it I Am the One Sent --

Sananda

I Have Stirred the Eth

Sanat Kumara Speaking:

Be ye blest this day - for Mine Hand is upon thee - and I say: "Be ye blest this day" - Let it be as I have spoken it -- For I have stirred the Eth - and I have caused the Eth to be moved - and I say unto thee - the Eth shall bring forth that which is unmanifested - and it shall give up the Secrets of the hidden - and the hidden shall be revealed - and no more shall there be any mysteries before thee - for they shall be revealed unto thee -- So be it and Selah ---

I speak that it be So - So let it Be as I have spoken -- I am come that the hidden be revealed --

So let it Be -

I Am Sanat Kumara

That Their Hearts be Cleft

Most Holy Father which hast brot us forth - I speak unto these Thine Children - as One of them -- As Thine Own "Will" I speak - as Thine Voice I speak - as Thine Hand I move -- I speak unto them in the tongue familiar unto them -- Yet I reach out and touch them - that they be quickened - that their hearts be cleft - that they might open up their heart unto Me - that I might enter in as Thine Own "Will" - that they might Glorify THEE and that they might Know Thee as I Know Thee. Place them upon Thine Right Hand - and place them upon Thine Holy Mount - Which is prepared for them -- Let them be brot forth as ones purified and justified ---

Let it Be Father - as Thou hast Willed it --

So be it I Am Thine Son

Sent that there be Light -

As One Which Hast Served

Beloved - I have gone before thee that the Way be prepared for thee -- Now it is given unto thee to go before Me - that the Way be prepared - that "They" be prepared to receive Me - that I might come in and abide with them -- Now let it be established that I - the Lord thy God - hast called thee forth - that Mine Work be done - for I have said: "I shall do a Mighty Work"-- The laborers are few and the harvest Great ---

I say: The Work at hand shall be done with great haste - and many shall hear the Word - and they shall respond - and they shall be lifted up - and no more shall they turn back -- No more shall they return unto the fields -- No more shall they return unto the places wherein they labor for bread - for they shall come forth as ones which have finished their journey in darkness –

NO MORE shall they be in bondage - for they shall be as ones illumined - and they shall walk in the Light -- Now ye shall be as One which hast served the Light -- Ye shall walk in the Light for ye shall be as One Illumined - for this have I called thee forth -- I have commanded thee: "Go feed Mine Sheep" - thou hast gone --

Now ye shall return unto Me unscathed - unharmed - for I the Lord thy God - hast sent thee forth as Mine Hand - Mine foot - and I shall bring thee forth - for I have called unto thee - and thou hast answered Me- and I am come that ye be lifted up - So shall it Be --

Let it be done as The Father hast Willed it

The Eternal Parent

Mine Children: Upon thine brow I place a Mark/ a Seal - each signifying a part/ a place/ a time - and it is given unto Me to know that Mark - and I am the Giver and the Taker -- I place it there - I take it away -- Yet the time beareth its fullness - the time brings its fullness - and at no time shall it be lost unto Me - for I Am thine Eternal Parent - I Am thine Father Solen Aum Solen -- I speak that ye be quickened - that ye be touched -- I speak the WORD and it is done -- At no time shall the Word be made void -- At no time shall ye be less for thine sojourn in bondage/ in flesh - for I say ye shall return unto Me unscathed/ unharmed -- So be it I have Sent Mine Beloved Son that it be done - so let it be -- For this have I sent Him --

Be ye as One blest -- I Am thine Parent Eternal—

There is a New Dispensation

Sori Sori -- This day I would say: Let it be understood that there is a New Dispensation - and it is for this that many have come into flesh - that it be fulfilled - as is planned in the beginning -- I tell thee: There are ones within flesh - in the world of man - which hast never before been born of Earthly Substance - neither have they been born of woman. I say that they have for the first time taken up the Substance of flesh bodies ---

Now while this is true - there are ones which have been born of woman many times! Which shall no more be born of woman - neither shall they be limited by flesh - for they shall be given bodies of Light - which shall not weigh upon them ---

Let it be known that there are ones amongst thee - which have the bodies of Light -- They are oft times within thine midst - unseen - unknown - while their presence is nonetheless real -- I say unto thee: Behold the Light - see that which is about thee - and know ye that ye are not alone -- Be ye as one prepared for the Greater Part - for I say unto thee: The Gates shall open up - and ye shall pass therein - so be it and Selah --

I Am The Lord thy God -

Sananda

They Shall Run After Righteousness

Be ye as the Hand of Me made manifest - and say unto them - as I would - that the time cometh swiftly - when they shall cry out for Light and they shall run after Righteousness -- They shall seek me out - and they shall fall upon their face and say: "Lord have Mercy - I come that I might have Light" -- I say - they shall come from afar crying for Light for they shall be sorely afflicted - and they shall be glad for Mine assistance ---

I say: They shall be glad for Mine assistance ---

Blest are they which cry for Light - for I shall touch them - and they shall be made to see -- So be it I see them - I Know them - I await their call --

I Am that I Am -

Sananda

The Great Light

Sanat Kumara speaking:

Wherein is it said that there shall be a Great Onrush of Water - a Great Onrush of Spirit - and It shall go forth as a Mighty Surge - and It shall move that which is before It -- It shall sweep them forward before it - It shall carry them forward as a great tidal wave - and they shall be as ones which are prepared -- There shall be others which find themself unprepared - and these shall find themself drawn beneath the Onrush - the Mighty waves of the tide ---

There shall be a GREAT WAVE go inland - and not one shall escape the Onrush - for no mountain so high - no valley so low as to be missed or overlooked -- For this is the day when the Light shall go forth into All the lands - and none shall escape the effects thereof ---

I say: "None shall escape the effects thereof"---

While some shall go beneath the waves and be seen no more - there are ones which shall arise from beneath the Mighty Surge Triumphant and Victorious - and these shall be the Victors ---

I say with The Mighty Host: Hail - Hail unto the Victors!!

Be ye as the Victor - For this have I spoken out -- I Am come that it be done So be it and Selah --

I Am Sanat Kumara

Let It Be Understood

Sori Sori -- Let it be understood that which I say - for it is given unto Me to see the many misunderstandings - the interpretations placed upon Mine Words ---

I tell thee for a surety - that I am the Lord thy God come that ye be lifted up -- Yet I say unto All men - Come - and as I say unto one - I say unto All - yet they move not - they are as ones with feet of lead - they move not - they have neither the ears to hear - neither the eyes to see ---

While thou hast picked up thine feet and come forth as a willing and faithful Servant - I have given unto thee in Great measure -- While it hast been for thine own self - it is for the Good of All mankind - and it is for their sake that I have given unto thee the many - many Words which have as yet not fallen on the fertile soil ---

While it shall come to pass that the soil shall be enriched - and the Waters shall be poured out - and the seeds shall take root and flourish. Long have We awaited the day when We should see the harvest come forth as a Great and beautiful Light -- There shall be Great rejoicing and much laughter - for again the Sons of God shall sing together as once They did -- And at that time there shall be the Great and Mighty City which shall arise from the ruin of many ages past - of many a civilization which hast gone into decay ---

Now I say unto thee: Be ye as one patient - and be ye not fearful of the days ahead - for I say unto thee: I Am at the helm of this Ship - and art thou not Mine Servant? - have I not brot thee thru troubled waters? Have I not baptized thee with the Holy Spirit - now shall I say more?

I Am Come that this be done - so let it Be as The Father hast Willed it ---

I Am The Sent of God The Father

Come Follow Me

Be ye as the Hand of Me and say unto them in Mine Name - that there is a Mighty Work to be done - and it is for this that I call unto them: "Come ye - follow Me" -- And it behooves them to come - for I say unto them: I have work which shall be done - and great shall be the reward of Mine Servant which gives unto Me of himself -- And his time shall be Mine time - and the labor of his hands shall be his reward -- For the reward shall be his - and no man shall pilfer it nor take from him his joy -- for work well done brings its own reward -- While I say:- That which I have for them - no man hast seen - until his work is finished - and he hast returned unto his rightful abiding place -- I say Come - Come All which will - and I shall give unto thee a part - and as ye are prepared - so shall ye receive -- So be it I stand ready to give unto thee that which thou art prepared to receive - so let it profit thee.

Hear ye that which I say unto thee this day –

WATCH! LISTEN! be ye as one prepared for the GREAT SPEAKING --

So be it I AM SPEAKING - and I AM NOT FINISHED -

Put Thine Feet on Higher Ground

Be ye as Mine Hand and record that which I say unto thee - that they might know that which I say unto thee-- By Mine own Hand shall it be for I have placed Mine Hand upon thee - and I have pronounced the Word which hast given unto thee the Authority to speak for Me / to speak in Mine Name ---

Now ye shall say unto them in Mine Name - that there is a time allotted unto the speaking - and a time of action -- And at no time shall anyone make a mockery of Mine Words - for I say I Am the Lord thy God - and at no time shall I mislead thee -- I am not a puny god - for I am the Sent of Mine Father that there be Light amongst men ---

There shall be Light - for this am I Come - so let it be -- While they but mimic Mine Words - and they but prattle Mine Sayings - they have as yet not been touched -- They have "thought" themself wise - and they have put their foot into a hole - and now the time is come when they shall take it out - for I say unto them: Pick thineself up - and walk ye as one sober - and put thine feet on higher ground - and at no time shall I deceive thee ---

I shall bless thee with Mine Presence - and I shall make of thee an humble Servant - and I shall go all the way with thee ---

Hallowed shall be the Ground upon which ye shall tread -- So be it I have spoken - and I am not finished -- Hear ye Me! And be ye profited thereby --

I Am Sananda

The Appointment

Mine Hand I have placed upon thine - and I have caused thee to record Mine Sayings -- And it behooves Me to say unto thee - that the time is come when I shall give unto thee in Greater measure -- And ye shall be as one prepared - for I the Lord thy God - shall place within thine hand a Great and Divine Part - which shall be designed to bring much Light unto them which seek the Light - which are of a mind to learn of Me. And unto these I say: Stand ye up and be counted - for I shall give unto thee as ye are prepared to receive -- And at no time shall I give unto thee more than ye can bear -- Yet I say unto thee Mine Servant: Thou hast been true unto thine trust - and I shall make thee Keeper of Mine Sobrieties - and at no time shall ye fail in thine appointment - for I the Lord thy God sustain thee --

I Am with thee unto the end --

I Am Sananda

The Time Includes the "Times"

Holy - Holy is The Word -- And it is given unto thee to Know the Word. Let it be understood that I the Lord thy God hast spoken - and I am speaking - and The Word shall go forth out of Mine Mouth - even as It hast gone forth from out Mine Father's in the beginning of thine going out -- Now it is come when I shall speak The Word - and It shall be made manifest before thee -- So be it that there shall be great changes within the time which is near - and it shall bring with it Great and Glad times -- For the time shall be divided into lesser times - and it shall be given unto thee to See the different times - as the lesser part in which many things shall be accomplished -- While the Greater time shall be beyond thine present comprehension - for it shall encompass the lesser times - which ye measure by clock and calendar - Watch - look – listen, be ye alert -- Walk ye with Me and I shall counsel thee - and guide thee thru the days ahead ---

So be it I Am Sananda

Sananda Speaks unto the Father

Most Holy Father - Father of Us which Thou hast Sent forth from out Thineself - as Beings of Thine Self made manifest -- O Father - We as Thine Sons stand before Thee - dependent upon Thine Love and Mercy Thou hast so generously extended Us -- Let it be the will of these Thine Children - to return unto thee purified and justified -- Let them put aside their own puny will that Thine be done in them - thru them - and by them - so may it be ---

Let them Know Thee as I Know Thee -- Let them be made to rejoice as I rejoice for Knowing Thee -- Let their hearts be made glad - let them be brot home even as I am --

So be it I have spoken unto Thee that they might Know that which I have said in Thine Presence Father of Mine - Father Eternal All Praise, All Glory unto Thee -- So may it Ever Be -

I Am Thine Son Sananda

Obedience

Sanat Kumara speaking:

There are many called and few are chosen -- Wherein is it said - "None enter into the Holy of Holies unprepared" - it is so - none enter unprepared - none come without the preparation necessary -- It is said: "They shall put on the WHOLE ARMOR OF GOD".

Thine Inheritance

Be ye as the Hand of Me - and record this Mine Word that they might know that which I say unto thee -- I say - It is the day long foretold - when there shall be great suffering - and great and swift change - let it be -- For this have I said: "Come ye out from amongst them - follow ye Me" - for I shall show thee great things - I shall deal justly with thee - and ye shall be given as thou art prepared to receive -- I say: "Prepare thineself for to receive the part which I have kept for thee" - for I have kept thine Inheritance for thee - it is not spent! No other shall claim it - for it is thine by Divine right -- Now I say Come accept it -- Yet ye have been given the law - thou hast been given the letter - and thou hast chosen the lesser-- Now I say : Choose ye the Greater - for no man knows the Greater Part - other than he which hast received it ---

I say: I Am qualified to say unto thee - it is a Great Inheritance - for I have received Mine in full -- So be it I shall give unto thee as I have received of Mine Father - when thou art so prepared ---

This day I say: Shake off thy lethargy - and come unto Me - for I Am the Light and the Way -- I Am the Life - I Am The One Sent -- So be it - I shall not deceive thee - I say ye shall profit thereby -- Let it be as The Father hast Willed it -- Come as one willing and obedient - Let it be - for I say unto thee -

I Am The Lord thy God -

The One Sent

Behold Me - sayeth The Lord thy God! Behold Me - Behold Mine Hand. See it move - Know ye that It moves -- I say - It moves and ye shall see it move - for I say unto thee: The Power of The Almighty God is That which moves -- And It shall open up the flood gates - for the Mighty Waters shall flood over the Lands - and it shall be washed clean, it shall be purified/ cleansed of all the debris -- For I say - there shall be a Mighty Onrush of Water - and there shall be some which shall not withstand the onrush - for they shall be swept asunder/ covered! I say: They shall go under and be seen no more -- No more shall they be seen for they shall be covered up ---

Let the poor in Spirit be enriched - let the deaf hear - the blind see. Let the hypocrite be- let the traitor atone for his unfaithfulness -- Let them come and be healed - for I say unto them: Seek Me out and I shall reveal Mineself unto thee - ask of Me and I shall do a Might Work -- I shall show thee that which hast been hidden - I shall reveal many things unto thee -- So be it I Am The Lord thy God - and I shall not deceive thee ---

Let them come inquiring of Me - let them find Me - for I am not afar off -- So be it I say unto them: Be ye as one prepared to receive of Me - as I have received of Mine Father ---

So be it I Am the One Sent of Him -

I Shall Overthrow Their Temples of Idolatry

Be ye as the Hand of Me - and say unto them as I would say - that the time is now come when the tidal wave shall roll over the land - and it shall take the debris before it - and it shall cleanse the land - and it shall leave behind it the signs of the Wave - for there <u>shall</u> be the signs -- Wherein is it said: There shall be changes? - And ye shall behold them for the mighty and the haughty shall fall - and the proud and profane shall be brot low - and they shall stand humbled - and they shall no longer hold in bondage a people which seek the Light --

I say: "They shall no longer hold in bondage a people which seek the Light" - for I shall reveal their wickedness - and I shall overthrow their temples of idolatry and hypocrisy -- I shall pour out Mine Spirit on the poor and just - and I shall lead them out of bondage -- I shall do these things and more - for I Am All that I profess to be - I Am The Lord God - Sent that there be Light - so let it be - LET IT BE! - For <u>this</u> do I Come!

I Am He - I AM HE!

The One Sent of God The Father

They Shall See

Sori Sori -- Hast it not been given unto Me to bring unto thee the Word. Hast it not been given unto thee to walk and talk with Me -- And I now say unto thee: Ye shall bare thine hand - and it shall be as none other - for I shall give unto them the privilege of seeing -- I say - they shall see and Know that which they see - for they have not seen - they shall be made to see -- I tell thee: Thine hand shall be bared - and they shall see for they have not seen -- Now let it be understood - that which I say unto thee -- They shall see that which they have not seen - for they have not seen that which animates thine hand -- So be it they shall see -- Be it so and so be it --

As Mine Fingers

Behold the Hand of God move -- See It move - for It doth move -- It moves with surety and perfection -- I say: Behold Its movements - for I Am the One qualified to say unto thee: IT MOVES - BEHOLD IT!! - And for that ye shall come to Know that which It shall do - for a Mighty Wondrous Work shall be done thru The Hand of God -- Now I say unto thee: Hold out thine hand and see that which hast been given unto thee AS THINE HAND - and know ye that I too hold out Mine - and as Mine fingers - there thou art as Mine fingers - and I hold thee as thou hold thine fingers - for thou art not separate from Me ---

I Am the Hand - thou art the Fingers - never hast thou been separate from Me - for I Am One with thee -- I Am One with Mine Father - even as thou art One with Me -- Let it be understood that I Am The One Sent that ye be made Whole - that ye might come to Know even as I ---

So be it I Am

Sananda

Time

Sanat Kumara Speaking:

Hear ye that which I say unto thee - and ye shall know that which I say - for I shall quicken thee - and ye shall have comprehension ---

Now it is given unto Me to be the Most Worthy Grand Master within the Inner Temple - and I Know the Workings of The Temple - I Know the plans and the preparation - for this is Mine part -- I have been long within this place - and I have held the records of time within Mine Hand - and I say unto thee - time is of no moment unto Me - for I am not of the Earth wherein ye reckon time by hours and moments ---

I say - time is of no consequence - for I am The One which holds within Mine Hand the records of time -- And the records shall be opened up unto thee - when it is come that thine part wherein ye are is complete/ finished -- Yet it should profit thee nought to see them now for thou couldst not read them - the records - for it is given unto thee to be under the veil -- I say - the Mist covers the records - yet it shall be rolled away ---

Bear ye witness of these Mine Words - and I shall bless thee with understanding and comprehension ---

So be it I have spoken and thou hast heard Me --

I Am Sanat Kumara

The Flood Gates...

Be ye the Hand of Me - and give unto them this Word - and let it be Known that It is The Word of God - for I The Lord thy God speaks this day unto thee - and none shall deny Mine Word - for I am Come that they be made to comprehend the Word -- So let it be as they are prepared ---

For this do I say unto thee: The time is come when the flood gates shall open wide - and the floods shall rush over the lands - and there shall be many which stand before the onrush - and these shall come thru the flood - washed and purified - Glorified -- Let it be known that the time is come when the Waters shall come - when the onrush shall come as a great tidal wave - and yet they look for signs and wonders - they wait -- And I say unto them: It is upon them - when the Son of God walks amongst them - and He hast revealed Himself unto the Ones so prepared to receive Him -- I say - there are Ones which have walked with Him - and counselled with Him - while others ask that He show His wounds ---

Nay! Nay! I say - never again shall I bare Mine wounds unto the profane and the unjust -- I say: They shall not put their fingers into Mine wounds again - for I bare not Mine side unto them -- Mine Hand

I extend unto them that they have assistance - yet their curiosity and unbelief shall not be part of Mine Work - neither shall I give unto them a part -- I shall let them be - and for that matter I shall give unto them nought -- For I say unto All: "Come and be ye made Whole" - yet I do not bring them against their will -- So be it I Am not a poor puny priest, I Am The Lord of Lords - The Host of Hosts - and I say: Arise! Arise ye laggards - ye slothful - shake off thine legirons and come - partake of Mine Cup - and rejoice with Me ---

COME ALL YE WHICH WILL and I shall give unto thee the Cup of Living Water - for I Am The One Sent of

Mine Father Solen Aum Solen --

None Other Hast Mine Part

Say unto them in Mine Name - that they shall be as ones alert - and prepared for the days ahead - <u>for there shall be days ahead</u> when they shall neither sleep nor slumber - they shall be as ones uprooted - and they shall find no place wherein to sleep - for I say unto them: There shall be no "sleeping" place -- For it is now the time of action and preparation -- It is now come when they shall become aware of their responsibility and of their need - for I say they are in need - in NEED I say! - For they are as ones impoverished - and they are as ones blind unto their need ---

While it is said: "They shall be brot out of bondage" it is said: "They shall will it so" and "As they are prepared so shall they receive" ---

Now I come that they might come to Know - that they might be prepared -- Yet they seek the ways of man - they look hither and yon - they run after strange gods - and I am not of them - for I Am The One Sent of Mine

Father that there be Light -- Let it be said that I Am He Which I was and shall Be - The Lord God - and none shall be given Mine Part - for I Am The One given this Part - and I shall not forfeit it -- For it is given unto Me to have received Mine Inheritance in full -- So be it I AM HE WHICH WAS THE LORD OF OLD - The One Sent of The Father Solen Aum Solen -- I Am NOW THE SAME - yesterday - today and forever -- Let them which deny Me - deny Me - for they know Me not they know Me not by <u>any</u> <u>Name</u> --

While I say unto thee: I Am now Come as Sananda - I Am no less than He Which is Sent/ was Sent of old -- While they accepted Me not. Now this day - they neither Know Me nor accept the Name which I bring unto them -- I have given unto thee the Name in the beginning thru thine hand in years past --

I announced Mineself as Sananda - I made appointment with thee - and did I not Come? - I say I came - and I went as I came - yet thine company received Me not - they were not concerned - they looked for great and glorious wonders in the Heaven - yet I gave unto them <u>NO</u> <u>SIGNS</u>! for I come not to satisfy their curiosity - I come to find One which sought the Light -- So be it I found One - and I gave unto that One many things which was new and strange - yet she wearied not of Me and Mine Sayings - neither did she turn back in the time of trial and persecution ---

Now I say unto her - well done - Well Done Mine faithful Servant I now have greater things for thee - and it is so - for she hast proven herself -- So be it and Selah -- I Am Come that it Be ---

So shall it be as The Father hast Willed it - let it Be ---

I Am He Which is Come - I Am Sananda The Lord - Son of God The Father - and so shall I be unto thee All that He would have Me Be.

Each in His Own Tongue

Be ye as Mine Hand made manifest unto them - and say unto them in Mine Name - that they shall bestir them - self - and they shall be given that which shall profit them -- For it is now come when the Word shall be proclaimed unto all the nations of the Earth - and they shall be given the law - and none shall be overlooked - for each shall be given in his own tongue - as he is able to comprehend - and he shall be as ones prepared - for I say - there shall go forth from out the Realm of Light - Ones which are prepared to do the Will of Mine Father - and they shall be as Ones well trained -- These that go forth shall carry Mine Banner and they shall be identified by their Works -- They shall walk humbly and gently amongst the children of the Earth - yet they shall walk Knowingly - and with surety --

I say: They shall walk gently and with surety -- So be it I Know them - and they are of The Order of Melchezedek - and for this have I given unto them passport into the place wherein thou art -- It hast been said - there are Ones which are refused passport - for these would be unto thee aggressors and transgressors - therefore I stand guard that they pass not -- I say there are ones which would enter into thine world as the oppressor and offenders - yet I have sent a Host unto thine aid - that they enter not into thine world - for I say unto thee: I Know them as the offenders - and I am watchful -- I Am at the Helm - and I Am not of a mind to give unto them passport -- Let them be - yet I say unto thee: Be ye watchful that ye might not be entrapt by them - for they are as the ones alert unto the way of man ---

I say: They know the weakness of man - and they play the piper's tune - and it behooves Me to say unto them which have ears: Hear ye Me - and Know ye that I Am alert - and I Know that which I am about. So be it I Am The Lord thy God --

Progress / Change

Be ye as the Hand of Me - and give unto them this Word: There shall be a great display of man's power - and ye shall see it and know it for that which it is ---

Yet ye shall not be confused nor confounded by it - for I The Lord thy God sees it and recognizes it for that which it is ---

It shall be as naught against the Power of The Almighty Allwise God - it shall be as NAUGHT! I say - as NAUGHT!! --

For it is given unto Me to see them building their great and grand edifices - and bowing down before them -- They come from afar to view them - yea - even touch them -- And it is given unto them to stand in awe - and be as ones confounded - as ones which have been enamored I speak unto thee that they might be prepared - So let it be -

I Am Come that it Be -

In Spirit:

I Thedra - looked into the heavens - and beheld some light fluffy clouds -- I looked again - and many "forms" appeared - round - long spear head shaped - Hoops -- And I called out in great joy: "Come - See"- and they came - we looked -- I said: I told you they would come The sky was filled with them -- We felt a great relief that the time had COME = One time ended - another come --

Karma - Justice

Say unto them as I would - that there is a Power which far exceeds that of man's - and man shall be disarmed of "his power" for he hast misused that which hast been allotted unto him -- He hast been given unto transgression and abortions - and adultery/ fornications/ and hypocrisy. He hast forfeited his inheritance - and he hast pilfered the "Word of God" - laying claim unto holiness - and he hast progressed not! - I say he hast <u>Not</u> <u>Progressed</u>! - For the last state is worse than his first state.

Wherein is it said: "He that hath been given the law - and doeth it not - is worse than the infidel"? I say - he is worse than the man which knoweth not the law ---

So be it I pluck out from amongst them - which are of a mind to follow Me - and these I shall set apart - and I shall do that which I will for I have said I shall do a Mighty Work - and it is so - so let it be -- And the ones which I have said are the hypocrites and the blasphemers I shall set apart - and I shall disarm them - and they shall be put in a separate place - and they shall be given as they are prepared to receive. The law is just - and it is exact! - I say it is <u>Justice</u> that they receive <u>Only</u> as they have prepared -- While each shall receive accordingly unto the law - the ones which find themself wanting shall lament and wail - and they shall have time - and it shall be long and hard - therein is their plight -- I say it is that which is just and lawful - for it is said: "As ye are prepared - so shall ye receive" - let it be - for it is the ONLY WAY OF PROGRESS ---

I say: The law requires a man to progress - yet they heed not the Word/ obey not "THE LAW"-- I tell thee: The LAW is given for his progress - let them then progress! Let them learn - let them prepare themself! I say - Prepare! Prepare! - and they turn their face from Me - O ye foolish ones - list unto Me - for I stand with out-stretched hands - I ask of thee nought save obedience unto the Law -- Come - Come - be ye made whole - for I Am the Lord thy God Sent of Mine Father - that ye be made Whole –

Let it be as He hast Willed it --

I Am The One Sent - Sananda

Needs vs Desires

Say unto them: There shall be great sorrow amongst the people - and they shall cry out for help - yet help shall not be found amongst them - for I say: Their help cometh from on High - their help cometh from the Great and Mighty Council – For it is given unto the Council to Know the needs of the people - and each unto his own - "<u>Each</u> <u>unto</u> <u>his</u> <u>own</u>"!

and at no time shall he be denied - I say at <u>no</u> <u>time</u> shall he be denied! For it is the way of the Council to fill the need - and as the need be - so is it met -- I too say: It need be met - the need is Great! and it is given unto Me to Know - for I am one which Sees - and Know that which is their need -- Now let it be said - that man's desires are not his needs -- His needs are not to be misunderstood nor mistaken for his desires - for his desires are his own downfall - prompted ofttimes of the dragon/ by man's opinions/ man's ambition - and he hast not the <u>will</u> to resist - neither the strength -- So be it that for the most part - they are weak of character - they are weak I say! - They are weak!! - and prone to sluggishness -- So be it I Am Come that they be strengthened - that they become alert - and that they be given the knowledge which shall profit them ---

Hold high the Banner which I give unto thee - and walk ye with surety - and give unto Me credit for Being That Which I Am -

For I Am The Lord thy God -

The Mask

Hear ye this day - that which I say unto thee - and be ye as the Hand of Me made manifest unto them which seek the Light - for I am Come that there be Light -- I bring the "Word" - I bring the Law -- And I have said that there are <u>many</u> to assist thee -- Yet I am He Which is the "Law Giver" -- I Am He - Which is The One Sent that ye might be brot out of bondage - I say - "That ye be brot out of bondage" -- Now - there are ones amongst thee which have come even as I - yet ye know them not by their appearance -- Ye see that which they <u>appear</u> to be - for they too wear the mask of flesh - ye but see the mask -- While I say ye but see the <u>mask</u> - I too say: Ye shall see beyond the mask - and know them for that which they are - for they shall be revealed unto them which are prepared ---

I say: They shall be revealed unto them which are prepared ---

Now ye shall see the ones which walk within flesh - as the ones which are of flesh - and ye shall see the ones which are <u>not</u> of flesh as different - they shall be as they are - yet ye shall Know them for that which they are - and thine thinking shall make of them no difference - let not thine eyes deceive thee -- For I say unto thee - these things shall be <u>revealed</u> unto thee - and revelation comes not by thinking - neither by thine eye - it comes thru the Hand of God - Which shall touch thee. So let it be - and be ye as ones prepared for the revelations which I shall make possible--

So be it I Am The Lord God -

The Host of Hosts -

Sananda

Fear Not Changes

Be ye as the Hand of Me made manifest - and say unto them in Mine Name - that the time comes swiftly - when One comes into their midst as One prepared to lift them up -- I say - One comes swiftly into their midst - which shall be qualified to lift them up - and for this does He come -- He shall have the Authority and the Power - and He shall be as

One prepared -- Now there shall be many changes - and they shall be according unto the law - for there shall be Great and <u>Mighty</u> Changes within a short time -- And no man can foretell the magnitude of such changes - for they know not --

While We of the Mighty Council Know - We are not disposed to give unto them which know not - that which they could not comprehend Yet let it suffice that I Know that which I say unto them - and it behooves Me to say: Prepare! Prepare! - for the days ahead shall be as nothing seen by man -- Yet I say unto thee: Fear not - abide in the Light - and give unto Me thine hand - and I shall lead thee aright - I shall not fail thee -- Be ye about thine preparation - and I say: Ye shall abide by the law -- Ye shall give unto Me credit for being that which I Am - and ye shall wait upon Me The Lord thy God --

So be it I Am The One Sent -

Amen and So Be it -

The Sleepers

Be ye as one prepared to give unto them this Word - and let it go forth as Mine - for I shall Author that which I will - and no man shall say nay unto Me -- I say: It behooves them to hear that which I say - and they shall do well to give unto Me credit for being that which I Am ---

It is now come when they shall go forth as ones prepared -or- they shall be caught up short of their course - for "Time" waits not! ---

I say: I Am Come - and I shall do a Mighty Work - and make Mine departure - even as I made Mine entrance - and the sleepers shall sleep on - knowing not that I have come -- I say: They shall awaken in a new place - yet they shall be in their own environment - and they shall be none the worse - none the better for the change - for they shall sleep on. I say: The sleepers shall sleep on! - Knowing not!! ---

Now I say unto them which are beginning to awaken: Listen! Look! See! that which I shall do - for I shall give unto them proof of Mine Word - I say - I shall give unto them proof - and they shall know!

So be it I Am The Lord God

The Place is Prepared

Say unto them as I would - that there is a place prepared for them which hast the will to go where I lead them - and it is given unto Me to have gone before - that it be prepared ---

NOW - - They shall come with Me - or - they may reject it - for I say: None bring them against their will -- NONE bring them <u>against</u> their will -- Yet - I say: None enter unprepared -- So be it that I come that they be prepared -- So let it Be as The Father hast Willed it -- I say: The Father hast Sent Me that they be brot out - yet I say: He gives unto them free will - and I shall not trespass upon it -- So be it that I Know the Law -- Let it be understood that they come of their own preparation and of their own will ---

While I stand with outstretched Hands to assist - it is given unto Me to see them reject Me and Mine assistance -- I say they reject ME - and

Mine assistance -- While I see them run after strange gods - and seek favors of them - I say: Behold ye that which I shall do -- Look ye - and see the Hand of God Move -- I Am not a "false god" - I Come as The One Sent of Mine Father Which hast given unto Us Being -- Let it suffice that I Am He - Come that ye be brot out of bondage -- So let it be as The Father hast Willed it -- HE hast provided for thine return - for He hast Sent ME to point The Way -- I Am called the "Way Shower" So it is---

Now I say: "Come follow where I lead thee - Come! Come!! - I say!!"---

Wherein is it said: "Ye shall pick up thine feet and follow Me"--

I Am Sananda

Thine Shield & Thine Rod

Sori Sori -- Be ye as one prepared to go all the way with Me - for I say unto thee: There are few which are prepared for that which I have for them -- They are NOT prepared to receive that which I have for them - yet they ask - and for that are they the unknowing ones -- For they could not bear that which I have for them - yet I give not unto babes - that which would choke them-- And yet they ask for the Greater part ---

Now it is come when Great Light shall flood the Earth - and many shall fall - many shall fear - many shall run to the mountains for safety. While I have said: "There shall be no safety save in ME" it is so -- So be it I Am thine Shield and thine Rod ---

I say: "I Am thine Shield & thine Rod" - and nothing shall come nigh unto thee to do thee harm - for I Am thine Protector in the time of stress -- So be it that I give unto thee passport into Mine place of abode -- Now I say unto thee: "Come unto Me - and be ye as One with ME - Come ye and be made Whole".

I Am Sananda

I Await

Say unto them - that the Way is now clear - and the time is Come when there shall be many which shall come in Mine Name -- Yet I say unto thee: "Hear ye Me - and Know ye the True from the false" -- For many shall come declaring that they are "He"- that they are the "Lord Jesus Christ" - that they have communion with Me -- Yet I say: "I give not Mine Jewels unto the bigots/ the proud and haughty" ---

I say: "Come as a little child" and I shall touch thee ---

Yet I see them puffed up - as ones prone to bigotry and flattery -- I say they are prone to bigotry - and they have not touched the Hem of Mine Garment - for they see not that which I have not revealed unto them ---

I say - I have not revealed Mineself unto them - for they are not as yet prepared to sup with Me -- So be it I await their preparation -- So be it I tire not ---

I Am Sananda

The Foundation

Say unto them: There are many which shall go out from the place wherein they are - as ones prepared to enter into the place wherein I abide --

Too - there are ones which shall go out unprepared - and these shall know much sorrow - and these shall be the ones which shall weep and wail - and cry: "Lord! Lord! hast Thou forsaken us"--

I have said: These shall be, as the traitors - it is so -- They shall be the ones which have betrayed themself -- Wherein is it said that I Am Come that they be prepared - So be it and Selah ---

I say: They which give not of themself that they be prepared - shall be as ones unprepared - and they shall be as the ones which have rejected Me - and Mine Word --

Now let it be known that I Am Come - that I have not rejected them neither have I forgotten them -- I Am as the One Sent that they be brot out of darkness---

Yet they receive Me not! -- So be it I Am He - and I stand at the Entrance of The Inner Temple - and I bid thee "Come" -- I say unto All "Come" - yet it is given unto Me to give unto them the Law by which they are to enter - and that is thru and by preparation -- I say: "Cleanse, thineself of all thine <u>pre</u> conceived ideas - thine hatred - thine puny ways - and give unto The Father thine Self - and ye shall be as One lifted up -- So be it I give of Mineself that this be done ---

I weary not of <u>Mine</u> <u>Service</u> - I weary not - for I am prone to patience - and I Am Love personified -- I come in Love - and I offend not -- I come that there be Light - So let it be -- And it is given unto Me to see them which are prepared - and them which are unprepared - and them which reject The WORD - these are the worst of the lot ---

I say: These are the ones which betray themself ---

So be it I speak again and again of preparation - for it is the foundation upon which ye shall build -- Be ye as the wise Builder - and as the one whose house shall stand ---

I say - let it stand the storms - Let it Stand! So be it I have spoken unto thee in parable which ye might understand --

So be it I Am The Lord God

Sananda

The Keeper of the Gifts

Say unto them in Mine Name - that they shall be as ones prepared for the part which I have kept for them -- And it is given unto Me to be The Keeper of the Gifts which shall be bestowed upon them which have prepared themself to receive them -- At last they shall come into their Inheritance - and they shall partake of the Manna - and they shall rejoice that it is come when they shall be given their Inheritance in full. So be it and Selah -- I say - they shall receive as I have - and they shall Know Great Joy - and they shall no more go into darkness -- So be it I Am Come that they which have prepared themself might be found and brot out --

So be it and Selah -

* * * * * * *

Beloved Ones:

I Am speaking unto thee as I speak unto Mine -- I Am speaking unto thee as Mine - for art thou not Mine? - I say thou art Mine - and no man shall say thee nay! -- For I Am thine Father from Which thou hast gone forth as an identity - an individuality/ an individual with free will --Now ye shall be reminded of Me - for I speak unto thee as One of thine own species - in thine own language - that ye might comprehend that which I say -- I say - ye shall comprehend that which I say - for ye shall be given the comprehension - and it shall be thru the Grace of Mine Sons Which have given of Themself that there be Light.- Let it suffice that I have Sent many to deliver thee out of bondage --

I say - I have sent many to deliver thee out of bondage - yet thou art as ones in flesh -- For this do I speak unto thee in thine tongue - that ye might come to Know that which I say -- Be ye as one which can hear-- I say: Yet thou art bound by flesh - thou seest the flesh - it weighs heavily upon thee - yet it comes to pass - when ye shall step out of the dense garment - and put aside all the heaviness and grossness of flesh and arise as on wings - and swift shall be thine flight -for no atomic weight shall hold thee unto the Earth --

Thine body shall be of Light Substance - and thine feet shall run and not be weary -- So be it that I have given unto thee the power and the Authority to claim thine Inheritance in full - as a Son of God The Father -- And when the time is come that ye return unto Me as One MADE WHOLE - ye shall be as One with Me - and ye shall Know All things - and ye shall do that which I give unto thee to do -- Ye shall Know that which ye have done - that which ye shall do - for there shall be no mystery - no longing - nothing hidden -- So be it I speak unto thee that thine longing be fulfilled -- So be it that I Am thine Father--

Solen Aum Solen -

Thine Eternal Parent

Their Weeping and Wailing Shall Avail Them Nought

Say unto them: There shall be Great weeping and wailing - and none shall find comfort within their wisdom - for their wisdom shall be as nought - for their knowledge shall not be sufficient unto them - for they shall take no comfort from all their knowledge - for they have misused their energy - and wasted their Substance --

Now it shall profit them nought - their weeping and wailing -- While I have called unto them - and given of Mineself that they be brot out of bondage - they have rejected Me - and they have fought against Mine Precepts - and against Me The Lord God -- They have made a mockery of Mine Sayings - and pilfered them-- They have gone the long way to persecute them which would serve Me -- And for this shall they be known - for this shall they reap that which they have sown - So be it and Selah ---

I say: They shall reap that which they have sown – So be it the Law. Wait upon Me - sayeth The Lord God - The Host of Hosts - and I Am Come that they might Know The Law - that they might have Light -- I say unto them: Bear ye Witness of Me - and I shall bring thee out of bondage ---

I AM HE -

THE LORD GOD KING OF KINGS -

THE HOST OF HOSTS -

Vain Image

Be ye as ones prepared - for I say unto thee: There shall be many come saying unto thee: "I am He which is Sent" - yet - let it be known that I shall announce "THE ONE SENT OF ME" - and ye shall know Him.

Now it is come when they shall raise up in great numbers - and they shall declare themself the prophet - and they shall think themself wise yet - I say unto thee: THEY ARE NOT WISE! They but image a vain thing! They but Image a Vain thing!! - And they are but the bigots - and the poor of spirit -- They shall be given as they are prepared to receive. And yet I say: I give not the babe at the breast that which he cannot assimilate and digest -- So be it that they have not in as yet partaken of the Bread which I have BROKEN for them - yet - they would fain sit at Mine board -- I say: they image a vain thing -- So be it I Am The Lord thy God - and I have Great things in store for thee -- Let it be as The Father hast Willed it -- So be it I Come that it be so - So - let it Be.-

I Am Sananda

Do Not Let Them Ride Thy Back

Sori Sori - Let it be said this day - that the time is come when Great shall be the Action - Great shall be the turmoil - and great the unrest -- And it behooves Me to say unto thee: Be ye at Peace -- Let not that which goes on about thee disrupt thine Work - for I say: They shall come crying and weeping - they shall wail aloud -- Yet ye shall give of thineself unto that which I have for thee -- I say: They shall be as their own porter - and they shall not ride thy back ---

Hold high Mine Banner - and let thine own Light so shine that they might see it from afar -- Yet ye shall give unto them nought which shall stumble them -- Give unto them only as they are prepared to receive -- So let them Come - let them Come -- While I say unto thee: Do not let them ride thine back ---

Keep thineself in readiness - that I The Lord thy God might speak unto thee - that they might receive Mine Word - and It shall suffice them -- Let it be said - that there is Greater things for thee -- I say: Greater things are in store for thee -- So be it they shall come asking - and these shall be given the WORD - and it shall suffice - that which I have given unto thee for them ---

They shall not bear down upon thee - for I have said: They shall stand on their own feet - or fall of their own weight ---

Let them be strengthened in their weak parts -- I have said - they are weak of character - they are frail of spirit - yet they shall ask - that they be strengthened - and they shall WILL it so - So let them be -- And I shall do a wonderful Work - and ye shall see that which I shall do -- Behold ye the Hand of God move - See It Move and rejoice ---

Let it Be as The Father hast Willed it --

I Am Sananda

I Wait

Say unto them: I Am Come that they might be prepared to go where I go - that they be given their Inheritance in full -- Now I say: They are as ones which have waited long that they be prepared ---

Yet the time is come when they shall prepare themself - for none other enter into Mine place of abode -- None enter save thru Me - for I Am He Which is Sent that they be prepared -- I have gone before them - and I have prepared the Way that they might follow Me ---

It is said - that there are few which have the strength of character to follow Me - for Mine Way is not easy -- Yet I say - it is the safe and sure Way -- So be it that I stand guard - and I protect Mine own - I say: "I protect Mine own" -- I Am the Protector - the Shield - and the Buckler -- I Am the Porter at the Gate - and I wait that they might come unto Me as ones prepared -- So be it I Am The Lord thy God -

Sananda

They Beat Their Breast – Yet ...

Sori Sori - Hast it not been said that I Am The Way - The Truth and The Light -- Hast it not been said that I Am The Lord God of old - the

Same today and tomorrow -- I say unto thee this day - I AM HE! - I Am Come - and I Am The One Sent that All might come to know Me For I Am the Way - I AM The One Sent of Mine Father - that they might return unto Him with Me - So be it as He hast Willed it -- Let them hear that which I say unto thee - for I say: "Come - Come unto Me as a little child" ---

Give unto them this Word - that they might be quickened - that they might be touched - that they might come to Know---

Many claim to know Me - many claim to Know ---

Yet they do not Mine Work - they mouth Mine Sayings - they beat their breast and call out - and yet they give no heed unto that which I say -- They put their fingers in their ears that they hear not ---

Now I say - they shall take their fingers out their ears - and listen unto Me - for I shall bring unto them that which they are prepared to hear -- I say they shall stand still and listen - for they shall be caused to listen -- They shall be CAUSED to listen! ---

Let them hear - let them See - for this have I - spoken -- Let them be as ones prepared to follow Me - for this have I Come ---

So be it I Am - Sananda

A Reminder

Be ye as the Hand of Me - and give unto them this Mine Word - and it shall be unto them profitable -- They shall receive it as Mine Word -

for I shall dictate each Word as it is recorded -- So be it - I say unto thee: Let them which will - come - and let them hear that which I say unto thee -- Yet I say: They which have not heard - shall be as the ones which receive not - for they shall be as ones which have their own will I say they will that which they do - and they put before their face their own hands -- Now - I say: They shall be reminded of Mine Sayings - and they shall be reminded many times! - For I shall say them yet many times - they shall come to Know them - and the meaning thereof -- I say: "As they are prepared - so shall they receive" - So be it and Selah. I have spoken that they be reminded - So be it and Selah --

I Am Sananda

The Rod of Power

Be ye as the Hand of Me - and record that which I say unto thee - that they might Know that which I say -- It is now come when the Light shall shine forth - and it shall be as nothing man hast seen - for thou art now come into the Age of Light - the Age of Maturity -- And it is given unto man to be yet in darkness - and it is said - he shall be brot out ---

For this have I spoken out - for this have I come -- I say: I Am Come that they be brot out - yet they which reject Me - shall be bound in darkness -- And at no time shall I reject Mine Father - for HE hast Sent Me - and for this have I been given the Authority and the Power to give unto them as I have received -- I say: I have the Authority and the Power which is invested within Me of Mine Father - and I am the One Sent with the Rod of Power -- And it is said - that the darkness shall flee before the Light -So be it and Selah ---

I Am He Which IS - WAS - and ever shall be -

The Lord thy God – Sananda

Humility

Be ye as the Hand of Me - and give unto them that which I give unto thee for them - and they shall reject it or accept it as they will --- Yet I say: Sad shall he be which rejects the Word of God - for no other protection hast he - NONE OTHER ---

I SAY - NONE OTHER!

By the Word shall he be made Whole - by the Word shall he be brot out of bondage - by the Word shall he be prepared to enter into the Holy of Holies -- So be it I say unto them - reject not the Word of God ---

I come that ye Know as I Know - for this do I give unto them the WORD -- And as they ask they shall receive - so let them ask of Me - and I shall give unto them - as they are prepared to receive -- Let them come as little children - humble of heart - and they shall not be denied for I shall Know them for that which they are --

So be it I Am Sananda The Lord God

As One Prepared

Sori Sori -- I say unto thee this day: Be ye as one prepared for the Greater Part - for it is now come when ye shall give thine whole time unto Me - for I have Great Work for thee - it is Mine Work - yet I have need of thee -- Serve All men even as I serve - yet I say unto thee: Thou shall be as one prepared for the Greater Part - let it be as The Father hast Willed it -- I say I have Greater things prepared for thee -- Let it serve thee well - and at no time shall ye be found wanting ---

Let it suffice thee that I Am with thee - and I shall give unto thee in Great Measure --

Let it be -

Let it Be --

I Am Sananda

I Have Unsheathed the Sword

Say unto them: Mine Hand is strong and I have within it the Rod of Power - and I have unsheathed the Sword of Truth - and I shall wield It - and no man shall stay Mine Hand - for I Am the Lord of Lords - the Host of Hosts - and I shall do a mighty Work ---

The time is now come when I shall speak out - and it shall be given unto Me to Know them which hear that which I say -- And too - I shall Know them which hear not -- And them which put words into Mine Mouth - these – I shall spew out - for I say: I shall cut clean All that which offends Me -- I shall separate them - and I shall give unto them as they are prepared to receive ---

Now I say unto them - they shall be as one responsible for that which they do - and they shall bear witness of Me - The Lord thy God.

I say I Am The Lord God -- I Am not amongst the dead -- I Live - I Am He Which Cometh -- Surely and swiftly I Come - I stand as One above thee -- I Am He Which is Sent that ye be lifted up -- I say - come ye up - stand with Me upon Mine High Holy Mount - and I shall show unto thee Greater things than thou hast dreamed of -- Put aside thine toys - thine puny things - and seek ye the Light Which I Am ---

Hear ye that which I say - and ye shall Know no sorrow --

So be it I Am Sananda

Thine Fortune

Be ye as the Hand of Me - and give unto them this Mine Word - and let them do as they will with it -- Yet I say - it behooves them to be mindful of Mine Word - and heed that which I say -- For I Am mindful of their every thot - and deed -- For this do I say: Be ye as ones mindful of thine ways - and let it be the fortune of Mine to give unto thee as I have received -- I say - I shall give unto them which follow Me - that which I have kept for them -- Is it not said - I'm the Keeper of thine fortune - and I Know that which I keep -- I Am the Keeper - I Am He Which Knows thine fortune - for I see as thou hast not seen -- So be it I shall touch them which follow Me - and they shall See -- So be it that I Am HE which Knows that which I See - And as yet thou seest not as I see for I stand upon Mine High Holy Mount - and I See as thou canst not see -- Boast not of thine fortune - for thou knowest not that which is in store for thee ---

So be it that I Am The Lord thy God -

Sananda

The Rites of Melchezedek

Say unto them: They do but betray themselfs - when they first accept their lying Spirit - before Mine trusted and ordained Servants ---

I say - they believe not Mine Servants which I have appointed and ordained - thru and by The Word of God - whereby I Am given All authority to ordain them in Mine Father's Name ---

I say unto them which do make of themself liars - they but betray themself - they have not the comprehension to know the True from the false -- I say: They are dupes of the lying Spirits - and they are entrapt within the web which they have spun for themself - for they but serve "self" - and they are wont to Know of "Self" - and they are bound within their own limitations ---

I say: Pity are the ones which serve "self" - for it is but the illusion and they lying Spirits deal with them - as they wont to deal with the Self -- They are easily deluded - and they are not prone unto the Light for they are not of the Light - therefore the Truth is not within them ---

I say: Seek ye not the "Spirits" of the Dead - for they are not more in one place than they were in another - until they be lifted up - OF THE LIGHT WHICH I AM ---

Now it is said: Ye shall first see the "Kingdom of Heaven and All things shall be added unto IT"- and it is So -- While it is given unto 'man' to run after strange gods - it is given unto him to be bound in darkness -- I say - he shall seek out the Light - and he shall be "Lifted up" - and then he shall be as one prepared to call himself "A SON OF GOD" ---

Let it suffice that I have lain Mine Hand upon Mine Servant - and I have pronounced "THE WORD" Which hast been according unto the Law Which is given unto Me - and thereby I Am prepared to set Mine Seal upon her which hast Qualified for the Priesthood of Melchezedek whereby I Am Come in Mine Father's Name -- I Am Come by Mine own free will - that I might be the Will of Mine Father which hast Sent Me -- So be it that I betray not Mineself -- I Am He Which Comes that MAN Know the true from the false -- I say unto thee O man: Bestir thineself - arise from out thine lethargy and seek ye the Light -- List ye and Know ye that I Am He Which hast thee within the Palm of Mine Hand -- Awaken unto Me - Awaken ye which slumber!

Awaken I say - Come forth and behold ye the Glory of God which hast given unto thee Being -- I say - Arise!! - Come forth and behold that which hast been forever thine Inheritance - Claim it! and ye shall be as one prepared to receive it -- Put on the "Royal Raiment" and let thine Shield be MINE Shield - thine Banner be Mine Banner - thine hand Mine Hand - thine Word Mine Word - and then ye shall be as one prepared to enter into the "Holy of Holies"-- Then I shall place before thee the Chalice of Living Water - and ye shall drink freely - and no more shall ye thirst ---

I say: NO MORE shall ye thirst ---

Be ye as one prepared to receive of the "Living Water" - and ye shall receive ---

Let it be said: "BLEST ARE THEY WHICH DOTH RECEIVE THE CUP OF LIVING WATER - FOR THEY SHALL NO MORE THIRST"

I Am prepared to give unto thee as thou art prepared to receive - So be it and Selah ---

I say: PEACE - PEACE - PEACE be upon thee O Mine Child - for I have so called thee out from among them - that ye be prepared to receive of the Rights of the Order of Melchezedek - and of The Order of The Emerald Cross -- I now bestow upon thee the Rites of the Order of Melchezedek - whereupon thou shall have full Power and Authority bestowed upon thee which shall give unto thee full Rites and Power to speak The Word - and unto Which thou shall eternally be bound -- I say: Ye shall be given full Rites and Power - and ye shall adhere unto the LAW - and ye shall be as One in full Command - and at no time shall ye betray thineself - and ye shall be fully prepared to receive the next Part prepared for thee -- And it shall be as None Other -- I say: Ye shall walk with Me - and I shall direct thee - and I shall be thine Shield and thine Buckler -- Ye shall wear the Royal Shield - and the Breastplate of the Order of Melchezedek - upon which shall be written the Name of The Son of God Which is The Master of the House -- Let it be Known that which has been said unto thee -- That which I have done in Secret I shall do openly - and they which are so prepared shall bear witness of that which I have said - and done in Secret -- I say: That which I say unto thee - I shall declare openly - that they might Know that IT IS SO -- So be it as I have spoken - for no man shall make void Mine Word - and no man shall shut Mine Mouth - for they have no power to shut up the Mouth of God ---

I say: "Place not thine hand against Mine Mouth - for it shall be as nought -- I Am The One Sent that this day be as none other - that the Kingdom of God be established upon the Earth ---

Wherein hast thou taken heed of Mine Words O man -- Wherein hast thou imaged ME a puny god -- Wherein hast thou made of Me an idol - wherein thou hast imaged a vain thing! ---

I say unto thee this day: Mine Hand is not shortened!

I Am He Which standeth on the Right Hand of Mine Father The Giver of Life - and no man can make of Me less - or greater - by his imaging ---

I say: He maketh ME neither Greater nor lesser by his vain imaging. Harken O ye men of Earth! I Am Come that All men be lifted up -- So be it I speak unto thee as of Old - thru and by a Servant Which hast been lifted up - and which I have Called and Ordained unto the Priesthood of Melchezedek -- So be it I pour out Mine Spirit upon Her and I shall Raise Her up to do a Mighty Work - and it shall be done unto the Glory of Mine Father Which hast Sent Me ---

Such have I said in The Name of Solen Aum Solen The Father Which hast given unto Us Being --

Amen it is so --

Sori Sori -- I have given unto thee that which I have kept for thee. Thou hast received the Rites - and thou shall go forth as none other - and thou shall attest unto this Rite Which I have bestowed upon thee - and no man shall stay thee -- No man shall be a hindrance unto thee - for I shall stand thee upon the High Holy Mount - and I shall place within thine hand the Rod and the Scepter - and it shall be as the Rod of Power which no man shall wrest from thee - neither shall he take from thee the "Word" which I shall give unto thee -- For "The Word" shall be neither written or spoken - It shall be engraven within thine heart - and upon thine forehead ---

Yet the profane shall not see it - neither shall they find it within thine heart - for it shall be hidden up from the profane and the unjust.

Blest art thou amongst women -- Blest art thou -- For this have I bowed low before thee - and called Thine Name Sacred before men -- I shall declare a time and a place wherein I shall give unto thee thine next Part -- I say: A time and a place shall be given unto thee - and ye shall be as One foretold and prepared -- So let it be as I have said -- So shall it be done according unto LAW ---

The Head of the Council

I Am He Which sits at the Head of The Council -- I Am He Which stands guard over thee -- I Am He Which awaits thine return -- I Am He Which hast given unto thee of Mineself that ye be strengthened - that ye be made strong ---

Now it is said that there shall be a Great Onrush of Water - and it shall nourish thee -- And the dry places shall be made to bring forth Great harvest -- For I say unto thee: Long hast the ground lain fallow - and the plowmen hast gone forth that the ground be prepared -- It is now prepared - and I say unto thee: Go ye forth as one prepared to sow where I have made ready the ground -- For have I not sent forth Mine Plowmen - and have I not given unto thee the Seed -- Have I not given unto thee the strength and the Knowledge of Mine Word -- Have I not set thee apart and prepared for thee a place -- And now ye shall set aside that place - and separate thineself - and I shall give unto thee another Part - and it shall be well with thee -- Prepare thineself - for I have called thee forth that ye do Mine bidding -- I have given of Mineself that ye be prepared -- and I have said unto thee: Mine time shall be thine time - So let it be ---

Rest in the Knowing that

I Am The Lord thy God

In Spirit

I - Thedra - sat high on a pile of snow by the side of a highway up a Mountain (Shasta) -- The road had been cleared of snow to the point where I sat as Sentinel -- Beyond that the clearing broke off abruptly - There were single file tracks continuing up the mountain - almost obliterated by the late snows ---

A strong stone wall lined the lower side of the road ---

I beheld a great abyss beyond the wall ---

An ultra modern "camper" truck came up at great speed -- It was the finest "rig" that could be bought or found <u>this</u> <u>day</u> -- I was watching with interest -- It came to a sudden stop - the door was opened - a man stept to the door and halted -- A. sleek black pig ran out between his legs -- It dashed over the wall and disappeared -- The "man" knew I had seen it - he was embarrassed -- He brushed his very fine clothes - and said to me - "They do make good bedfellows"-- The scene changes to a small jeep full of young fellows intent upon making the Mountain top - ignoring the snow -- Their vehicle swerved quickly to the right - and over the wall from sight ---

= = =

The broad cleared highway lies ahead and behind -- many there be that travel to the Mountain - never attaining its heights -- There is a "Time" when the character of man is tested - exposed - revealed -

A place where he leaves All behind to enter "Single file" on his upward climb -- This part of his path is not well beaten by the "Machinery" of men -- The Trailblazer - The Wayshower has gone before to show the Way-- Time has almost obliterated the tracks - but to the "Observer" they are seen - The <u>brashness</u> of youth has not assisted them in their journey -- Lacking wisdom - discernment and humility - they are turned aside to be seen no more ---

Ye Shall Be as the Living Word

Beloved One : - Let this be recorded which I have shown unto thee - and it shall be liken unto Mine Word -- For I have given unto thee to

See and to Know that which ye See - and that which ye are to do -- Now ye shall be as Sentinel - ye shall keep watch -- Ye shall guide and direct them which come unto thee inquiring the Way -- Ye shall be at All times the Light -- Ye shall be as the Living Word made manifest unto them -- Ye shall hold high the Banner of Light which I bring -- Ye shall know the Joy of serving a people which is to be brot out of darkness ---

Let it suffice that I Am The Director -- I have gone before thee to prepare the Way before thee -- So be it ye shall follow in Mine Footsteps -- Let it be a day of Great Joy - for I say unto thee - thou art One with Me - and I shall lead thee aright ---

I Am Sananda

The Father of Perfection

Holy! Holy! Holy! is the Name of Solen Aum Solen - for He is The Father of Us – the Sum Total of All perfect things - All that We shall yet become -- By His Grace We are Perfect -- Even in His Image have We been given that which is Ours by Inheritance -- For He is The Donor of All Perfect Gifts -- And none receive of themselves - for The Father is The Giver -- He is The Giver of Perfection - for in Him are All things made perfect - even unto the smallest! yea - even unto the smallest!!

I say: In Him All Perfection rests -- In Him All things perfect are created perfect - and outside Him no thing can <u>be</u> -- All outside Him is illusion - and has no existence -- Be ye as ones which can Know the illusion from the Perfect thing which He hast brot forth - that He might be Glorified ---

I say: He - The Father of Perfection hast Glorified Himself in His Creation -- So let it be brot back unto Him perfect - even as it went out. I say - even as it went out ---

Praise Him for His Word Which hast brot forth such Perfection as is His -- For this hast it been said: Look! See! Behold the Hand of God move! For it shall bring forth that which He hast Willed - and the illusion shall pass ---

It is said: Arise from thine sleep - and come follow Me - and ye shall Know that which I Know - and there shall be no more darkness. I say: <u>Let</u> <u>there</u> <u>be</u> <u>Light</u>-- <u>Let</u> <u>there</u> <u>be</u> <u>Light</u> - <u>and</u> <u>there</u> <u>Is</u> <u>Light</u> -- Walk ye in <u>IT</u> and ye shall <u>not</u> fall --- I Am Sananda

Pay Heed

Be ye as Mine Mouth - Mine Voice - and say unto them in Mine Name that they shall pay heed unto that which I say unto them -- They shall heed the Word - and they shall be as ones quickened unto It - and it shall be for the Good of All that I speak -- For it is the Way of The Lord thy God - and none shall be given a Part within the place wherein I am beforetime -- I say - each in his own time - and according unto his preparation ---

So be it I come that All be lifted up - and it is given unto Me to see them as ones bound and crying out in their darkness -- Now ye shall prepare thineself to be as Mine Hand made manifest unto them - and they shall accept Mine Gifts or reject them as they will -- Yet I speak forth this day that they all be prepared to enter into Mine place of abode. So be it and Selah ---

I am now prepared to accept them which are prepared to come -- I say: "Come" and they which come shall be forever blest -- So be it and Selah ---

Sananda

How Long?

Mine Beloved: - While I say unto thee there is but a short while in which to do thine part - I say it is in this short while that Great and Mighty Work shall be done -- And it is for this that I have set aside a time and a place - and it is now come when ye shall be as one prepared to do that which I give unto thee ---

Now ye shall give unto them the Word as it is prepared for them - and it shall be as they have not had -- They shall be as ones blest to receive it - and ye shall be blest to receive it -- So be it that I shall bless thee ---

Let thine Voice be Mine - and let thine hand be Mine - and I shall do a Mighty Work -- So sayeth The

Lord thy God -

I Am He -

The Heavens Shall Open

Be One with Me and I shall declare unto thee: "The Heavens shall open wide the doors - and ye shall pass thru as One with Me" -- Open - Open I say - and the Gates shall swing wide -- I say unto thee: The gates shall bar not thine way - for I shall say unto them: "Open" - and they shall open - and it shall be as they are not -- I say - the Gates shall be no more for I say "Open" and it is done -- Hold ye fast - fear not - and wait upon Me The Lord thy God- and I shall bring unto thee that which I have for thee -- So be it and Selah ---

I Am He Which holds within Mine Hand the Key - and it is thine - it is Mine -- Be ye One with me and We shall be eternally One -- Hold not thineself from Me - for I Am The Lord God - and I bid thee enter into Mine Holy Place of abode -- Rest in the Knowing that I am with thee -- So be it I shall not forsake thee ---

Hold high thine head - and walk ye with dignity - for I Am with thee -- Let it ever Be --

I Am Sananda

Acceptance

Say unto them: The day approaches when there shall be Great Light - and no man shall be as the shadow - for I say: The shadows shall be removed - and man shall no longer walk in the shadows - for there shall be no shadows - it shall be LIGHT! ---

Now ye shall walk with Surety - Knowing that there is Freedom - there is Light -- And man's thinking shall make it no less -- So be it that the Light shall be so bright - it shall dispel the darkness - and man shall no more be bound in the darkness -- Now while it is said: "He shall no more be bound in darkness" - it is said: "He shall seek the Light"-- For this am I come - for this am I come -- It is the Coming of The Light which shall dispel the darkness - and I say - I AM COME --- While they which have closed Me out know not that I Am Come - I say unto thee: Thou hast seen the Light -- Thou hast accepted ME - and thou hast been true unto thineself - thou hast been obedient unto the Law -- Now ye shall walk with surety and Know as I Know -- So be it that I Am The Lord thy God -

Walk With Caution

Be ye as the Hand of Me made manifest unto them which seek the Light and say unto them as I would - that they shall find that which they seek and no man shall hide it from them - for it shall be revealed unto them. I say - "They shall seek - and they shall find"- So let it be ---

I am Come that it be given unto every man as he is prepared to receive -- I say that I am Sent that they have Light more abundantly - and they shall <u>first</u> seek - and it shall not be withheld from them ---

Now I say unto them which have come this far with Me - that there is but a little way yet -- Altho it be short - it be perilous - and therein lies great yawning chasms wherein he might step -- Therefore it behooves Me to say unto him: WATCH! WATCH! WATCH! See - and be alert unto thine way - and at no time shall ye walk alone -- I say: At

<u>no time</u> shall ye walk alone -- And therefore I say unto thee: Be ye aware of thine own part - and of thine own way - and let not thine foot slip ---

For it is given unto Me to See them which hast become puffed up and willful - and them which have wearied of Mine Sayings - and them which have taken unto themself great glory and great praise - and them which are wont to take unto themself all the praise and the glory. I say: I see them - I know them - and yet I say unto them: Beware! Beware! Lest thine foot slip!!

I say unto them: Beware of the Law - for it is sure and swift -- Turn not a deaf ear unto Me - for I am aware of thine every act/ word/ and deed -- I am aware of <u>all</u> thine ways -- Forget not that I Am The Lord of Lords - The Host of Hosts - The Lord thy God - and be ye as ones respectful of the Law -- Hold thine tongue - and pilfer not Mine Sayings! ---

For "I Am a jealous God"! -- I Am Mine own Porter - and I care for Mine own - I say: Mine Hand covers Mine Flock - and I watch with diligence -- I sacrifice not Mine own unto the One of darkness - yet I say Come! Follow ye Me -- And I am not to be discounted - I am not to be put aside - for I am not a puny priest - neither am I amongst the dead - crying out from the tomb---

I Am The Risen Christ! - I Speak as The Christ -- From out the Realms of Light I speak ---

I know whereof I speak -- <u>Nothing</u> is hidden from Me - and I say unto thee: I Am He Which is Come this day that Life might become that which is Eternal -- I say that All Life be made Pure: - and be as The <u>Christ</u>---

I say: That All Life be made Pure - that All misqualified energy be made Clean and Perfect -- For as the Great Power which I Am - which is invested within Me - is of Mine Father - and I Am One with Him - it is given unto Me to have the Power to Cleanse and renew that which hast been tarnished/ adulterated and made unholy ---

I say it hast been given unto Me - the Power to make Clean that which hast been made un-holy -- By His Grace hast it been so -- By His Grace hast it been given unto Me to walk amongst men of Earth as One prepared to lift them up -- So be it I pronounce THE WORD and it is done - yet I say not The Word until it is given unto Me to say ---

For Mine Father hast The Word - and He hast the Authority to give It unto Me that I give it unto anyone whomsoever is prepared to receive It ---

I say: It shall not be withheld from anyone whosoever is prepared to receive it -- So be it I have spoken unto thee of preparation - and THIS IS THE DAY OF PREPARATION - and no man shall be as one prepared by another ---

First - I say: Prepare thine own self - then I shall touch thee and ye shall be as one prepared to stand in the Presence of The Most High Living God -- So be it and Selah ---

I Am Come that ye be prepared --

So let it Be as He - hast Willed –

Responsibility - Lay Up Treasures

Be ye as the Hand of Me made manifest - and say unto them in Mine Name - that the time cometh when they shall have the part for which they are prepared - and they shall see that which they have stored up as their fortune - and they shall be as one which have been responsible for their own fortune -- They shall be as ones responsible for all their joy - or torment -- I say: They shall see that which they have stored up - and it shall be their <u>own</u> - and no man shall add to or take from it ---

They shall look well into the secret place wherein they have hidden their fortune - and they shall Know that which they have hidden there and it shall be theirs and none other -- For this is it said: "Lay up thine treasures in Heaven" - and it shall profit thee - for all thine Earthly Goods shall profit thee nought---

I say - it shall profit thee naught ---

Let it profit thee that which is Eternal - where rust and corruption enters not -- So be it I have spoken for the Good of All men --So be it I Am Come that they be profited ---

I Am Sananda

Blest are They

Blest are they which do Mine Work -- Blest are they which are Mine Servants -- Blest are they which Know Me -- Blest are they which are the Servants of The Lord thy God --

* * * * * * *

Be ye at thine post of duty - for I shall Call unto thee in the hours ahead and it shall be for the purpose of putting within thine hand a Portion which shall profit thee -- So be it I Am He which hast brot thee hence- and I have given unto thee abundantly -- And now I shall give unto thee in Greater Measure --

So be it and Selah --

* * * * * * *

Be ye as one prepared this day for to receive that which I have for thee for I shall give unto thee another part for the Book of Life - and it shall profit thee to receive it --

So be it and Selah --

The Seal - Hand - Heart - Head

Sori Sori -- Hear ye this day that which I say unto thee - and bear ye witness of Me -- Give unto them that which I give unto thee for them - and fear not - for I say: I Am He Which holds thee within the Palm of Mine Hand - and I say unto thee: The time is come when I shall make Mineself Known unto them which serve Me ---

I have called thee out from amongst them - and given unto thee the Authority to speak in Mine Name - and I have Ordained thee and named thee -- I have placed upon thine head Mine Hand - and I have placed

MINE SEAL upon thine forehead -- I have written upon thine heart that which no man shall pilfer or destroy ---

I say I have placed upon thine head in Holy Benediction Mine Hand and Sealed thee - for I say: Thou art Mine - Mine - and no man shall deny Mine Word - neither shall the forces of darkness swallow thee up. I say: No more shall the forces of darkness confuse or hold power over thee - for I Am the One Which stands watch - and I say - I Am The Lord thy God - and I am not of a mind to surrender Mine Own up unto the forces of darkness -- I Come that they be delivered up -- So be it I have brot forth the Prophets - and I have given unto them in abundance and they have been persecuted and martyred - condemned unto death.

Now the traitors shall come to Know the parts which they have played in the past - and they shall be as ones prepared to be their own judge - for they shall stand before the High Court and see their records and all that is written therein -- I say: All that is recorded therein shall be revealed unto them - and they shall judge themself - for there is none other -- I say: All shall be revealed - and they shall stand as ones condemned - or as ones justified ----

Let it go on record that thine record is clear - for this I have placed Mine Seal upon thee -- For this have I given unto thee the Authority to bear Mine Name - for this have I given unto thee thine Name and thine number -- I have given unto thee Mine Hand - and thou hast held on to it -- For this have I lead thee - for this have I given unto thee strength and peace -- Mine Peace I give unto thee - and I bid thee rest in Me -- Know ye that I Am thine Shield and thine Buckler - and I am as One prepared to go all the way - for I turn not Mine Face from Mine Servants.

I say: I turn Mine Face not from Mine Servants -- I now say unto thee Mine Beloved: It is come when I shall put within thine hand a Portion which shall profit them which have the mind to receive it – so be it it shall bless thee for that matter ---

Ye shall be thrice blest that ye .receive it first - and then they which reach out shall be blest -- And they which are yet unborn shall receive it - for Mine Word shall not perish from the Earth - for IT is imperishable -- And thine Name shall be forever written in the imperishable records of time - so let it be -- For this have I given it unto thee ---

Let it be said - I Am with thee this day that this be done - finished - and a Greater Work shall be done ---

= = =

Sori Sori -- Thine time is come when ye shall walk and talk with Me - and ye shall be as one prepared -- I say - I am with thee that ye be prepared - so let it be ---

While I say I Am Come - I too say: I am with thee that ye might receive the Greater Part - so shall it be - for I Am not of a mind to turn from thee - for I have long awaited this hour - when I might make manifest Mineself - and that ye might Know that which I have done -- I say - I shall do a Mighty Work - and ye shall Know that which I have done --

So be it and Selah --

The Unknown Shall be Known

Be ye as the Hand of Me made manifest - and say unto them: There is One amongst them which is the manifestation of The Word - and He walks amongst them as man - and He walks as man which is the manifestation of The Word -- And it is now come when they shall awaken unto that which <u>is</u> - that which they have not seen - that which they have not Known -- I say: They shall awaken unto that which they have not known -- For it is now time that these things be revealed unto them which are prepared to receive -- Therefore I speak unto them in ways in which they might comprehend - and it behooves Me to give them that which they <u>can</u> comprehend - therein is wisdom ---

Now I say: There are many which shall deny Me and Mine Words. Many shall accept Me and The Word -- Yet I say: Each unto his preparation - each in his own tongue - and it is for this that I have given unto them the power to speak - and the power to act -- I say I have given unto them the power to speak and to act - even as they will -- Yet it behooves them to Know from whence the power cometh -- I say - it is by Mine Grace that they have been given the power to speak - and they go so far as to deny Mine existence! ---

I Am the One Come that they be lifted up - yet they move swiftly unto their own destruction? - or unto their own salvation? ---

They move surely! - For there is only movement - Spirit moveth -- It is said: "Spirit is not stagnant" and it is so ---

They move as with the Sea - they are restless - knowing not from where they cometh - neither where they goeth -- I say - they are as ones forgetting -- Forgotten? Never!! are they forgotten - for this have I come - that they might remember their fortune - that they remember their inheritance - and return unto their rightful place ---

I Am Come that they be found and returned --

So be it and Selah --

Protection

Be ye as the Hand of Me - and give unto them this Word - for it is a part which shall be added unto that of the "Book of Life"- and it shall go down in history for the generations yet unborn -- It shall bear Mine Seal - and I shall bear testimony of thee - for I have given unto thee Mine Cloak of Authority - and Mine Shield shall be thine protection - and I shall hold over thee Mine parasol - for I say: Nought shall touch thee which is not of Me -- For I say - I am thine Shield and thine Protector -- I Am He Which is Sent that this day bring forth Great Light. And for that matter I bring with Me a HOST - and They too Come with Me that there be Light ---

So be it I say unto thee this day: There shall be a Great Light flood the Earth - and they which have the eyes to see - shall see - and these shall walk therein -- So Great shall be the Light - that the ones which have not eyes to see shall fall and perish -- Therefore I cry aloud - Awaken! Arise! LOOK! SEE! COME FORTH! - - - WALK YE UPRIGHT ---

Follow ye Me - for I Am The Lord thy God - Sent of Mine Father that ye perish not -- Arise O man of Earth -- Come out from the darkness which thou hast created - for I bring unto thee Great News.

Listen unto Me - and I shall deliver thee up --

So be it I Am The Host of Hosts - The King of Kings - Lord of Lords - The Lord thy God -

Sananda

* * * * * * *

Hear ye this: - I say unto thee: Ye shall stand as One which hast Mine Hand upon thee - and ye shall bear Mine Sign - Mine Signature -- Mine Name shall be written upon thine forehead - and ye shall be Known as I am Known -- So be it and Selah -- I say Hail! Hail and well done!

Sananda

Testimony - Sananda

Be ye as the Hand of Me and record that which I say unto thee -- It is Mine Part to give unto thee this Word - and thine Part to record it - that it go on record - that they might Know that which I have said unto thee.

It is for this that I now give unto thee this Word -- Ye shall be as the One to receive it - yet many shall see it and Know that which hast been written---

While it is for the Good of All that it is written - I say it shall be for thine own Good that ye record it well within the records -- Ye shall say unto them in Mine Name that there are many which profess Mine Name and call themself Christ-ians - yet they know Me not - neither do they follow Me -- I say - they follow Me not -- For I Know the Way which I have gone - and they go not in the Way I go ---

I say - they go not the Way I go - for I go unto Mine Father Which hast Sent Me -- They make for themself images - They set up temples and place therein their images - and they fear that which man might do or say -- I say unto thee: "Fear no man – be ye as one fearless - follow Me - and I shall be thine Shield and thine Buckler"---

Bless thineself and ask nought of man - save obedience unto the law -- Give unto him no power to take from thee thine Peace -- Rest in Me - and I shall lead thee -- Be ye as One with Me and call upon ME THE LORD THY GOD - and I shall hear thee --

Take ye heed of Mine Words and make ye ready for thine Greater Part - for it behooves Me to say again: Prepare thineself for the Greater Part -- Rest not on thine "Laurels" for I say - there is yet Worlds beyond thine own to conquer! ---

Let it be for thine own sake that I speak - yet it is for the Good of All -- So be it that I am no respecter of persons ---

I Am Come that there be Light --

I say unto ALL: "Come follow ye ME"--

Let them Come --

Let them Hear --

The Master Architect

Be ye as the Hand of Me - and write within the "Book of Life" that which I now give unto thee - and place thine Seal beneath Mine - for as I give it unto thee - ye shall give it unto them - for it is for this that I now give it unto thee in this manner -- Put thine hand in Mine - and together We shall deliver unto them this Word - and it shall be called the Foundation - I say - it shall be called "The Foundation"- and it is The Foundation upon which ye shall stand - and it shall be sure and safe -- I say ye shall be sure of thine footing upon <u>this</u> Foundation - for I have lain it - and I Am a Builder of Means -- I Know that which I build to be of Good timber --

I Know that which I have done - that which I shall do - for I AM THE MASTER ARCHITECT - and I Am The Master Craftsman -- I build upon the Master Plan - and I Am Come that I find the Pillars of The Temple which I shall build -- I say: I shall tear down and build anew -- I shall throw down the decayed and sordid - the rotten - and I shall replace it with the New and Good Material -- For this have I called Mine Servants/ Mine Hand Maidens - and for this have I given unto them that they prove themself worthy - I say - that they Prove themself worthy --

I Am Come that they be made ready - for the time cometh swiftly - when the last trumpet shall sound - and a Great Sound shall go forth - and a Mighty Light shall appear from out the East - and each one shall be as one prepared to go forth as One - and they each shall have a Part - and All Parts shall be brot before Me as a Living Testimony - and they shall bear Witness of Me - and The Word which I have spoken -- And then they shall sit with Me at Mine Board - and We shall Counsel and Commemorate that "Last Supper" - for I say unto thee: It shall be the

Great Feast which shall be given in commemoration of the Services rendered --

So be it I have spoken of Service - Now I say it shall be the Great Day for which thou hast waited - when each one shall hear the Word "Well done Mine faithful Servant - be ye forever blest"---

So be it I have spoken - and I am speaking unto them which have ears to hear -- Let them hear then - that which I have said - for unto them which hear - let it be understood -- Let it be - for this is it given unto thee ---

Be ye blest this day --

'Time' Shall Be Shortened

--Coran

Sori Sori -- For the first time I shall bring unto thee One Which hast His Hand in Mine - and He shall speak unto thee in thine own tongue - and He shall give unto thee a Part which shall be for the Good of ALL mankind -- He shall say that which He will - and I shall allow Him His Will - for He Serves well in His capacity -- So let it be for the Good of ALL that He speaks unto thee --

= Coran =

For the first time I greet thee - Beloved One of Mine Father: - For I am come in His Name -- I bring with Me a Host which are wont to speak - yet there be wisdom to withhold Their Speakings -- I say - I bring with

Me many of The Light - Which would give unto thee Greetings - yet it is wise that They speak not at this time - for I come to say unto thee: There is One which walks within the world of men - prepared to bring forth Great Miracles - Great Parts -- Great shall be the Parts which shall be put together - and they shall be as the Testimony of The Mighty Host, The Great and Mighty Council-- I say - the Parts shall be put together as One Whole - and they shall comprise the Whole of the Great and Mighty Message unto Mankind -- I Come that Mine Part be added unto the Other Parts - that I might add Mine Testimony - that I might bear Witness of Mine Father thru Whose Grace I am permitted to come unto thee at this hour -- I say - I am Come by The Grace of Mine Father and by the Consent of The Great and Mighty Council Which hast blest Me with this Privilege ---

So be it that I say unto thee: I Am amongst the Ones Which have held out a Hand unto thee in the hours of thine travail - and I have watched thine going and coming -- I have concerned Mineself not with thine coming and going - yet I rejoice with Mine fellow "Partners" - Mine Brothers - that thine progress hast been swift and sure - and thine feet hast been swift to do the Work which hast been allotted unto thee. I say: Great shall be thine reward - and Great thine joy ---

Let thine time be spent in thine Work - and let no man deter thee from thine appointed Course - for Great things shall be accomplished in a short while -- Rest in the Knowing that the "Time" shall be shortened-- I tell thee: The "Time" shall be shortened - and it shall be for the Elect's sake -- I say: The Elect hast drawn close unto Them which are the Messengers - and the Ambassadors - and the Emissaries I say - They have drawn near unto Thee - and They form a Great Guard, a Shield and Protection about thee - and They tire not of Their Guard -

Their Watch - for They Know that Their efforts are not in vain -- I say They Know thine worth - They Know thee - and thine worth --

They are alert and They are about The Father's Business -- So be it I too - come as One Which hast Guarded thee in Love and Holy Benediction -- I say unto thee: Be ye as one prepared - for Great shall be thine accomplishments - So be it and Selah -- Hold thine head high and let thine Light so shine that All might walk therein -- So be it I have said that which I have said - that I might add Mine Testimony unto that of Mine Fellow Brother -- So be it I take Mine leave with Love and Peace unto thee -- Let Mine Peace rest upon thine dwelling place --

Peace - Peace - Peace -

I Am - Coran

Mine Father's Will

Say unto them: Mine Hand bringeth forth the fruits of the field - and I shall do with them that which I Will - and I shall garner into Mine place that which is Mine - and I shall do that which I Will --

For is it not said: I Am The Will of Mine Father made manifest - and it is so -- And at no time shall one wrest from Me Mine Power which is given unto Me of Mine Father -- At no time shall I forfeit Mine Inheritance - for I Am One with Mine Father -- And I say unto thee Mine Beloved: I Am Come in His Name that His Will be done -- So let it be---

I have given unto thee Signs and Wonders - and I have placed before thee Mine Works - and thou hast tested them and found them Good --

And it is said: As thou art of Good Account - I shall do even Greater things - which shall confound the wise ---

So be it I Am not finished --

Light vs Darkness

Be ye as the <u>Word</u> - and the Word shall go forth as a Mighty Power - and a Mighty Light shall raise up out of the darkness - and great shall be Its Power -- For it is said: "There shall be Great Light" - and It shall be unto them a Sign -- And it is said: "The darkness comprehends not the Light" - for the darkness is "The Darkness" - opposite Light - the opposite of Light - therefore it knows not its opposite -- While I say unto thee: "Great Light shall go forth - and the darkness shall be dispelled!"---

So be it I have spoken -- So let Mine Words be made manifest in thee --

Preparation

Be ye as One on whose head I place Mine Hand -- And I speak unto thee as Mine Own which I have called out from amongst them - and I say unto thee: Thou hast heard Me and answered Me - saying: "Here I am - take me and Glorify Mine Father that His Will be done on Earth as it is in Heaven"-- Therefore I The Lord thy God decree - that ye be placed in a place new unto thee - and ye shall stand arrayed in White Linen - upon which shall be Great Gems of Light Substance which hast not any comparison - and nothing shall be known unto man which shall compare unto them --

Let it be recorded in the Book of Life - that which I now say unto thee - and at no time shall they say unto thee nay -- For eye hath not seen the fullness of the Glory of Heaven - neither have they the eye to see - for they are blinded to the Glory of Our Father Which hast Sent Me -- So be it I say unto thee: Come ye forth that ye might dwell with Me in the Upper Regions and wherein there is no darkness ---

I say unto thee: Behold the Glory of The Kingdom of God The Father - The Source of thy BEing -- So be it I have spoken unto thee and thou hast heard Me - yet they too shall Know that which I have said. That which I say in Secrecy shall I say openly -- So let them which have ears to hear - let them hear - and these shall bear witness of Me - and Mine Words -- So be it I Am He - I AM HE Which cometh into the world of darkness - that man be lifted up -- So as he is prepared - so shall he receive -- So let it be --

Amen and Selah

Mission Statement

Give the truth to the world. Let it be received where it will. Many will read the messages. Some will accept the truth, others will read through curiosity, a few will ridicule. Yet to all is the truth given, and to all remains the power of choice.

The hope of the world in these times is in spiritualizing all forms of activity---promoting understanding through love and service. These must be the watchwords if the world is to come into lasting peace. We are trying to influence a world that is going astray and could cause undreamed of suffering. We are trying to overcome the thought of materialists and to bring a spiritual outlook into the earthly life. We need the help of all on earth who can think in spiritual terms. The great battle to be fought now is between the spiritual and the material, between idealism and carnalism. You can help by spreading the word---we are asking that you help because the battle may be long and the victory far away.

Halls of Light is not allied with any sect, denomination, political entity, organization, neither endorses nor opposes any cause. There are no dues for membership. Halls of Light is self-supporting through its own voluntary contributions. Halls of Light has but one purpose: to help through encouragement and understanding...

To contact the publishers or to obtain copies of our other books, please contact us at

Email: goldtown11@gmail.com

Web: https://whoamiandwhyamihere.com/shop/

Sananda's Appearance

Be ye as one which hast heard Mine Voice and responded unto it - for I speak that ye hear, and I say that which is wise and prudent.

Let it be known that 1, the Lord thy God hast spoken and bear ye witness of Me, for I have made manifest Mineself that ye might know Me - and for this wast these manifestations made.

I say that I have made Mineself manifest that ye might see Me with thine mortal eyes; that ye might bear witness of Me. Yet thine companions saw and believed not; neither did they hear, for they were selfish and unprepared - yet, did I deny them?

I say; I came that they which would might see and hear. I went and came again unto Mine own. So be it that I have found; I have given unto the found that they which know not might know; that they might come to know as thou knowest.

Yet, how many hast turned from Me and persecuted thee for Mine Word. It is said, "Woe unto them which persecute Mine servants." is it not the law which they set into motion?

Yea Mine beloved, I say they bring about their own downfall. So be it that I am a compassionate one, and I would that they know what they do. So be it they shall learn well their lessons. So let it be, for this is the mercy of God, the One which hast sent Me.

So be it. I AM The Wayshower, the Lord thy God

I AM Sananda

About the Late Sister Thedra

Since the later part of the last Century, the Kumara wisdom has begun to reemerge into the world. This process began with the late Sister Thedra, whom Jesus Christ appeared physically to while on her deathbed and spontaneously healed her of cancer while she was in the Yucatan, where she had gone to accept her fate and the will of our Lord Jesus Christ.

That is when something miraculous occurred. Jesus spoke to her saying, "My name is Esu Sananda Kumara" and then sent Thedra down to the Monastery of the Seven Rays in Peru to learn the Kumara wisdom. After five years, Thedra was told to return to the United States where she founded the Association of Sananda and Sanat Kumara at Mt. Shasta in California.

While heading this organization, Thedra channeled many messages from Sananda and taught the Kumara wisdom. He introduced himself to her by his true name, "Sananda Kumara" And it was by his command that Sister Thedra went to Peru but eventually left upon being told that her experience there was complete. She then traveled to Mt. Shasta in California and founded the Association of Sananda and Sanat Kumara. A.S.S.K.

You ask, Is There a difference between Jesus and Sananda? Our Lord's name given at birth by his Father Joseph and his beloved mother Mary was Yeshua, thus being of the house of David and the order of Yoseph, he would be called Yeshua ben Yoseph. The Roman Emperors placed the name of Jesus upon the sir name of Yeshua after the Emperor Justinian adopted Christianity as the official faith of Rome and ordered that the sacred books be compiled upon approval of a specially appointed counsel appointed by the Emperor into a recognizable and uniform work titled "The Bible". Prior to this, there never was a Bible per se.

There existed until the time of the Emperor's edict, a selection of many Sacred texts that were employed in the Sacred Teachings, many of which were copies of what the Greeks had transposed from the original texts in the Libraries of Alexandria which were originally compiled by Alexander the Great, and were destroyed by Julius Caesar, fearing that they might prove dangerous to the rule of a Caesar, an Earthly God.

In addition, it was to keep the knowledge of Alexander's Libraries out of the hands of the Ptolemy's who were said to be descended from his bloodline. At the time, Caesar had no way of knowing that vast portions of the Library were already in the Americas, in the Great Universities of the Inca, and in possession of the Mayans.

Yeshua spent many years in the East after his ascension. The Good Sheppard, upon his appearances to the Apostles after his ascension, told them that he was going to tend to his Father's other sheep; which meant, plainly, that he was continuing upon his sacred journey. As The Ascended One, Yeshua took to himself the name of Sananda, meaning the Christed One, and Sananda was thus embraced forevermore by the Great Solar Brotherhood. To many of you this is all new, to others it will be received as a welcome easing of the wall that has so long separated two sides of the same coin. This is being placed into the ethers and the matrix of thought at this time, as it is the time of The Great Awakening, and the Christos is already emerging into the new consciousness.

Authority to use the name of Sananda was given to Sister Thedra when Jesus, (Sananda), appeared to her in the Yucatan and cured her instantly of the cancer that had taken over her body. Further, he allowed a picture of his countenance to be taken at that time that she might realize the occurrence was more than a dream. Thedra had a large format camera called a 620 that she used to take the picture of Sananda.

Sanada's Message to her by Sister Thedra: "Sori Sori: Mine hand I have placed upon thine head, and I have given unto thee the authority to use Mine name. Give unto them the name Sananda, by which they shall know Me as the Lord thy God - the Son of God, sent that ye be made to know me, the One sent from out The Inner Temple that there be Light in the world of men. Now it is come when ones which have the will to follow Me shall come to know Me by that name which I commanded thee to give unto the world as Mine New name.

There are many that shall call upon the name of Jesus, yet they will deny the new name as they are want to do. Unto thee I give assurance that I am the One sent that there be Light in the world of men. Now let this be understood, that they that deny Mine New Name deny Me by any name. So be it I have appointed thee Mine spokesman; I've given unto thee the power and authority to speak for being that which I AM. And I say unto thee Mine child whom I have called forth and anointed thee with the Holy Spirit, thy name shall be as it is now called, Thedra, that name I spoke unto thee from out the ethers, and thou heard Me and accepted that which I gave unto thee; and wherein have I deceived thee? Wherein have I forgotten thee, or left thee alone?"

I say unto thee: "Mine hand is upon thee and I shall sustain thee and you shall come to know that which I have kept for thee. So be it that I have kept thy reward, and at no time shall it be dissipated or scattered, for it is intact. So let this Mine Word suffice them which question thee - let them question, and I shall bear witness for thee. For do I not know Mine servants from the traitors? Do I not reward Mine servants according unto their works or merits? I speak that they might know that I am mindful of Mine servants, that I am not a poor puny priest who has forgotten his servants.

"I say unto them: Mine servants shall be glorified above the crowned heads of the nations which have set themselves apart, and denied Me Mine part of Mine word for they have turned from Me in their conceit and forgetfulness. Now let this go on record as Mine Word, and I shall give unto them proof, which are of a mind to follow Me.

So be it as I have spoken and I am not finished; I shall speak again and again, and I shall rise Mine Voice against them which set foot against Mine servants, and they shall be as ones cast out. So let them ask of Me and I shall enlighten them. So be it I know whereof I speak. Be ye as ones blest to accept Me and know Me for that which I AM." On Saturday, June 13, 1992, at exactly 10.00 PM, at the age of 92, Sister Thedra made her final transition from the comfort of her own bed. When the time arrived, she simply took one small breath and slipped quietly away, without pomp or fanfare.

She left as she had lived: as a humble servant for the greater good. The messages included were given to Sister Thedra shortly before her transition. They are compiled here to give you some idea of the significance of her passing and of the expansion of the work, as she is now free of the physical limitations and the pain of the past. Her work now in the higher realms will simply be an extension of that work.

Divine Explanations

Part - I

The following explanations and definitions of terms used by Sananda (Jesus) and the various Sibors were given by Sananda through direct revelation. They are not alphabetical. These explanations should be read over and over.

- - - - - - - - - - -

My Beloved Sibors please give us plainly the definitions of the following words that there may be no error on our part." - Thedra.

THEMSELF? What is the explanation of your terminology of "Themself" – "themselves"?

I (Sananda) say unto thee mine beloved: they which would be unto thee a vessel, unto thee a sibor, unto thee teacher, are as ones enlightened of the Father, enlightened of the Father for the light is in them.

They know their parts well, they have their memory, they have mastered the elements, they can do all the things which I do and they take unto "themself" no credit for they have overcome self. They are self-less. Now I say unto them: them which work with thee are the Selfless ones. They ask nothing for "themself." Now while this is true they are as one.

They are within the great brotherhood of the Selfless Ones - the Ones clothed in white. They are as the Royal Assembly - and each unto his own, yet each for all and all for one. Now while in thy world, they (of thy world) are <u>selfish</u> and they are not for the whole - they ask for self and I speak of these as the selfish ones. I speak unto them in terms which they shall come to know and therein is wisdom.

I say that they shall be responsible for 'themselves' and as a world of me I say they shall be responsible for their society; they 'themselves' have created it. Now I speak unto thee mine beloved, I say "ye shall be responsible for thyself. He shall be responsible for himself. They as a whole shall be responsible for that which they have created, while thou art responsible unto thyself for thine part - and not held accountable for theirs. Be it so."

BELEIS? "Mighty is the word and great the power thereof. I say unto thee this word carries with it the part of surrender. The word is the release of power - that which is sent forth by the one which asks of the Father His blessing. It is the surrender of the self - the complete surrender of the personal will and letting the Father's will be accomplished in all things through thee. "<u>So be it</u>" - it the accomplishment, the acceptance of the Father's plan."

SELAH? - "The word carries the Seal of Truth - meaning it is without error - no mistake - it is the verification of Truth - not subject to change.

SIBET? – "The Sibet is one which has offered or presented himself as a candidate for the greater learning and for the greater initiation. He comes as an empty vessel that he may be filled. So be it."

SIBOR? - "I am the Sibor of Sibors." - "The Sibor is one which has been illumined of God the Father. He has returned unto the Father purified. He has gone the Royal Road - which means he has overcome death. He has mastered the lower elements - he controls the elements. He can raise the dead - heal the sick - he can create like unto the Father <u>for</u> he has finished his course and won the victory and returned unto the Father the Victor. So be it."

"I am the Sibor of Sibors. I am the first born of Him which hast sent me. Sananda."

LEGIRONS? - "Beloved - I say unto thee: thy opinions and thy dogmas are not the least of these - neither thy creeds. Be it ever that these are great and heavy ones. Now let it be understood that a leg-iron is something which holds thee bound. It is something which holds thee, it keeps thee fast, wherein progress is not possible. Now that progress be made possible, ye shall cut away the legirons.

Knowest thou these bound by legirons? These are to be pitied, they drag them with them, impeding their progress - and they are as ones bound! They are not free - are they? While they serve their sentence - they are as ones bound - they are bond-men - they are bound men - men bound. Now let me say I too am a "bondsman." I came that they may be free. I say I bring unto thee the law which thou shall obey - unto the letter - then I shall give unto thee that which I have kept for thee. Be ye as one prepared for that.

PREPARATION? Now - preparation - what do you mean by "preparation?" "This my beloved is the part which they shall do - the part of preparation is: cleaning thyself of all the opinions, indoctrinations of man. The cup must be emptied. This is thy part, the becoming the "'little child" un-opinionated, unscathed and unmarred with or by their doctrines, creeds and crafts. I say the child is unindoctrinated and un-opinionated and is the virgin mind – (yet it does not remain so long in this world). While the little child represents the empty cup - the empty vessel, the Virgin Spirit, it is given unto the child to be one which has come from other realms and to have been in many embodiments, many times: yet the symbol of virginity. Wherein is it said there are none innocent among thee?

WHEREIN I AM? - "Now while thou art yet within the world of men - I am within mine Father's realm, the place wherein there is no darkness, wherein <u>ALL</u> things are known. I say wherein <u>ALL</u> things are known, wherein there is <u>No</u> mystery.

And too - I say when thou hast attained unto thy Royal Road, when thou hast become part of the Royal Assembly, thou shall know as I - thou shall be as I - thou shall be brought into the place wherein I am, for I say unto thee this is attainment. This is the day of Attainment, the day of "becoming," the day of thy salvation. Know ye that this is Mine day - the day for which thou hast waited? I say unto thee: "This is the day of fulfillment. This is Mine Day. Mine Day is come ---"

What is meant by "ALL THE LANDS OF THE EARTH?"- "This I mean, all the lands of the Earth. I have said it, I mean it as I have said it and there is no mystery of or to it."

ALL MANKIND? "This is Mine people - Mine children - Mine flock - Mine Church - Mine brethren - Mine congregation unto whom I shall minister. By Mine own hand shall they be fed and led. These have I came to find. Are not all <u>hu</u>-man beings considered "Man kind"? by thine own standards. Yet all men are not of me."

WHAT DO YOU MEAN - "WILL IT SO"? - "There is power in the "WILL" and the power which they use to create their own torment and confusion is misused energy. Yet they will this - they will it so. Now when ye will to serve me ye give unto me thy undivided attention, the whole heart - thy heart - thine ALL. Yet I say that they which doth attempt to serve me with one hand and the dragon with the other has not willed to serve me. They are not of me - they are not of Mine flock. I say they are either with me or against me. I cannot accept the one hand while they reserve the other for the dragon. They are not wholeheartedly mine.

I make no compromises with the dragon. Mine shall come out from them and surrender unto me themself - their all - without reservation. This is willing it so - for they will the Father's will be done in them, through them, by them. They leave no energy that the dragon may use. They use all their energy to serve me. This is mine word unto thee."

WHAT IS DARKNESS? - "Thine Un-Knowing - thy darkness comes from the fall of man - which one was with God the Father perfect which didst have his memory blanked from him when he didst transgress."

MAYAS VEIL? - "The result of such unknowing - the darkness which man has brought upon himself. The part he has created for himself."

WHAT DOES IT MEAN TO <u>BETRAY</u> <u>ONES</u> <u>SELF</u>? - "This is the sad part for first the 'fall' came from his betrayal - and it hast resulted in the fall - in the veil of Maya - the "illusion" and in thy un-knowing - in thy own darkness."

WHAT OF BETRAYING "HIS OWN TRUST"? - "The plan is all inclusive and includes <u>all</u> - yet there are ones unaware of the "plan" - (and they are not as included in this temple as yet) - no personal reference unto the ones within this temple. Now when one becomes aware of his part, he is given the law and it is provided for his own good and he has the law clearly stated, plainly recorded, and he turns his face away - that he may hide from it. He puts his fingers into his ears that he may not hear it. He gives unto his benefactors the bitter cup and he goes his own willful way.

He has betrayed himself for he shall be caught up short of his course. When he has been given a chance - a "part" within the plan and he has committed himself, he has the responsibility given unto him for that "part" and should he be so foolish as to betray his trust he shall be like unto one which has thrown overboard his <u>own</u> life belt - poor foolish ones!"

WISDOM? - What is meant by the word "Wisdom?" - "Wisdom is that which is light, the knowledge of the law and its proper use. The right use of the law - and this Mine children is Mine part. I come that ye may BECOME wise! Wisdom is thy divine gift - not of man, for man of Earth is foolish indeed - and he is nothing save that which the Father has endowed him. All else is of the world of "illusion" which shall pass into nothingness in the Light which I Am."

WHAT IS THE "PEARL OF GREAT PRICE, THE PRICELESS PEARL? - "That which I offer thee - thy freedom, thy salvation from bondage - thine inheritance in full - Mine word which is not purchased with coin - not bought, neither is it sold. It is the wisdom of which I speak. Mine offer unto thee is without price - it is the 'pearl' - "Mine Pearl."

WHY ARE MIS-SPELLED AND GRAMMATICAL ERRORS USED IN THESE SCRIPTS? – Sananda: "I am not a conformist. I am not concerned with the letters of man for I am He which has come that they be unbound by their fetters. I say unto them which desireth the letter - unto them the letter.

I say unto thee: be ye as ones free from such bondage. I stand ready to free thee from thy bondage. Unto thee I say - give unto the letter no thought. <u>Hear</u> what I <u>say</u> for I shall say it in many ways as becomes me and serves mine purpose. I say I am no stranger in thine midst. While they know me not, I know them. I see them bowing down before the Golden Calf - and they worship at the shrines which they have set up. (Their own standards of education.) They guild them and bring unto them burnt offerings - yet they close me out.

Be ye not so foolish. <u>Be ye not so foolish</u>! I am come that ye might have Light - Wisdom - Freedom which is the Father's will. While the letter changeth and passeth away - and the letter is not the law - the letter is of no consequence other than to cause thee to see the "Word." The word is the power which shall provoke thine mind into action and thy mind shall be free from the letter. See what is meant within the Word, and let thine mind be staid on <u>me</u> - the Light, the Way - Truth and Wisdom."

"I am He which hast come - that ye be free: forever free. I am Sananda - Son of God. Once known as the Nazarine, He which was born of Mary, Ward of Joseph.

Recorded by Thedra

Part - 2

THE WHITE BROTHERHOOD AND THE EMERALD CROSS.

THE MANY QUESTIONS ABOUT THE WHITE BROTHERHOOD AND THE ORDER OF THE EMERALD CROSS MAY BE EXPLAINED IN A FEW SIMPLE WORDS.

ONE HAS TO EARN THE RIGHT TO BECOME A MEMBER - EITHER IN THIS LIFE OR OTHERS BEFORE OR AFTER - NONE ENTER UNPREPARED.

THE WHITE BROTHERHOOD - or - THE ROYAL ASSEMBLY is of the Realms of Light---not of Earth. The Ascended Masters have proven themself in the school of Earth (THE SCHOOL FOR GODS) who have trodden the path of INITIATION - overcome the trials and temptations of the mundane world - who have gained their freedom and ascended as the Lord Jesus Christ (Sananda). They have gone the ROYAL ROAD.

Knowing the path of the Initiate -- and its pitfalls -- and sorrow, they extend a hand in Fellowship - LOVE and WISDOM - NEVER depriving the candidate an opportunity to learn his lessons well -- for this is His salvation -- for this do they proffer their hand, NOT to do our part for us, but rather that we become strong and free by our own strength.

The Royal Assembly or the White Brotherhood have known all of the heartaches, the longing, crucifications, temptations and JOYS of the aspirant -- the candidate -- the Master -- the Sibor -- herein lies their strength, their understanding, their great love for us on the path.

Their love and understanding knows no bounds. They give help when necessary for our progress. They also withhold it wisely - should it deprive us of our lessons. The candidate on the path of initiation shall become self-responsible for all his actions -- all the energy allotted him throughout his whole EARTHLY existence - and make atonement for all his misused energy, for therein is his salvation.

There is no one else which will ever make this atonement for us (the candidate) on the path of unfoldment. While the host of "WHITE BROTHERS" Brothers of LIGHT are ready to assist, the candidate shall (MUST) put forth every effort to overcome all the forces of darkness which would deter his progress and earn for himself his freedom from BONDAGE.

THE EMERALD CROSS

THE EMERALD CROSS is a company – and an order of beings who work within the Brotherhood of MAN - and the Fatherhood of God - for the good of all mankind --- And at the head of this group is one known as MOTHER SARAH, the personification of love -- embodiment of all MOTHERS. That is: the LOVE of God made Manifest - in MOTHERS. The blessed Mother Sarah is the head of this Order of the Emerald Cross. And when one earns the Divine right and privileges to associate themselves with this Order, it is the joy of all the Orders - and Brothers of Light. I speak for the Order - for I am known as Merseda. (As told to Sister Thedra of the Order of the Emerald Cross).

COMANCHE - which is the porter at the door - which doth keep out the unworthy, the unjust, the unclean. The Door Keeper - the one responsible for the Temple Gate.

BITTER CUP - that which you would not like to partake of - that which poisons thee, that which is not good, that which torments thee - that which ye have given unto thy brother to torment him which returns unto thee as a boomerang to torment thee - which ye shall receive multiplied - which has accumulated in its swift flight. I say prepare not for thyself the bitter cup for ye shall drink of the portion which thou doth prepare for thy brother. Be ye not foolish - make it not bitter.

BLEST OF MINE BEING - I have given of Mine self that Mine beloved has being.

BLEST OF MINE PRESENCE - Have I not gone the long way? I have gone out from Mine place of abode that I might bring light unto the Earth that she might be lifted up - that the children thereof might be delivered of all bondage - that they might return unto the place from whence they went out. And have I not come unto thee many times that this be accomplished? Have I not done all which has been given unto me to do? Wherein have I failed thee? Have I not done all that I have come to do? - While it is not as yet finished, I shall not fail. My mission shall be finished ere I return unto Mine abiding place. Shall I not be unto the true and shall I not return the Victor?

GAVE OF HIMSELF - Did I not give of Mine Self - hast thou? Have I not been true unto Mine trust? Have I asked aught for Myself? Have I not done that which I have promised? Have I not given Mine All? Have I not come on a Sacrificial Mission? What more have I to give - other than myself?

PORE - The physical body - vehicle which thou dost use.

<u>INITIATION</u> - Thy preparation for the inner temple. Each step is an initiation. One step at a time - the overcoming of self - the world - the becoming that which I am.

<u>COSMOS</u> - That which is unseen throughout many universes by thy eyes. Great is the expanse of the Father's Kingdom and the total thereof is referred to as "throughout the Cosmos."

<u>LORD'S STRANGE ACT</u> - This I shall reveal in Mine own time.

<u>WALK WHICH WAY THY CROWN TILTS NOT</u> - as a Son of God. Do honor unto thy Father Mother God - and thou shall be as one which has the Royal Raiment upon thine shoulders - and ye shall wear it in honor and with dignity.

<u>WHEN IT SAYS IT IS RECORDED - WHEREIN IS IT RECORDED</u>? - In the secret place - in the eth - and within the inner temple - and wherein thou art are many things recorded - which I do speak of. Ye shall see these recordings when thou doth enter into the secret place of Mine abode. I say ye shall read the records wherein are written the records of all thy travels from the time ye left the Father Mother God until thine return unto him.

<u>WHAT IS MICHAEL'S FLAMING SWORD</u>? - "The "Sword of Truth and justice."

Recorded by Sister Thedra

Other Books by TNT Publishing

Who am I and Why Am I Here?

The Significance of Existence

Death and the Incredible Life After

Fear of Death Removed

Paradise Regained

Spiritual Laws Revealed

Unseen Forces

Too Good to Be True

The Truth of Life in the Spirit World

He Who Has Ears

The Great Awakening, Volumes I thru VII

The Great Awakening, Volume VIII,
THE WHITE STAR OF THE EAST

The Great Awakening, Volume IX,
I THE LORD GOD SAY UNTO THEM

The Great Awakening, Volume X,
MINE INTERCOM MESSAGES FROM THE REALMS OF LIGHT

The Great Awakening, Volume XI,
THE BOOK OF THE LORD

The Great Awakening, Volume XII thru XV,
TEMPLE TEACHINGS FROM THE HIGHER REALMS

Transfiguration Volumes I thru Volume VIII

The Part of Counsel

The Book of Wisdom

The School of Melchezedek

Hail! Hail! Unto the Victors

The Book of Light

The Book of Life

The Golden Scripts

Seven Minutes in Eternity

No More Hunger

Contact us at

Email: goldtown11@gmail.com

Web: https://whoamiandwhyamihere.com/shop/

www.ingramcontent.com/pod-product-compliance
Lightning Source LLC
LaVergne TN
LVHW051540070426
835507LV00021B/2343